Of Moral Conduct

In this book Robert Audi presents an original ethics of conduct, spanning moral theory, practical ethics, and theories of obligation and value. Conduct is determined not just by *what* we do, but also by *why* and *how* we do it. To integrate these dimensions of conduct, Audi clarifies the relation between intention and obligation, explains the difference between moral rightness and moral worth, and describes myriad manners of human actions. He also clarifies major moral standards such as justice, fidelity, beneficence, and liberty, and explores ethics from the perspectives of the theory of action, the epistemology of moral principles, the metaphysics of normative properties, and the value of human experiences. His concluding chapters offer a theory of reasons and values and propose an original theory of value.

ROBERT AUDI is John A. O'Brien Professor of Philosophy at the University of Notre Dame. He is Editor of *The Cambridge Dictionary of Philosophy* (3rd edition, Cambridge University Press, 2015), and his many publications in ethics include *Reasons, Rights, and Values* (Cambridge University Press, 2015) and *Means, Ends, and Persons* (Oxford University Press, 2016).

T0371094

Of Moral Conduct

A Theory of Obligation, Reasons, and Value

Robert Audi
University of Notre Dame

CAMBRIDGE
UNIVERSITY PRESS

Shaftesbury Road, Cambridge CB2 8EA, United Kingdom

One Liberty Plaza, 20th Floor, New York, NY 10006, USA

477 Williamstown Road, Port Melbourne, VIC 3207, Australia

314–321, 3rd Floor, Plot 3, Splendor Forum, Jasola District Centre, New Delhi – 110025, India

103 Penang Road, #05–06/07, Visioncrest Commercial, Singapore 238467

Cambridge University Press is part of Cambridge University Press & Assessment, a department of the University of Cambridge.

We share the University's mission to contribute to society through the pursuit of education, learning and research at the highest international levels of excellence.

www.cambridge.org
Information on this title: www.cambridge.org/9781009266963

DOI: 10.1017/9781009266987

© Robert Audi 2023

First published 2023
First paperback edition 2024

A catalogue record for this publication is available from the British Library

Library of Congress Cataloging-in-Publication data
Names: Audi, Robert, 1941– author.
Title: Of moral conduct : a theory of obligation, reasons, and value / Robert Audi, University of Notre Dame, Indiana.
Description: First edition. | New York : Cambridge University Press, 2023. | Includes bibliographical references and index.
Identifiers: LCCN 2022052550 (print) | LCCN 2022052551 (ebook) | ISBN 9781009267014 (hardback) | ISBN 9781009266963 (paperback) | ISBN 9781009266987 (epub)
Subjects: LCSH: Ethics. | Conduct of life. | Responsibility. | Values.
Classification: LCC BJ1012 .A83 2023 (print) | LCC BJ1012 (ebook) | DDC 170–dc23/eng/20230328
LC record available at https://lccn.loc.gov/2022052550
LC ebook record available at https://lccn.loc.gov/2022052551

ISBN   978-1-009-26701-4   Hardback
ISBN   978-1-009-26696-3   Paperback

To Malou

Contents

Preface

Ethics has always focused on actions, but morality reaches further than action. It also concerns why we do the things we do, thus our motivation, and how we do them, thus our manners of acting. Human behavior viewed in all three dimensions, action, motivation, and manner, is *conduct*. The concept is most easily seen by thinking about someone's doing the right things toward a friend, but for purely self-interested reasons or in a hostile manner. A comprehensive ethics should offer an account not just of right and wrong action, but also of good and bad conduct as incorporating action, motive, and manner. This book is the first full statement of an ethics of conduct.

To understand conduct requires more integration between ethics and the theory of action than is at all common in moral philosophy. Action theory addresses what action is, how it is explained by our beliefs, desires, and intentions, and what significant range of manners it exhibits. To appraise rightness and wrongness, we need standards of obligation. And to justify those standards, we need an account of how they may be known. This requires explaining how they may be based on apprehension or perception of genuine facts. In developing a comprehensive ethics of conduct, Part I is devoted mainly to action-theoretic aspects of ethics: to what action is, its relation to motivation, and the moral importance of its different aspects. Part II mainly concerns normative ethics, Part III the epistemology and metaphysics of normative principles, and Part IV the theory of reasons and values. Part IV frames a moral theory that reflects both the results of earlier chapters and some of the best elements in other theories.

The book takes account of much in the history of ethics and many important contemporary writings, but it is not a critical study of existing literature. Its aim is to present and defend an overall ethical theory that is an advance over alternatives, including major theories whose best elements it seeks to preserve. These are particularly the virtue ethics of Aristotle, the deontology of Kant and Ross, the consequentialism of Mill, Sidgwick, and Moore, and the intuitionism discernible in moral thinkers from antiquity to the present.

Every effort is made toward clarity and concreteness to enhance readability, and this book should be intelligible to not just moral philosophers and advanced students of ethics, but also professionals and some students in ethics as taught or practiced in law, bioethics and other branches of applied ethics, political theory, and religious studies, including theology. Many non-philosophers, including undergraduates studying philosophy, can learn from the examples, especially the many narrative ones in Part II. These and other examples introduce many of the concepts and distinctions important in ethics. Part II is accessible almost entirely independently of the others, and teachers of ethics might assign it for undergraduates even without leading them through earlier or later parts of the book.

Part I is self-contained and will hold most interest for readers in moral psychology or the action-theoretic dimension of ethics; and, given the introduction and some use of the detailed table of contents and the index, various chapters might be read separately from others or omitted from a reading guided by special interest in one of the main elements of the overall view. Particularly for readers who may choose to read less than the whole book, the introduction is a guide. The table of contents and detailed index should also help in locating topics of interest.

As a whole, the book presents an ethical theory that aims at representing the importance of action theory and epistemology in ways no other wide-ranging contemporary works in ethics do. Part II, by contrast, is not mainly in ethical theory as distinct from "practical ethics." It presents a detailed pluralistic ethics that reflects – sometimes also refining or correcting – commonsense normative standards proposed, though in very different ways, by Aristotle, Kant, Mill, Ross, and others. I do not, then, construct an ethical theory in abstraction from the historically leading moral philosophers, and I regret that space permits only limited discussion of – among other things – action theory in Aristotle, obligation in Kant, intrinsic value in Mill and Moore, and intuitive knowledge in Ross. Both action theory and epistemology are crucial for understanding not only obligation, moral creditworthiness, and virtue, but also moral education, which I view as an important source of data for ethics as well as a testing ground for its major claims. Where space permits, I consider ethics developmentally with a view to understanding how moral standards are learned, role modeled, and appealed to in decision-making and in appraising action. Given this developmental concern, which requires accounting for elementary and spontaneous moral conduct, I try to avoid intellectualism in understanding thought, motivation, and action. Actions for good reasons, including right actions having moral worth, need not be based on an intellectual process or even an inference from a moral rule. Morality may be manifested as well in spontaneous human relations as in reflective deliberation.

Acknowledgments

This book presents an ethical theory that substantially advances my previous work in ethics. Among my books that provide major elements that – often in revised forms – appear here are *The Good in the Right* (Princeton, 2004), *Moral Perception* (Princeton, 2013), and *Means, Ends, and Persons* (Oxford, 2016). Many of my papers have also been important for the book and some are on the reference list. No chapter, however, simply reprints any of those, but Chapters 3, 7, and 10 have appeared (with some revisions), respectively, in *Ratio* 34 (2021), 56–67, DOI: 10.1111/rati.12286 (as "Acting Rightly: Three Dimensions of Moral Conduct"); in *Res Philosophica* 97, 1 (2020), 69–92 (as "Toward an Epistemology of Moral Principles"); and in *Noûs*, DOI: 10.1111/nous.12377, 2022 (as "Are Reasons Normatively Basic?"); and a paper close to Chapter 9 is appearing approximately simultaneously as "The Explanatory Role of Moral Facts and the Case for Moral Realism," in Paul Bloomfield and David Copp, eds., *The Oxford Handbook of Moral Realism*. I am grateful to the editors and publishers of these sources for allowing presentation of much of the content of those papers.

The book was written over several years and has benefited from comments by and discussions with friends, colleagues, students, and anonymous readers. I cannot name them all or the many people with whom I have had valuable exchanges in presenting some of the ideas in the book to one or another conference or university audience, but I should mention a reading group that explored an early version in 2020, attended by Notre

Dame graduate students, Isabel Canfield, Rachel Dichter, Lucia Dikaczova, Stephen Evensen, and Dominic LaMantia, as well as (in part) my colleagues Brian Cutter and Michael Zhao. These discussions considerably helped me, and Cutter and Zhao both commented helpfully on specific chapters. Beyond this, I benefited from comments on at least parts of earlier versions from Karl Ameriks, Selim Berker, Mario De Caro, Fred Feldman, Noah Lemos, Christian Miller, David Phillips, Declan Smithies, Joshua Stuchlik, Elizabeth Tropman, and Abigail Whalen. For both comments on a full earlier draft and valuable, often extensive, discussion, I am particularly indebted to Roger Crisp, Garrett Cullity, and Mark Timmons. Their writings have also been of great value in my thinking about the issues.

It has been of immense help to have discussions or correspondence (often both) with all the colleagues so far mentioned, particularly Ameriks, Berker, Miller, and Smithies, but also, and sometimes going back to very early stages of composition, Paul Audi, Feraz Azhar, Paola Bernardini, Paul Bloomfield, Gwen Bradford, John Broome, Sarah Buss, Anjan Chakravartty, Ruth Chang, Nevin Climenhaga, Tony Coady, Earl Conee, David Copp, Terence Cuneo, Jonathan Dancy, Stephen Darwall, Richard Feldman, Stephen Finlay, William FitzPatrick, Rainer Forst, Berys Gaut, Brad Hooker, Thomas Hurka, Karen Jones, David Kaspar, Thomas Kelly, Pauline Kleingeld, Christopher Kulp, Clayton Littlejohn, David McCabe, Kristopher McDaniel, Sarah McGrath, Gerald McKenny, Jefferson McMahan, Michael Moore, Patrick Murphy, Thomas Nagel, Onora O'Neill, the late Derek Parfit, Rik Peels, Jean Porter, Michael Rabenberg, Massimo Renzo, Sonja Rinofner-Kreidl, Robert Roberts, Richard Rowland, Jack Sammons, T. M. Scanlon, Russ Shafer-Laudau, Walter Sinnott-Armstrong, Michael Smith, William R. Smith, David Sosa, Ernest Sosa, Nicholas Southwood, James Sterba, Philip Stratton-Lake, Eleonore Stump, Christine Swanton, John Tasioulas, Nandi Theunissen, Jens Timmermann, René van Woudenberg, Ralph Wedgwood, Paul Weithman, Oliver Williams, Susan Wolf, Mark Wynn, Linda Zagzebski, and Lorenzo Zucca.

At the Press I had good advice and considerable help from Hilary Gaskin, Thomas Haynes, Abi Sears, and, in the final stage, Vinithan Sethumadhavan, project manager. For expert copyediting, I also want to thank Rose Bell.

Introduction

E thics has triple vision. It looks to the past and concerns what we have done, why we have done it, and how we did it. It also views our ongoing activities in three dimensions of what we do: its *what*, *why*, and *how*. What we do (our "deeds"), why we do it (our motivation for acting), and how we do it (the manner in which we act) are morally important. Beyond concern with all this, ethics requires us to choose well among our options and, so far as we can, to realize good ones, to do so for good reasons, and to do it in the right ways. From the moral point of view, what kind of person we are is evidenced by our past actions, manifested in our present conduct, and confirmed or disconfirmed in our future conduct. All three basic dimensions of conduct – our deeds, our reasons for doing them, and the manners in which we do them – are explored in this book.

The most salient dimension of our behavior is action. Actions are the central focus of standards of right and wrong. But *why* we do what we do is also morally important. This motivational foundation of action is crucial for determining its moral creditworthiness and, more broadly, our moral character. The third dimension of conduct, the manner of our actions, is determined by how they are performed – not in the sense in which 'how' concerns means to ends, but in a sense in which manner is closer to behavioral styles and includes diction and body language. The manner of actions is independent of what is done – the deed – and, in principle, of why it is done.

These points are abstract, but they are readily illustrated. Think of the world of business – including large organizations. Imagine a manager, Fred, terminating the employment of a salesperson, Jesse. Suppose Fred has hired Jesse several months before the termination, has clearly communicated to Jesse what the day-to-day procedures are, and has done the usual amount of mentoring for Jesse. Fred reflects on how to communicate the termination. He wants to be honest yet firm, but also prudent in producing no avoidable distress or cause for retaliation. The company is a furniture showroom. The city is small enough for word of the dismissal to reach many businesses to which Jesse might apply. Fred has never come to like Jesse but thinks his dislike has not affected the termination decision, which was approved by the owners. Fred thinks about how to conduct the meeting. He concentrates on what to say. He presupposes taking a professional but broadly sympathetic tone, as in past terminations. He plans to review the record, then move to the communication of the decision, and conclude with the terms of release and an assurance of willingness to provide a reference that stresses lack of "fit" with the sales tradition of the company.

Fred has a positive self-image. He presupposes that in conducting the meeting he'll be motivated by his managerial responsibility. Given his experience in performance reviews, he doesn't worry about whether he might be influenced partly by his dislike, but is aware of his desire to get rid of Jesse as someone who is a bit loud and talks with others to the point of distracting them. Fred has no need to think about speaking rudely or even patronizingly, because that manner of communication does not represent his character and he never falls into it.

Plainly, Fred has a huge range of verbal actions to choose from in communicating the termination – too many to consider all of them in advance in any normal case like this. He is not writing a letter of termination – though even prose has an authorial voice that is not determined just by diction and content. Still, ethically, Fred is at best less creditworthy in making the termination decision if dislike of Jesse is a major factor motivating it, say strong enough so that without the dislike he would have delayed termination – though we may assume that he also would not have terminated the employment without good grounds. Moreover, the dislike might affect the manner in which he acts in the interview. Is Fred's review of past performance, for instance, sympathetically given? Compare saying, with a pained expression, "*Unfortunately*, you allowed credit to a friend who never paid the $6,000 bill" with saying, as Fred does dryly, "*Against our policy*, you gave credit to a friend of yours who didn't pay the $6,000 bill." Wording in such cases might be pre-planned. Even the facial expression and intonation might be, though for many people planning in that much detail is less likely. Both wording and intonation may still be affected by dislike (or some "implicit bias"), which can be an important influence on conduct quite apart from motivating particular actions.

Perhaps only some quite consciously moral people understand the ethical demands of such a situation well enough to block the influence of biases or negative emotions. These can affect both word choice and manner of speaking as manifested by intonation and gesture. Manner of expression is often affected by word choice; and, in two-way communication over time, changing motivation may affect both wording and manner.

The termination case indicates many options and many ethically relevant choices. It also pictures an activity rather than a momentary action; and, given the stages an activity may go through – sometimes unforeseeable in number or complexity – conscientious preparation may be limited in anticipating and controlling performance. But consider other activities: classroom teaching, working with a colleague in making a joint decision, describing a landscaping job to someone hired to do it, and – often fraught with conflicting concerns – cautioning adolescent children.

The literature of ethics has too often concentrated on what acts are right or wrong at the expense of neglecting the manner of their performance. One manifestation of this imbalance is the widespread use of 'acting rightly' and 'acting wrongly' to refer to the types of act in question and not behavior conceived in terms of (at least) act-type *and* manner. This is illustrated in the termination case (and will be explained in detail in Part I). The manager might clearly do the right thing in terminating, but fail to do it *rightly* because of a hostile or offensive manner in communicating the decision. *By* doing the right thing, Fred acts rightly at the level of deeds conceived as act-types; but *in* doing the right thing in the wrong manner, he acts wrongly at the level of concrete behavior. Morally, his conduct is mixed.

Moral philosophers have given far more consideration to the motivation of action than to its manner of performance. Where the literature of ethics has addressed the moral importance of motivation, it has often inadequately dealt with certain of the issues raised by motivating reasons as elements in moral conduct. Chapter 2 partly fills this gap. How motivation affects manner of action is suggested by the case of Fred and Jesse. How manner of action is to be conceived and why the agent is morally responsible for it are related topics that need philosophical discussion and are explored in Chapter 3.

It should be clear by now that my approach to ethics is informed by a theory of action. That theory has been developed in many of my books and papers, but a major application here is taking the *agential perspective* as mainly future-directed. Action has a broadly teleological structure: we act in order to bring things about. This view has been prominent since Aristotle's *Nicomachean Ethics* and underlies the naturalness of consequentialist ethical theories – though Aristotle's ethics is one indication that consequentialism as usually understood, and as epitomized in classical utilitarianism, is not a necessary commitment of integrating a teleological perspective into an ethical theory. Not everything we bring about is something caused by what we do (for reasons that will be brought out especially in Chapters 11 and 12), and not every concern of ethics is with our *doings*. On this point, the Kantian tradition reflects the concern, prominent in Aristotle, Aquinas, and many contemporary philosophers, with the "moral worth" of our actions – clarified in Chapter 2 – and the constitution of our character. Here ethics focuses mainly on our past or present action. It remains true, however, that the point of view of practical reason is future-directed – governed by standards *to be realized*.

From the point of view of action theory, our basic practical commitments are represented by intentions, and intentions are future-directed. Even intending to do what I am "now" doing is directed toward a "present" understood as moving into the future. Our morally most important intentions have objects that include the distant future as well as our next steps, and I find it fruitful to posit, for at least rational adults, a kind of *vital itinerary*: its destinations are one's intended future actions and activities. An itinerary will not get us to its destinations apart from a map, and here practical reason depends on theoretical reason – particularly on perception – as basic in giving us a map of our world. That map is comprised mainly of beliefs, especially those that reflect what we learn from perception and from inferences that draw on its deliverances. Rational action is both belief-guided by certain elements on our map and end-directed toward choice-worthy destinations on our itinerary.

Moral conduct depends on theoretical reason – and especially on perception as a source of rational belief – for a conception of the range of good itineraries in human life. It also depends on theoretical reason for the understanding, even the identifiability, of choiceworthy destinations, and on a conception of the good to guide selecting those destinations. In these matters, ethical theory depends on moral epistemology, the main focus of Chapters 7 and 8. It also depends on certain metaphysical ideas. I have in mind the widely accepted view that normative properties, including both deontic ones such as obligatoriness and axiological ones like intrinsic value, depend on, indeed are grounded in, "descriptive" properties, roughly the kind that, in the basic cases, are accessible to perception. This view is illustrated and defended in Part III, which concerns both the epistemology and the ontology of moral and other normative properties. The overall work of the book, then, represents ethics from the point of view of the theory of action, the epistemology of normative principles, the metaphysics of normative properties, and the value of human experiences.

At various points I draw on major works in these fields. Some ideas of Aristotle, Kant, Mill, Sidgwick, Moore, and Ross are considered at various points. There is some detailed discussion of Kant in Chapter 2, and Chapter 4 makes extensive connections with Ross and, in some cases, revises and extends his ethical view. Ross is easily among the leading intuitionists in moral philosophy, and *The Right and the Good* (1930) is increasingly considered among the most important general works in ethics of the twentieth century.

The outline is this. I begin, in Part I, with a short account of action as it is best understood from the point of view of ethics and will proceed to an account of motivation and its place in determining the moral worth of actions and to an explanation of the moral significance of manners of action.[1] Given the action-theoretic account of conduct and its constituent elements of act-type, motivation, and manner, Part II presents a set of intuitively plausible moral principles. These commonsense standards of action are in a certain way basic, and they are clarified by narrative examples and shown to play a constitutive role in moral conduct. Chapters 4 and 5 formulate and illustrate a common core of moral principles, and Chapter 6 explores how a life in which they are internalized may be structured. Readers who know Aristotle, Kant, utilitarianism (especially in Mill and Sidgwick), and Ross will find many elements of their ethics reflected – and sometimes refined or replaced – by what I consider preferable formulations.

Part III defends a realist and moderately rationalist view of morality,[2] and clarifies the epistemological and metaphysical status of the principles. Chapter 7 outlines a conception of our knowledge of the kinds of moral principles considered in Part II,

1 Important aspects of the action theory I bring to bear trace to my *Action, Intention, and Reason* (1993a) and *Practical Reasoning and Ethical Decision* (2006b), which connects my account of action with normative ethics and moral psychology. The account is extended in "The Practical Authority of Normative Beliefs" (2013c). The kind of intellectualism I resist, especially in moral psychology but also in epistemology, is described and assessed in my (2017a).

2 The epistemology in question is presented in (among other works), *The Structure of Justification* (1993c), *The Architecture of Reason* (2001b), and *The Good in the Right* (2004).

with examples of their role in inference and moral discourse. Chapter 8 presents a theory of moral perception and explores the possibility of moral knowledge and justification for singular moral judgments. With this epistemological framework in view, Chapter 9 presents a case for a moral realism that supports both the epistemology of the book and the normative ethics of Part II. That chapter clarifies the explanatory power of moral statements and shows how it depends on their relation to natural facts but does not require the reducibility of moral properties to natural properties.

Part IV both supports and builds on the earlier parts. Chapter 10 offers an account of the normative basis of reasons for action. In that light, Chapter 11 frames a comprehensive account of intrinsic value that extends to moral value as a distinct kind. The account is three-dimensional: it introduces a kind of non-instrumental value that differs from intrinsic value as best conceived but, unlike instrumental value, is a source of *non*-instrumental reasons for action. The overall contribution of the book is a comprehensive pluralist ethical theory that has advantages over any of the major kinds of theory we know in the traditions of virtue ethics, Kantian deontology, and utilitarianism. The theory reflects significant merits of all of those but is not a version of any of them. It also owes much to the intuitionist tradition, but it is more systematic and more comprehensive than any intuitionistic ethics so far developed. It preserves the distinction between deontological and consequentialist theories, but it transcends the dichotomy between them. It does not eliminate their important differences but shows that these have neither the magnitude sometimes claimed nor bar agreement on major normative standards.

Part I

Dimensions of Moral Conduct

1   Action and the Will

It is natural to think that what morality mainly requires of us is to do the right things and avoid doing the wrong ones. The "things" we ought to do are actions. But actions are not merely things we do. A plausible view is that actions (as actual events expressing agency) are doings that have a description under which they are intentional. When people act, they do something; and if what they do is not mere bodily movement of the kind illustrated by snoring while asleep, it is (with a few possible exceptions) action. To see how actions should be conceived, we should clarify not only what actions are, but how and to what extent they are under our control; how they are understandable in terms of our system of beliefs, desires, and intentions; and the manners in which they may be performed.

1   Action as a Kind of Doing

Usually, asking what someone did presupposes that the doing was an action, but snoring is behavior that is also something a person does, yet isn't action. It could be cited by a light-sleeping host in answering 'What did he do that so annoyed you?' But snoring is not a straightforward example of action. Snoring of a kind *can* be action. An actor can do it in a sleeping scene. In any case, not all doings are actions. Sneezing can occur during a formal lecture and might be described as what someone did that explains the visible annoyance of the speaker. Unlike snoring, however, sneezing is a kind of doing that cannot be intentional: even if an actor impeccably mimics sneezing, the behavior is not genuine sneezing. Still, unlike knee reflexes, some sneezes are not mere movement. Unlike certain reflexes, sneezing, though not action, may be suppressible with effort – thus *negatively voluntary* and in that way under the control of the will.

What, then, distinguishes actions from doings that do not count as actions? If we consider something a person does an action, we presuppose some answer to 'Why did you do that?' where we can offer a description of the doing under which it is voluntary and, at least normally, may intelligibly be viewed as intentional.[1] If it is voluntary, as is spontaneously stretching an arm upon waking, it is under the control of the motivational system (and normally suppressible at will), and we can ask why the agent did it. One answer is 'I just felt like it'. Here one might call it done "on impulse" but not intentional (though also not *un*intentional, as with stumbling). One might also call it voluntary and incidental rather than purposive – it is normally no part of any plan or project.

It may be debatable whether we should consider such voluntary doings intentional, but we may surely call them actions as opposed to mere movements or, especially, reflexes. It is important that we see voluntary doings as under the agent's control, since this makes clear that the agent may be held morally responsible, prospectively or retrospectively, for doing the things in question. Compare these two cases. I am sitting on a stone wall above a picnic table with a pitcher of juice just close enough so that, if I impulsively swing my foot forward I will knock it over. In

---

1 Conceiving actions as doings to which a kind of why-question applies seems central for Elizabeth Anscombe (1963). My conception of intentional action is similar in representing action as explainable in a certain way (detailed in Chapter 10), but is not built around such questions. The suggested intentionalistic view does not entail that every *doing* has a description under which it is intentional. As noted in the text, snoring need not, and sneezing cannot, have one: a "sneeze" that is intentional stands to the doing-type much as a wink stands to a blink. Mere doings may be indirectly but not directly voluntary, though they can be under direct negative voluntary control, as with suppressing a sneeze. On both those counts, we may be morally responsible for them. For Goldman (1970: 18–19), all actions of the most basic kind are intentional.

one case, I haphazardly do this while excitedly telling a joke. In another, a prankster hits my knee with a hammer just so as to make the knee reflex produce the same motion. My hosts may count me careless in the first case but not in the second. There the prankster is blameworthy for the spill. Much that we are responsible for is voluntary but not intentional. This includes many of the manners in which we intentionally do things, as the Introduction illustrates with Fred and Jesse.

What we have seen regarding doings suggests that even if there are actions that do not have a description under which they are intentional, it is at least characteristic of action to be rooted in intentionality as an element in the psychological structure of the agent and often indicative of moral character. The point is important for ethics. If action were not generally rooted in intentionality, most typically in intentions but also in desires, emotions, and hopes, it would be difficult to appreciate the adage, "Actions speak louder than words." As that adage reminds us, although self-descriptions may tell us much about someone's motivation and character, a pattern of deeds (including speaking, of course) very often more reliably indicates intentions and plans. Intention not only underlies virtually all our actions; it also embodies motivation of a kind that represents some aspect of the will. Good will has great moral importance, and it is at least largely constituted by governing, generally long-standing altruistic intentions.

Many intentional actions are expressions of a "prior intention," an intention to do some deed before actually doing it. But not every intentional action occurs in this way. It is perhaps easiest to see this when the agent has only a slight hope of success, but aims at something and succeeds. Someone who shoots at a threatening drone with only a slim hope of hitting it may, upon succeeding, intentionally hit it.[2] More common are cases in which one acts instantly in order to prevent something, say blocks a running child who is about to fall down the stairs. One might here posit

2 This is argued in my (1973) and supported further in my (1986).

an intention *in* action, and that is possible without the existence of the intention *prior* to the action. What is crucial for a doing to be intentional is its explainability as something the agent does on the basis of a twofold psychological state: wanting to bring about something and having an appropriate belief guiding the action appropriately toward that end.[3]

2   Act-Types and Act-Tokens

So far, action has been characterized in a way that indicates its moral importance as connected with intention in a way that, partly by representing the agent's will, manifests good or bad character. To understand action sufficiently for moral theory, it is also essential to keep track of two distinctions: one between act-types and act-tokens, the other between basic and non-basic actions. The latter distinction presupposes the former, and I begin with types and tokens.

In typing, I am acting. I'm doing something in time – in space too, if the action is physical. I could have typed the same letters in the same way earlier, and others can also type them. My typing the letter *t*, here and now, is a concrete event; but there is also the act property, *typing the letter t*. In typing a *t* for illustration, I intended to type a *t*. *What* I intended, the content of my intention, was *typing a letter t* (also expressible as 'to type a *t*'). A different concrete doing, however – a different *act-token* – would have fulfilled the intention. One agent can do the "same thing" – token the same act-type – at different times; and multiple agents can do the same thing simultaneously or at different times.

Moral principles characteristically call on us to *do* things, say keep our promises. These principles implicitly refer to act-types and are internalized only when we form stable intentions

---

3 There are myriad complexities besetting the analysis of action. The conception of action sketched here is akin to Anscombe's in (1963), Davidson's in (1963), and Goldman's in (1970); and I have developed and defended my conception in detail in (1986) and later works. Related work bearing on the issue is von Wright (1971), McCann (1998), Ginet (1990), Tuomela (1995), and especially for discussion of intention in relation to planning, Bratman (2018).

regarding the appropriate types. Stable intentions are sometimes created by or expressed in vows, promises, or resolutions, to do the things in question. Our intentions to do things are *type-directed* and *token-realized*. Full-scale appraisal of actions performed by actual people must take account of act-tokens – not just what type of thing we do but our *doing* of things. We can do the right thing (token the right act-type) for the wrong reason, at the wrong time, or in other ways that incur criticism. To be sure, if we say someone did a good deed, e.g. putting out a brush fire, we would normally presuppose that both the type and the token were morally appropriate. That twofold presupposition shows not that the deed we refer to is not a type but rather that the *doing* of the deed instantiates – tokens – an act-type appropriately good in the circumstances.

3   Basic Action, Levels of Action, and Voluntariness

The second distinction, between basic and non-basic actions, can now be clarified. Consider the point that one types a *t* by moving a finger but (normally) does not move a finger by doing anything else. We do it *at will*, in the sense that it is directly voluntary, by contrast with typing a *t*, which is indirectly voluntary, done by moving a finger. Here distinguishing the directly from the indirectly voluntary becomes crucial.

The voluntariness of act-types is doubly relative: to both agents and times. What is voluntarily done by one person may be involuntarily done by another. The voluntariness of act-tokens, by contrast, is fixed as to both agent and times. My signing a check is by me and at a definite time. In broad terms, to indicate what *kind* of act-type can be voluntarily tokened (instantiated) by an agent *S*, "directly" or, in more common terminology, *at will*, we need a characterization like this: (1) an act-type, *A*, is directly voluntary for an agent, *S*, at time, *t*, if and only if, at *t*, *S can A* at will, i.e., without *A*-ing *by* instantiating any other act-type (can *A basically*, in one sense). This formulation concerns agential potentiality. By contrast, direct voluntariness may also character- ize actual behavior – act-tokens. Thus (2) *A*-ing, at *t*, is directly voluntarily *performed* (instantiated) by *S* if and only if, at *t*, *S* *A*-s at will.[4] We normally can do at will things like moving a finger "just because we feel like it," *and* without doing something else by which we do it.

In the example of extinguishing a fire by using a hose, 'by' is instrumental in a causal sense. But there are other by-relations, including many in which one violates a standard. A wrong might be done by lying or by hitting. This relation between lying and doing a kind of wrong is constitutive, not instrumental. That kind of wrong might be said to be constituted, rather than caused, by lying (a distinction that will be important in Chapters 11 and 12). Another constitutive use of 'by' is non-moral: the pleasure of playing a piano piece is partly constituted by playing it, but the relation is not moral, pleasure is not an action, and playing it is not an instrumental means to that distinctive pleasure. The playing is essential to the pleasure of playing, whereas extinguishing a fire is possible by other means than firehoses. Various kinds of constitutive relation are considered in Chapters 2 and 3, but it should now be clear enough how the by-relation is important for understanding action and relevant to ethical theory.

As to mental action, I can at will call up an image of the spruce in my backyard. This is a basic mental act for me, and the act-type is normally under my direct positive control. I can also muse to myself that a proposition (*p*) seems implausible, and I may thereby (sometimes) bring about withholding belief regarding *p*. If the withholding is achieved by my thinking about the proposition (which I can do at will), it may evoke a sense of falsehood. This

---

4 Often, 'at will' is used with the suggestion that one can do the thing readily and pretty much every time an occasion arises on which one tries. The general notion, however, allows for cases in which a basic action is difficult, say raising an injured arm. Even if one struggles and sometimes fails, the action may still be basic. Moreover, I do not take 'at will' to imply either an "act of will" or something naturally called trying. The notion is illustrated by many of the things we do in familiar unimpeded activities such as cooking, gardening, and indeed speaking. These are commonly intentional but not executions of will-ings, tryings, or even intentions formed prior to the actions in question.

case illustrates indirect negative control. Control also has degrees: I can normally raise an arm easily and at will; whether I can produce withholding a proposition by considering it critically varies greatly with (among other things) the content of the proposition.

These notions of control of our actions are important in ethics for a number of reasons. First, we normally cannot even intend to do what we believe we lack the power to do and thus conceive as not under our control. Second, we normally do not intend, or at least do not *plan*, to do something when we cannot see or presuppose that we can do it either at will or *by* doing something at will. (We may presuppose this simply by presupposing that we know how to do it.) Third, we are normally either not morally blameworthy or are less blameworthy than otherwise for not doing something when we lacked at least indirect negative control over it. Fourth, moral rules and moral imperatives must be understood to apply to types of acts that can be intended by those who are to be guided by those rules and imperatives. What you cannot intend to do you cannot put on your itinerary.

Philosophers differ regarding the types of acts we can perform basically ("at will"). On one view, all we ever do is move our bodies; the rest is up to nature. On a Cartesian view, one might say instead that all we ever do is move our wills; the rest is up to nature.[5] Fortunately, the distinction between basic and non-basic action is neutral with respect to the difference between physicalistic (say neurophysiological) and mentalistic (say Cartesian) views of the category of basic human actions. But ethics partly concerns activities of mind, particularly those that manifest motivation and cognition or influence the role of either of these in moral character and intention-formation. For ethics, then, our

---

5 Davidson (1971/1980: 59) has expressed the physicalist view. The mentalist view is certainly the view of C. I. Lewis: "Every governed act begins as a mental process ... The commitment [to act] is that inscrutable fiat of the will, the 'oomph' of initiation, which terminates the mental part and is the bridge to the physical part of the act" (1955: 43). "An action ... is an activity of willing some change (Pritchard, 1949: 193). Cf. Mele (1997), which presents papers exploring basic action and does so in his informative introduction to them.

mental lives are immensely important. A moral directive may concern mental life and call for mental action. The Bible has widely known examples. Take 'Thou shall not covet' (Exodus 20; Deuteronomy 5). This seems directed toward the internal dimension of lust – though its external manifestation in trying to get the desired thing is implicitly also proscribed. Clearly, planning to fulfill a lustful desire, even if the planning is only in silent premeditation, is prohibited. Here direct negative control is presupposed: one can – by and large – at will prevent one's planning such things. If at some point the prospect assails one and is like a roar one cannot quiet, the only resort may be to turn to something like vigorously playing an instrument to drown out the offending voice. This would illustrate indirect voluntary control.

It is often held (plausibly) that we cannot produce desires at will, by contrast with, say, fasting all day, which produces desire *by* doing something else. This contrast shows how the scope and power of the will is ethically important. Can we, at will or even by some technique, create morally good desires in ourselves? And, when a selfish desire is served by doing something also obligatory, can we, at will, do the deed only *for* that moral reason? Kant among many others, thought we cannot do this at will but also that actions *not* done for morally appropriate reasons lack moral creditworthiness. This issue will be examined in Chapter 2, but a prior question is how to conceive *what* we are obligated to do in the first place.

4   Obligations as Potential Contents of Intentions

The case of lust shows not only that the mental realm is within the reach of moral directives, but also that they presuppose our having a kind of regulatory control of our actions. The control may, as we've seen, be indirect and imperfect, but our having it represents our voluntary ability to regulate our conduct. Such control is a power of will. The Biblical example illustrates an important point: that obligations – whether expressed in principles, imperatives, or other directives – are, in content – act-types, including activity-types. The content of obligation is determined by the specified act-type(s): schematically, the obligation is *to A*, where '*A*' represents action (including activity); and the type is represented as *to be instantiated* (though not necessarily in those terms, or even subvocally).

This view does not entail that act-tokens cannot be obligatory in a derivative sense. An act-token, such as saying 'yes' if asked to do a job, may (especially in retrospect) loosely be called obligatory, but only by virtue of its tokening some obligatory type, such as agreeing to do a job. Tokens, like types, are individuated very finely. Even if one promised to say 'yes' at 10 a.m., in English, and at a certain volume, so long as the specification is not so comprehensive as to cover every possible way in which concrete acts may vary, more than one token can fulfill the obligation. One can do it in writing, in speech, in song, etc. The content of moral obligations is not essentially tied to particular tokens.

Do exceptions occur where an intention is *de re*, as when it is directed partly toward a particular? I can intend *a friend* to convey a message or intend my joke to amuse Rosaria. There is no doubt that such intentions concern something concrete. But surely their content is still a type, say *to ask her son to convey the message*. The content of both intentions is a type, though in the second it is a type "embodying" a singular reference to a person. To be sure, unbeknownst to me, Rosaria may no longer exist, but I leave aside whether this must in every case make a difference in the content (as opposed to reference) of the intention. The important point for ethics here is that if the content of either intention corresponds to that of an obligation, its content is best construed as an act-type.

———

Moral principles, then, and for similar reasons, statements of specific moral obligations, express requirements *to do* – to instantiate an act-type. Our assertions of obligation normally presuppose that the agent(s) in question can do the obligatory deed. Actual deeds, such as saying 'yes', may be considered obligatory in virtue of the agent's having an obligation to token the obligatory act-type they instantiate. Obligation, however, is far from the only morally important property we must consider. Suppose I say 'yes' to doing something, not because I promised to (which I did) when asked to do a favor, but entirely for a profit motive. This is fulfillment of an obligation for the wrong reason – or anyway not a moral one. It fulfills the letter but not the spirit of morality. It may be hypocritical, but it may also fail to be moral even where the promissory obligation is felt but, given what the agent really cares about in assenting, not motivating. What is required to act morally in the fullest sense of that phrase is a matter of great complexity. This will be illustrated in a number of ways in Chapter 5. A prior task is to explore what it is not just to do something that is obligatory, but to do it on a basis that makes our doing it morally creditworthy. This brings us to Chapter 2.

2   Moral Worth

The title of this chapter may call to mind Kant's view that actions not performed "from duty" have no moral worth. Much can be said about exactly how he meant this. On the face of it, the view seems paradoxical: a risky rescue of a child from a fire might be right, even admirable, but (for Kant) would have no moral worth if done just to impress the mother. If there is paradox here, it is reduced in the light of what has emerged so far. Whatever moral worth is in the Kantian sense, it is a property not of act-types but of act-tokens. A type of act, such as keeping my promise to say 'yes' to a request, is not necessarily instantiated "from" any specific motivation. An act-token (as intentional) is motivated by some specific element(s), even when agents cannot tell what has motivated them. A mere doing, such as "automatically" moving one's feet under a table, might occur without motivation and be neither intentional nor unintentional; but normal fulfillments of the obligations expressed in moral principles are intentional.[1] If, however, moral worth is a property of

---

1 Why just normal fulfillments? I could fulfill an obligation to pay a bill by unintentionally signing a check in practicing my signature. Someone knowing the habit could deftly slip a check under my pen in just the right way to get my signature. Moreover, the merely non-intentional need not be unintentional. I might increase someone's reading light by turning on a ceiling light as I leave a room, though my aim is only lighting my way. Increasing the reading light may be foreseen but not intentional or, like accidentally flipping the switch, *un*intentional.

act-tokens, how are we to account for the apparent fact that there are morally good deeds understood as act-types?

1   The Objects of Moral Worth

Given the possible diversity of usage of 'moral worth', the wisest course here is to take Kant's deservedly insightful discussion of moral worth to be so well known that we should use some other term to account for the different though closely related concept that concerned both Kant and other moral philosophers from Aristotle to many contemporaries.[2] I refer to *being creditworthy*, a positive status roughly equivalent to meriting a positive assessment. This applies primarily to actions and, largely on that basis, to persons, whereas 'moral worth' is at best potentially misleading applied to persons. Ethical appraisal should be guided by an understanding of when concrete actions are or are not morally creditworthy, say in being praiseworthy or in some other way positively reflecting the agent's character.

We also need a way to understand how moral education and moral life should be structured to elicit not just our doing the right things but also our doing them for reasons that are, on the one hand, morally appropriate and bespeak morally good elements of character and, on the other hand, support confidence in our future conduct. This makes kind and degree of our control of our actions crucial for a full-scale ethics.

As a matter of normal English, there is no question that regardless of your motivation, you may be said to do a morally good deed in rectifying an unfair distribution of important resources, say medical supplies to the needy. We may also ask someone to do a good deed of this (distributively just) kind in the future. This is a request to do something of the indicated type. It does not precisely indicate a highly specific act-type or call for any particular motivation. People unfamiliar with the literature of ethics might even call

---

2 For Kant's best known statement of his view see Section 1 of the *Groundwork* (1785/1997). A useful comparison is Book 2 of Aristotle's *Nicomachean Ethics*, esp. 1105a–1107a26.

such action – which should, after all, be encouraged – morally praiseworthy quite apart from what motivates it. If, however, rectifying an injustice is motivated wholly by a desire for promotion, many of us would not call it morally praiseworthy, and Kant would deny that the action (the act-token) has moral worth. The best thing to say is probably that the agent did a good deed, but for a reason that prevents the doing (tokening) of it from being (morally) creditworthy.

The term 'creditworthy' is doubly useful because, though applicable to particular actions, it also applies to the agent, who may be creditworthy for the act-token in question even given a mistake in considering the act in question a good deed. Suppose a physician makes a very well justified estimate of a medicine's good effect but is mistaken and thereby delays a patient's recovery. The physician's moral record may or may not be improved by such action. But as a *person*, such an agent might still merit some moral credit.

If, as argued in Chapter 1, the contents of (action-directed) intentions are act-types, some defenders of Kant might hold that the scope of intentions can include a purposive element, say a reason for the intended act.[3] If it can, then even if moral creditworthiness is a property of tokens, the contents of motivational element(s) making moral creditworthiness possible might be thought to figure in the act-type the agent is obligated to

---

3 Mary Glover argued for a similar view in (1938). My (2015b) appraises her case, and I here show why we need not attribute the view to Kant. More recently, Korsgaard has formulated the conception of action I reject (as does Ross): taking "the basic form of a Kantian maxim" to be "I will do act-A in order to promote end-E," she says that if one dances for the joy of dancing (which I consider a double-barrelled behavioral description), "*dancing* is the *act*, and *dancing for the sheer joy of dancing* is the *action* ... it is the action that is the object of choice." See her "Acting for a Reason" (2008: 219). Cf. Nelkin: "On the Kantian picture, a choice of maxim is a choice to prefer a particular action for particular reasons in particular circumstances" (2011: 88), which leaves open what belongs in the content of *S*'s relevant intentions. For a contrasting treatment that takes account of Ross's view, see Stratton-Lake (2000), chs. 3–5. Even if Kant is read as committed to the view that there are duties to act from duty, he need not have taken all duties to have that form. Indeed, how can we know our duty is to *A*-from-duty-to-*A* if we lack a prior conception of duty to *A*?

perform. To understand this odd view, consider intentions whose objects appear to be acts purposively described. Suppose I promise to help Bernie organize his library in May and by then he inherits a fortune and does not need my help. Asked why I still intend to take the trouble now that Bernie can hire someone to help, I might say: 'I intend to help him because I promised to'. This is familiar phrasing, but it is ambiguous in a way that prevents assuming that it expresses the kind of view in question. It might mean roughly (1) 'The reason why I intend to help him is that I promised to' – an explanatory statement we readily understand – or (2) the self-ascription 'I intend this: to help-him-because-I-promised-to', where the hyphenated element ostensibly specifies the *content* of the intention and not *why one has it*.

Can intentions have such apparently motivational content? Suppose I intend to assist Camilla in planting a vegetable garden. Asked what I will do, I might reply: 'Whatever she needs me to do'. Isn't this an intention with the content, *to do what she asks when and because she asks it*? The case is probably best seen as one of conditioned intention: what I intend is to do what she asks *when* she asks it. I presuppose that her asking – the triggering condition – will occur, but my intention, though higher order in the sense that the act-types eligible for me are to be determined by a future request, contain nothing concerning *why* I will do whatever this is. Granted I may also *presuppose* that I will be acting for reasons of, say, fidelity to my word. But this does not show that I have an intention with the content, to-do-her-bidding-from-fidelity-to-my-promise. Would anyone think that I did not do what I promised to do (or never intended to do it) if it turned out that when the time came, I was offered such a great reward for assisting her that getting it dominated my motivation and made me act mainly from self-interest: in order to get the reward? Surely I still kept the promise. As before, we must distinguish the contentual question of what is intended from the motivational question of why the agent intends that or, in realizing the intention, does the intended deed.

There is a sound point that expresses part of what underlies the motivational-content view. I can intend, subjunctively, *that* my helping be explainable by my promising. But this is no ordinary intention. It is not action-directed and not realizable at will: the explainability of my future action by my promising is not an action, though in principle I can intend to do something that will *bring about* a future action's being thus explainable. I might, then, have indirect control over whether I achieve this double goal: good-deed-for-good-reason. The supposed intention in question, however – to-do-her-bidding-from-fidelity-to-my-promise – is sometimes conceived as act-directed. But the subjunctive that-clauses in question specify no act-type and indicate no intention to do anything determinate. A subjunctive intention might reflect a plan to do something that *causes* that explanation-relation to hold. In principle, I could, e.g., get my brain manipulated to guarantee this effect. But subjunctive intentions (which will be considered further in Chapter 6) are motivational place-holders for ordinary act-directed intentions.

Recognition of subjunctive intentions is important both for action theory in general and for appraising agents. These range only indirectly over acts and commonly are not realized at will, but they are important for understanding how we realize ideals and, especially, virtues. Nonetheless, the possibility of intending that (e.g.) one's promise be kept solely from a sense of obligation does not answer the question whether the kind of thing one wants to bring about, '*A*-ing for *R*', where *A* is an action (or activity) and 'for *R*' indicates an explaining reason, reports an act or activity. Surely this phrase, like '*A*-ing from a sense of duty', is a double-barrelled report. It indicates items in two very different categories: an action, which is an event, and a reason as a motivational element (e.g. resolution to fulfill my duty), which is not an event but a disposi-tional psychological property that does not entail any event. The importance of this difference will shortly be evident.

2 Reasons, Intentions, and Morally Significant Act-Descriptions

One might think that 'keeping a promise from a sense of obliga-tion' does simply report a kind of action, since knowing a reason for which someone A-s may provide a different description of A-ing, as with 'killing for money', which invites describing the action as murder. Granted, a hired killer may be said to intend to murder someone. But surely what is basically intended (if there is a definite plan) is one or another *kind* of killing. What the killer intends is in any case not a compound behavior-type such as shooting-for-money. The killer may believe that the intended shooting will *be* for money, but (as we'll see) this does not entail an "intention" to-kill-for-money. The term 'murder', as used in statements of the form $\langle S$ murdered $X\rangle$, does not specify (though it presupposes) any lethal act-type, such as shooting, much less *the* lethal act-type that the murderer tokens.

It is true and important that knowing a reason for an action or an intention underlying it may yield a different description of the action, say of a killing. Moreover, 'murder' (like various other terms) restricts the range of eligible reasons for the action designated. They must, e.g., in some way imply intentionality – and with murder, the action must be for some non-self-defensive purpose. A general caution here is that we must avoid letting the difference between *what* is done (e.g. killing) and *why* it is done be obscured by our desire to view ourselves as able to act for the right kinds of reasons (or our preferred kind). If 'murder' were not complex in bringing both elements – act-type and eligible range of explaining factors – into play, juries might have less difficulty in arriving at verdicts. The difference between what is done and why it is done may also be obscured by the sound point that an act-token may be given different descriptions when the context makes it desirable to refer to it so as to indicate for what sort of reason it is performed – as where a killing should be described as a murder to avoid any thought that it is, say, accidental.

Circumstances may also come into behavior-descriptions, as with 'assassinate', but given our often being able to control in what circumstances we act, this does not present the challenge comparable to trying to understand how one might intend (e.g.) to kill-from-a-desire-for-revenge. The desired *place* for doing a deed can clearly figure in the content of an intention to prefer it, and without raising the problems we shall soon see. It is also true that we may properly *say* we intend to A for R (or to bring about some event for a particular reason), where this is supplying two related kinds of information. But that duality should in most cases be represented as already illustrated: expressing an intention to A *and* an explanation of why one has it is one thing; putting a motivational explanation of A-ing into the very content of intention to A is quite another. Note that we may also say such things as that we intend *to be* attentive listeners, and this plainly does not imply that 'being an attentive listener' designates action. It is elliptical and leaves open how we intend to bring about the desired condition. We cannot understand either intention or action by assuming that every grammatical completion of 'S intends' expresses an act-type.

This point should be still clearer if we ask whether complex behavior such as keeping-a-promise-from-a sense-of-duty, even *can* have a description under which it is intentional. There is no question that such phrases indicate *behavior-types*. Nor is there reason to doubt that a morally self-conscious person may say 'I know it's in my interest to keep my promise to pay the bill, but I intend to keep it *not* from self-interest but from obligation (as a fulfillment of duty, to live up to my promise, or the like). One point I could be making here is that if, at the time to act, I feel self-interest intruding, I will wait for a better occasion.

It is also possible for some agents to believe, regarding something they ought to do, that they will do it *from* obligation or, say, *because* they promised to. Indeed, tending to believe such things seems normal for conscientious agents keeping promises. But this does not support the motivational-content view of intention. Compare intending to turn on a radio when one knows it's time for a newscast. If the question arises why one will be turning on a temperamental radio, one would normally believe – if the matter comes up at all – that one will be doing it in order to hear the newscast. But this is not a belief one *need* form just to act in the normal way by turning it on when noticing the time for the newscast. That may be purely habitual. In any case, forming the intention does not imply the further cognitive element, taking the act to be one of (say) turning-on-the-radio-from-a-desire-for-news.

Do normal agents even know how to bring about 'turning-on-the-radio-from-a-desire-for-news except by just turning on the radio in the normal way *when* they want to hear news? If there is a competing reason to turn it on – say to annoy someone intently reading – I can imagine self-manipulation to be sure I'm not acting from that motive. This, however, would simply be a case of doing something else – trying to *cause* myself to avoid acting for a bad reason. There is no need to deny that one can sometimes achieve that, but I have no idea how to find a way to be at all sure of success, and success would in any event not show that there is an *act*-type, A-ing-for-R.

It should be evident, then, that as important as it is why we do things, and as common as it is to believe or presuppose that we will do them for certain reasons, *what* we will do and what we intend is not of the form $\langle$to-A-from-motive-$M\rangle$. We can intend to *cause* this motivation-action complex, but it is not itself an act-type. It is, to be sure, a behavior-type, and some action-verbs – e.g. 'avenging', 'punishing', and 'favoring', imply both an (unspecified) act-type and a motive. As illustrated with the case of murder, this complicates our descriptive vocabulary, but it does not undermine the framework proposed here.

3   The Limits of Our Control Over Our Motivation in Acting

Should we make an exception for the special case of basic acts for which we have two or more reasons? Might we intend to bring about, at will, our performing them *for* one of these reasons in particular? This would indicate a power of will whose exercise would sometimes lead to acting for a creditworthy reason and thus to being morally creditworthy to that extent. It may seem here that our work would be only ruling out an unwanted influence. But can we do this at will? We can *indirectly* bring about A-ing for reason R provided that we can A *and* our only way to A is on the basis of R, as where my only reason to shake your hand is to greet you. In some contexts, it might be psychologically impossible for me to shake your hand for any other reason. But this is really bringing about A-ing for R by A-ing. At the time, there is only one reason available for A-ing, it is performed at will, and here A-ing *at all* guarantees traversing our only route to that performance.

Imagine, however, that I have a reason of self-interest *and* a promissory reason to help someone. Can I at will bring about my doing it for the promissory reason – directly harnessing that reason to the action?[4] I don't know how. I can think of my promissory reason as I act, but this does not entail that I act for that reason. Such a focus could indeed be a self-deceiver's white-wash. Suppose, however, that I could harness a motive, M, for acting, to an action and thereby make the action explainable by citing M. It does not follow that this behavior is an action.

Imagine that it is an action. Then, given the desirability of doing, for an appropriate reason, what we ought to do, one might think that we not only have primary obligations to do the right deeds but also a secondary obligation to do-the-right-deeds-for-appropriate-reasons. In that case, we can not only intend to do such complex things but, surely, can do them intentionally, hence for some reason. If we want our actions to be morally creditworthy – say, to be done in order to fulfill our moral obligations (as opposed to just avoiding censure by a Kantian observer), then A-ing-for-R should be no exception. We should be able to be obligated, and so able to intend, a higher-order action, say to A-*for*-R-*for*-R_2, where R_2 is a second-order reason, for instance: to satisfy-my-

---

4 Kant would not claim this: "I ... admit that even most of our actions are in conformity with duty; but if we look more closely at the intentions and aspirations in them we everywhere come upon the dear self ... and [in such cases] it is on this that their purpose is based, not ... duty" (1785/1997: 20). Granted, he spoke as if we had a duty to act-from-duty, but not in a way that permits taking him to posit *direct* obligations to bring about at will acting "from duty." I have explored limitations in our direct control in a number of works, including ch. 3 of my (2006b). My view is more sympathetic to Kant's than is Ross's, but Ross makes valuable points supporting my view – particularly on the content of duty – in (1930: 4–6) and (1939), esp. 114–121. He noted that if a duty to A [say to pay a debt] is to-A-from-duty, then the moral worth of *that* "act" demands that one A-from-duty, *from* duty.

Kantian-father-by-doing-*from-duty*-a-lucrative-service-from-a-motive-of-duty-rather-than-profit. But this complex behavior, if an action, could *also* be performed for an appropriate reason or not. Then it, in turn, is morally creditworthy only if "performed" *for* an appropriate reason. On the plausible assumption that intentional actions are actions for reasons, we now encounter either an infinite regress – assuming that "actions" of the form ⟨*A*-ing-for-*R*⟩ are intentional – or, for agents with finite minds, a point at which there is an action that is for a reason but not intentional. Surely these are consequences we should not be committed to if there is no reason to think that we can, at will, perform actions properly described as instances of *A*-ing-for-*R*.

So far, I've been assuming the intelligibility of taking '*A*-ing-for-*R*' to be an action-report and arguing that, on plausible assumptions, so construing it leads to a regress. We should now ask whether, quite apart from regressive implications, the presumed kind of intending, namely to *A*-for-*R*, even makes good sense. As indicated already, I can resolutely say to myself, 'I will do this not for money but solely in order to keep my promise'. But it does not follow that I intend this complex behavior or, if I do, that what I intend is an action. Perhaps I might intend (subjunctively) *that* my doing this be solely in order to keep my promise. Perhaps I can get my brain manipulated to justify expecting that I *will* do the deed for the preferred reason. But expectable behavior is not thereby intendable; and intending to *cause* oneself to *A* for *R* does not require having an intention whose content is to-*A*-for-*R*.

A quite different way to see that motivation should not be absorbed into descriptions of action is to consider how questions figure in individuation: in determining what counts as a single action rather than two or more different ones. The normal way to determine what single action an agent performed (in a context that limits options) is to ask 'What did *S* (the agent) *do*?' (There might be more than one relevant doing). It is significant that answering '*What* did *S* do?', leaves open importantly different answers to motivational questions, say '*Why* did *S* do that?' Clearly, an item cited as answering the former question should not normally be identified with an item cited as answering the latter. This is especially evident where the answers specify entities in different ontological categories, here actions, which are events, and desires, which are not events but dispositional in character. 'What did S do?' is not directly and specifically answered by 'S A-ed for R'. In the context of a courtroom, for instance, a judge might respond: I didn't ask *why* S did it; just tell us whether S hit her. If A-ing for R is an action, then what S does in performing it is constituted by both an event, a doing, and a dispositional element (such as a desire) that explains why S did it, thus by *some* relation to a causal basis. This is a categorially mixed type; *A-ing for R* places such complex behavior outside the category of doings: tokening this behavior-type takes *both* a doing and a realization of an explanatory condition for that doing.

Perhaps one source of confusion here is that in calling something S did an action, one presupposes that there *is* some intentionalistic explanation, thus that there *is* a mixed behavior-type, say defrauding from greed, which both reports and partially explains action. But far from entailing that act-tokens are constituted in part by what explains them, this point surely confirms that the constitution of those concrete actions leaves *open* what explains them. Similarly, 'For what reason did S A?' is properly answered by 'For R' – that S A-ed is presupposed, and various reasons are eligible. Such erotetic (question-theoretic) individuation is important: When, in the way illustrated, a statement constitutes a proper and direct answer to one question and not to a second, and vice-versa, this strongly suggests that the two statements report different kinds of thing. It may certainly indicate that we should not assume a statement that entails answers to both questions designates an entity of just one of the kinds, as would 'S A-ed for R' taken as a single-barrelled act-report.

4   Moral Creditworthiness in the Appraisal of Action

The view proposed here should clarify elements in Kant's ethics. But it also provides a much clearer understanding of moral obligation and moral appraisal than we would have if we allowed as obligations, and thus as contents of intention, elements of the form $\langle A$-ing for $R\rangle$ and similar motivational forms. Suppose I promise to sign a check and am thereby obligated to do so. If my obligation is also (or instead) to sign-the-check-from-duty, one cannot even tell observationally whether I have fulfilled (done) the duty – acted "in conformity with duty," in Kantian language. If my duty entails signing-from-a-motive-of-duty, we would need to know both that I have an appropriately moral motive and that it explains the action.[5] These should be separately understood.

In stressing the importance of taking obligatoriness to be a property of act-types and taking moral creditworthiness – in its main sense applicable to behavior – to belong to act-tokens, I am not suggesting that there is no behavioral term that applies to both types and tokens. Indeed, what I am developing is an overall theory of moral *conduct*, which encompasses three quite different things: act-type, motivation for acting – thus the psychological basis of act-tokens – and manner of action, thus a behavioral dimension of them. Manner is, however, specifiable at the level of types when it is an object of intention as well as at the level of tokens when it is a specific way in which they instantiate the "mannered" type. Let me illustrate.

Nothing said here in distinguishing what we do from the more complex case of acting for a reason diminishes the importance of the latter for understanding moral creditworthiness. Imagine that I know someone who rectifies an unjust distribution of medical supplies and I realize the deed is being done to facilitate a promotion. Entering the scene, I can see that the agent is (uncharacteristically) making notes that can confirm the corrected distribution and is also being sure to be noticed. This is apparently hypocritical. With, say, a nephew, I might privately say, 'Your

---

5 We can of course characterize a *person* as obligated to A, but this ascribes the property of *having* an obligation, and that is to be understood in terms of a relation between the agent and an act-type (including activity-types). What that relation is will be clarified in much of what follows, but it is uncontroversially normative in implying that in some sense one *should* fulfill the obligation.

conduct was manipulative, and if you get what you want I hope you'll live up to it'. Suppose he replies, 'I admit that I was trying to get the promotion, but I wouldn't have done the redistribution at all without thinking it was the only fair thing to do'. This response suggests a complexity we must account for. People often act for more than one reason. Where there are two or more reasons, each may have a different role in producing the concrete action to be evaluated: each may or may not be necessary and may or may not be sufficient but not necessary; they may be jointly sufficient but not individually necessary; and some reasons may be stronger than others whether necessary or sufficient or neither. How to determine creditworthiness in such cases is a matter of casuistry.

Some philosophers have thought, as Ross clearly did and Kant likely did, that the best motives to act from are of moral kinds.[6] If so, then the limitations we have seen on what we can do at will also apply to what moral good we can produce at will, even in fulfilling obligations. One could hold that moral motivation has this kind of *paramountcy*, as it might be called, and still consistently maintain that an act is morally creditworthy provided that first, it is not morally wrong (a plausible if controversial condition[7]) and, second, it has appropriately moral motivation that at least suffices to explain it. This condition is in a way stronger than the one suggested by the nephew's self-defense: that he would

---

6 Ross (1930), ch. 7, e.g. 164. For clarifying discussion of Kant on this and related points, see Stratton-Lake (2000) and Timmons (2021), e.g. sec. 5.4.

7 If the agent has good moral reason for an act that is nonetheless wrong, one could say that although the action-token is not creditworthy, either the agent is creditworthy as conscientious or, if this is not so, then since the agent tried to do something right, there is a description of the act, say 'trying to keep my promise' under which the action *is* creditworthy. Cf. Sidgwick on "formal" and "material" rightness (1907: 206–207) corresponding roughly to what is now called "subjective" vs. "objective" right. I am also using 'right' objectively. On some views of Kantian moral worth, Kant considered an action's being motivated by duty to suffice for moral worth even if it is not objectively right. See, e.g., Isserow (2020: 531). This in any case seems implicit in her pluralist view of moral worth, which is relevant to assessing the paramountcy thesis (introduced and discussed in my 2001b: 103–104).

not have done the deed without a moral reason. That allows that his moral reason was not strong enough to yield the deed without the help of non-moral considerations, whereas that reason's being sufficient implies that no non-moral consideration is necessary. But if, other things equal, one would have done the deed without a moral reason, can it be morally creditworthy?

There will be disagreement about this, and I leave open just what motivational role a morally appropriate reason must play if the deed is to be morally creditworthy. Here I find particularly interesting a case drawn from the ethics of love, which may be significantly similar to an ethics of care on the case in question. Suppose I help someone I love with a nasty task, such as cleaning a house that has been closed for a year. I might have a strong enough sense of duty to act from that alone and also strong enough love to act from that alone. If I act for both reasons, I cannot properly say just 'I'm doing it from duty'. But I also cannot say that love is my only motivation. Is the act morally creditworthy? It may be. We could say that the act is both morally and affectionally creditworthy. Affectional creditworthiness is highly consonant with moral creditworthiness but may derive from emotions independent of or unconnected with the sense of right or wrong.

It might be thought that such combined moral and affectional motivation makes the action less morally creditworthy than where (other things equal) the motive of duty is both necessary and sufficient. But consider this analogy. Several people together clear a field of poison ivy. Judy does most of the job; Karl does about a third, and Timothy does about a tenth. Judy should get most of the credit but the others should surely get some too. In a similar way, we can distinguish (as Kant could have done consistently with his overall view) between actions done *purely* from duty and those done sufficiently, mainly, or partly from it. We can then take actions to have different degrees of moral creditworthiness depending on what "proportion" of their explaining motivation is appropriately moral. This variability in proportionate influence leaves open the range of moral motives. They may or may not, for instance, embody moral concepts, say that of *obligation*. They might be, e.g., simply desires to relieve the suffering of war victims.

May agents be creditworthy for doing something wrong if they had excellent reason to believe it right and all the motivational requirements are met? This is controversial. I am assuming here that the *rightness* of an act in a set of circumstances is not relative to the agent's (in principle accessible) evidence (this will be discussed later in relation to excuses and mitigation). Creditworthiness, however, may depend on whether the agent's sense of the evidence is sufficiently reasonable. Where it is highly reasonable, the natural view is that given appropriately moral motivation, there can be a degree of creditworthiness in the doing in question.

A guiding consideration here is implicit in the ethics of belief. Assume, plausibly, that there are moral requirements – applicable to normal adults throughout their lives – that govern seeking, appraising, and cognitively responding to evidence, especially regarding consequences of action. It would seem that an agent who, in determining whether an act is permissible, meets a high standard in this moral dimension and, for good moral reasons, makes a mistake in thinking A-ing to be right, may still be significantly creditworthy in A-ing. This may be unlucky rather than uncreditworthy.

One possibility is that the creditworthiness accruing to the agent on either motivational count – moral reasons or reasons of love – is very roughly determined by two elements: first, as illustrated, their proportional causal roles as relevant moral or affectional motivating reasons in yielding the action; and second, their absolute strength. Thus, a predominant motive weights more heavily in creditworthiness than a minor one; and perhaps an absolutely very strong motive, say, of duty, counts more toward creditworthiness than it would if barely sufficient to yield the action. Perhaps, however, the absolute strength of a motive may by itself be a credit to the agent, but does not add to creditworthiness for acting on it except in relation to its role in producing or sustaining that action. One problem in appraising these views is that we apparently lack an adequate "measure" of strength. It is doubtful that we have such a measure except possibly in special cases. Desire strength might seem measurable by ascertaining how much pain a person will endure in order to satisfy the desire. But how can we measure degree of pain? Not by strength of electric shock, for people differ in how much shocks of various strengths pain them. There are other possible measures, such as self-reports. But these are fallible and differentially accurate depending partly on who is reporting. There are also other obstacles to exact measurement of motivation, but our purposes do not require pursuing this difficult empirical matter.

In some cases, we apparently do judge the strength of desires and other motivational elements. We can make sense of such morally significant phenomena as, for instance, wanting too strongly to do justice to a certain person, where this interferes with fulfilling other obligations. It would be better to speak of moral creditworthiness as roughly proportional to (or at least as rising with) the *fittingness* of the degree of moral motivation to the moral importance of the act in question.[8] Such fittingness is best understood in relation to what other actions the agent has good reason to consider moral competitors, and this, in turn, is partly a matter of the obligations of the agent and what is at stake in the context. One could not only want too strongly to do something that is right yet of minor importance, but also want too weakly to save a life one can easily save. Saving a life from a motive of duty when one's motivation is so weak that a slight distraction would have derailed one might not be highly creditworthy. The fittingness conception also takes account of the kind of evidence an agent has. Having good evidence that one might be wrong in A-ing could reduce one's motivation to A but still leave it strong enough to entitle one to moral praise for the action (where it is not wrong), even if that motivation is weak and barely suffices to sustain the action.

---

8 The notion of fittingness figures at various points in this book in ways that should be adequately clear, but I offer a detailed partial account of it in "Normative Priority, Fittingness, and Grounds of Normativity" (forthcoming). See also Price (1787/1974), Broad (1930), and Cullity (2018).

Normative ethics must deal with myriad cases involving determination of creditworthiness, as well as with a multitude of variables determining what is obligatory or wrong in the first place. In each of these domains of moral concern, both act-types and act-tokens are crucial. So is the kind and degree of control we have over our behavior. I have so far indicated limitations on our direct control of motivation. This is important because our motivation, ranging from momentary impulses to slowly passing desires to long-standing intentions, is a factor in our control of our actions. Our indirect control of our actions, particularly our prospective actions, is extensive in scope. Taking medication for anxiety can give some people wide indirect control by eliminating or reducing certain actions that would be produced by that emotion. As this suggests, in some dimensions of our indirect control, we need specialized psychological knowledge to achieve effective control of our future behavior. As psychology progresses, both moral education and moral responsibility may be strongly affected. The better our ability to control our behavior, whether direct or indirect, and the easier it is for us to exercise control of it in our actions, the wider, and in some cases the greater, our moral responsibility for what we do. This applies to prospective responsibility for accomplishing the relevant deeds as well as to retrospective responsibility for having done them. My emphasis here is on what can be said about those matters from the perspective of general knowledge of human action. Such knowledge is extensive and, in many cases, confirmed by psychological findings.[9]

———

From the point of view of ethical theory, whatever we say about the moral creditworthiness of actions (for their agents), it is a property of act-tokens, not of act-types. This is not to deny that

9 Here one might consider literature including Haidt (2001) and discussions of that by Railton (2014) and Sinnott-Armstrong (2006a), which discuss Haidt's social intuitionism in detail. Murray (2020) ranges widely over empirical literature on our control of our actions.

any kind of value is attributable to act-types, but 'creditworthiness' and 'moral worth' are misleading terms for the kind of value that is. Moreover, although there is much we can do in self-direction to bring about the kind of virtuous dispositions that tend to yield creditworthy actions, our control in such self-direction is mainly indirect. We cannot, at will, produce motivation, harness or unharness it from a prospective act, or determine its relative strength in producing or sustaining something we actually do. These limitations partly explain why such complex double-barrelled behavior as keeping-a-promise-from-a-sense-of-duty cannot be brought about at will. We have also seen reasons to think that the very constitution of actions as doings of a certain sort precludes taking any one kind of reason for which they may be performed as essential in their constitution. In any case, it is at best doubtful that such behavior as keeping-a-promise-from-a-sense-of-duty represents a content of intention. The questions of what we (morally) ought to do, how we should be motivated in doing it, and in what manner we should do it are very different. This will become still clearer in the next chapter.

3   Manners of Action

S o far, I have partially presented a three-dimensional conception of human conduct. Its constitution is determined jointly
by doing something of a certain type, being motivated by one or
more elements that figure in explaining it, and doing the thing in
question in one or another manner. Conduct, then, might be said
to have a three-M structure determined by the matter of the
"central" action, its motivation, and its manner. What is still
needed for a good understanding of conduct is an adequate
characterization of the dimension of manner. Whatever we do
is done in some manner, and the manner of an action is often
important, whether intended or not.[1]

The theory of manner concerns part of the highly diverse
adverbial dimension of action. One reason for the diversity is that
some adverbial modifiers of action, including some that are morally important, do not indicate manner. Doing something *vindic-
tively*, for instance, indicates a kind of motivation but not a
manner of performance. Doing something *immediately* (say, upon
seeing something) specifies a temporal relation but leaves manner of performance open. Moreover, manners of performance,
even of intended actions, need not themselves be intended.
Intention is not closed even under believed consequences: I can
intend to serve a guest wine and believe that this will cause a
headache, yet not intend to cause a headache and wish I could

---

1 For discussion of adverbs in action theory see Davidson (1980, esp. 105–148).
  A more formal treatment of adverbs is in Parsons (1970).

avoid causing it. I can intend to ask permission to miss a meeting, believe that I will ask it guiltily, but not intend to ask it guiltily. In both cases, I have a kind of responsibility for what I foresee – an action in one case and a manner of action in the other – though causing a headache may be significant and asking guiltily may not be. Manner can also be important when it has unforeseeable effects. One could ask a question of a friend softly and delicately, with no way of knowing that one's manner of speaking would revive in the friend an old memory that produces shivers of remorse. Assessment of moral creditworthiness in actions and even of the character of agents depends partly on appraisal of manners of action.

1   Are Manners of Action Reducible?

Does ethics really need to represent manners of action as distinct from acts of a certain act-type? One might think that acts described by an adverb of manner are simply acts simpliciter (of a complex kind) and that therefore intending to *A M-ly*, where *M* is a manner of acting, reduces to intending to *B*, for some act-type *B*, identifiable without such an adverb.[2] Certainly doing something in a certain manner is a kind of behavior and, in the abstract, there is a corresponding behavior-type. Moreover, if, in ethical thinking, we can distinguish between simply doing a deed and doing it in a certain manner, and if we can also adequately connect this difference with differences in intention, obligation, and moral responsibility for conduct, then it may seem not to matter whether we consider *A*-ing *M*-ly a different action from simply *A*-ing or instead take the adverb to concern, as it appears to, the character of the action. Chapters 1 and 2, however, provided good reason not to take every behavior-type to be an

---

2 This schema does not imply that just any act-modifying adverb is an adverb of manner; 'prematurely' can modify 'informing' and indicates *when*, not a *manner* in which, or even *how*, the action is performed. Also excluded are intentional verbs, e.g. 'purposely' – though they are important in ethics.

act-type. Let's explore whether a similar resistance to reduction is reasonable for manners of action.

Suppose that (a) refusing a request peremptorily and (b) refusing it (simpliciter) are considered different act-types. There is, after all, a difference indicated by 'peremptorily', and it could be morally significant (the agent might have promised to make the refusal seem difficult, so it should have been given, say, reluctantly). A natural way to represent a difference of this kind is by construing 'refusing' to ascribe a property to the *agent* and 'peremptorily' to ascribe a property to the act-token. On this conception, act-types represent agential doing properties and adverbs of manner represent behavioral properties of doings. This conception of the difference is expectable given the significant fact that 'refusing', as reporting S's *behavior*, properly answers questions of the form ⟨What did S do?⟩ and 'peremptorily' properly answers questions of the quite different form ⟨In what manner did S do it?⟩ where 'it' designates the concrete action (the act-token) cited as what S did. Given the proposed distinction, although 'S refused peremptorily' does not *fail* to answer the question what S did (since it specifies refusing), it does this by describing that *and* S's manner in refusing. This is not a direct way to answer it, and it might raise concerns not appropriate to answering it. In any case, from the fact that a single simple (non-compound) declarative sentence can answer two questions, we should not conclude that the two questions do not concern importantly different kinds of thing.

It is also instructive to consider manners of action in relation to intention. Whatever intended actions are taken to be, they are entities that, by being of the intended type, can realize intentions. Now even if A-ing (say, refusing) is behaviorally equivalent to B-ing (say, declining peremptorily), it does not follow that *to B* is the content of the intention to A. Intentions characteristically have a definite content that would be altered or lost by any substitution that lacks exactly equivalent content. Even (1) intending to draw a circle – which is itself provably equivalent to drawing a plane figure whose circumference is pi times its diameter – is not equivalent to (2) intending to draw a figure whose circumference is pi times its diameter. A student asked to draw a circle may form the intention to draw one and carry it out; but the same student might have no notion of the theorem for determining circumference from diameter and so could not form the intention to draw a figure whose perimeter is pi times its diameter; and a teacher who calls for the drawing would not think it could be expressed indifferently for pre-geometry students and for those who know the theorem.

Moreover, in principle, just as any act-type can be instantiated by different tokens that each have a different motivational explanation, any act can be performed in more than one manner. In some cases, providing an act-name that absorbs the adverbial modifier (as 'screaming' absorbs voicing in a certain loud tone) can be misleading. Even when the encapsulation is not false, it may conceal an important dimension of behavioral assessment. Take screaming. We can ask 'Was it in words?' to determine whether the action was linguistic. If so, this categorization provided by 'screaming' leaves manner open in ways that do not apply to a mere outcry as someone falls into an icy lake. By contrast, 'Was it done angrily?' is normally aimed at determining a dimension of manner of performance. The range of angry manners is so diverse and so variable with context that devising an act-type designator like 'angressing' would yield an open-ended description and be at best an occasional linguistic convenience.

2 Manners of Action as Manifested in Performing It

A further difference between actions and manners of action goes with what I have called the secondary status of manners: they depend on actions in a way actions do not depend on them. We cannot do a thing in any given manner without doing it. The manner of action is indeed exhibited *in* the doing of it, but a given manner of A-ing need not be exhibited by A-ing, since there may be many ways to A in some other manner. Stopping a bike by braking may be done quickly, silently, or dangerously, but need not be done in any of these ways. Here manner is left quite open, though there are actions, such as pointing a visibly loaded revolver in a stranger's face, that usually call for a particular adverb of manner, e.g. 'threateningly'. The manner of an action seems best conceived as an aspectual property of a token that has that manner. By contrast, what we do *by* doing something is characteristically instrumental. There can be overlap in the references of 'in' and 'by'. One might break a rule of silence both in and by speaking; but, with these uses of 'in' and 'by', no manner of speaking is specified.

The in-relation that goes with the aspectual 'in' of manner is constitutive in a way the by-relation in question is not. We decline peremptorily because our manner *in* declining constitutes a manner of being peremptory; we lift a log *by* using a crowbar because the crowbar is our means; it does not constitute lifting it – we might have used a rope and pulley. Here the 'by' is instrumental and contrastive, rather than constitutive. To be sure, one could break a speed-limit law by speeding, where 'by' indicates no contrast, but there are still differences from the case of manners of action. One difference is that speeding is a constitutive means of law-breaking, which is entailed by speeding. But the manners of what we do, though partly constituted by the tokening of some act-property we instantiate, are not necessarily fixed by our simply doing it, nor is what we do a necessary means, especially a causal means, to realizing its manner. The manner characterizes the doing.[3]

Given that basic actions are performed other than by performing some different action, might we say that acting in a particular manner is never basic? This would go too far: we can at will move our limbs quickly, as in running. We need not run by doing anything else – though it is in moving our limbs in a certain manner (rapidly) that we run. It seems, however, inessential to basic actions that we do the things in question *in* doing something

---

3 Here Goldman's account of "level-generation" (1970) is instructive, though my points differ in being framed in relation to a coarse-grained conception of act-tokens by contrast with the fine-grained view he takes there.

else. We may move our limbs in a basic way, neither by nor in doing something else.[4]

More generally, then, we may say that doing something in a particular manner, even if this is basic in not being done in that manner *by* doing something else, is, by virtue of the in-relation, always dependent on basic action. This ontologically secondary status does not diminish the importance of manners of action – particularly given that manners may be intentional and may have important effects. But it is clarifying to distinguish types of action from manners of action, and doing so facilitates both comprehensiveness and accuracy in making moral appraisals.

There is a type-token distinction for manners of action, as there is for action itself. But this does nothing to show that manners of action are reducible to kinds of action. There is a type-token distinction for sentences and many other things, but this does not count toward any significant kind of reduction.[5] Broadly, manners of action are modifications of action and, as our examples indicate, impossible without it as the thing that admits of different adverbial modes.[6] This way of viewing manners of action makes it natural to take some adverbial modifiers of action to express higher-order behavioral properties. Consider ordering a meal *angrily*. This does not entail being angry (one could be practicing for a part in a play). But it does imply speaking with a certain air of annoyance, and it may have ethical significance. If there is a particular action that is an ordering, then 'angrily' likely provides a higher-order act-description, not a psychological description of the agent's state; and if ordering is a property instantiated by the agent in acting,

4 If basic acts should turn out to be volitional (a kind of willing), the same point would hold there; they are instantiable in a basic way.

5 Robert Frost's poem, "Stopping by Woods on a Snowy Evening," closes with two tokens of the type, *And miles to go before I sleep.* Since the second token apparently refers to death, it can be important in recitation that they be tokened in different manners. The type-token distinction was originally made for sentences, and this example illustrates how manner can be important even if act-type and motivation are held fixed.

6 This is meant to hold for single actions, not cases in which the manner of doing something like greeting warmly, can be achieved by two simultaneous independent basic act-sequences.

'angrily' seems to modify that action. It may be indicated by voicing, gesturing, glaring, or a combination of these.

Manners are intendable separately from the actions that manifest them. Wanting to wake someone, one might intend to do something noisily. Later one might decide to play a piano chord noisily. Doing something noisily, moreover, differs from simply making a loud noise. Screaming, being essentially noisy, is a case of doing something noisily; but screaming does not reduce to making a loud noise. One can do that by quietly causing a machine to make a loud noise. Reducing the manner-involving intention to simply intending a certain act-type obscures the intuitive difference between what one intends to do and the manner in which one intends to do it.

3   The Range of Manners of Action

Perhaps the point needed most here is that even if, on the one hand, whatever we do is done in some manner or other, we need not, in everything we do, aim at doing it in any particular manner. Indeed, the *non*-intentional manners in which people do things may often be morally more important than their intended manners of action. Related to this point is that many adverbs of manner simply specify a position on a dimension in which the action *must* have a place whether or not the agent aims at doing the thing in some manner. Running must have a speed, and this may make 'running fast' seem a good candidate for a single behavioral property of the agent, say running at n feet per second. Even if we may conceive running at n feet per second as a "single" act property, this reductive strategy will not work for adverbs that, like 'warmly', 'angrily', and 'arrogantly', specify a manner that is *not* on a continuum like speed or in a dimension such as bodily behavior, in which the primary predicate, for instance 'greet', 'run', or 'sing', has its referent. Singing must have a volume, as running must have a speed. But the former can be done soothingly or threateningly in alternative ways, whereas running cannot occur without a speed. Even if every action is done in some manner, a dimension like speed, in which some acts must have a position, need not be a manner. These cases suggest that many manners of action that have moral significance can normally be suppressed at will. Whether adverbs – or some of them – are best taken to express higher-order properties need not be settled here, but the view has enough plausibility to take as a working assumption.

Other adverbial modifiers are motivational and should not be viewed as indicating manner of action. Some adverbial modifiers are, like 'rightly', normative. Here 'acted inexcusably' is akin to 'acted wrongly' in being both normative and open regarding whether the error is in act-type or in manner or both. It is significant, moreover, that 'wrongly' can apply where *only* the manner is morally criticizable. A request in courteous diction can be made so flatly as to rise to acting wrongly toward a new employee. Such duality of interpretation also holds for 'offensively'; but this, in addition, is a consequential adverb implying that there might be a morally important effect: offending. Both cases indicate how 'acting wrongly' may apply on the basis of the manner of an action rather than its type.

This is not the place for a comprehensive theory of behavioral adverbs.[7] My positive point is that we should take account of the role of many adverbs of manner, together with the distinction between *intra-dimensional* adverbs, such as 'fast', 'loudly', and 'heavily' – which must apply to some degree to actions of certain kinds – and *extra-dimensional* ones such as 'angrily', 'reluctantly', and 'elegantly', which, for many kinds of action, need not apply to any tokens of those kinds. It is at best unwise to regard adverbial modifiers as simply indicating a more "fine-grained" act-type. They do indicate *property* types – behavioral ones – but behavior-types include more than act-types. The flutter of eyelids may be significant behavior without being action.[8] With

---

7 For a quite general treatment of adverbs from the point of view of linguistic theory, see McConnell-Ginet (1982). Her account seems consistent with taking adverbs of manner to represent higher-order properties.

8 In e. e. cummings's poem, "since feeling is first," we find: "the best gesture of my brain is less than/ your eyelids' flutter which says/ we are for each other."

ingenuity, we can devise predicates that, if only by stipulation, incorporate the force of any given adverb in a single behavior-describing term. But devising such predicates may reduce clarity under a rationale of simplification rather than enhance it by revealing ineliminable and sometimes morally significant complexity.

There are acts that simply must be done, with their manner of performance making no morally significant difference. Signing a check may sometimes be of this kind. Nonetheless, every concrete action is performed in some manner or other. Suppose we take behavioral reports of the form ⟨A-ing M-ly⟩ to be action-reporting, in the sense that they designate actions. Must each such action be intentional? Manners of action may be intentional, but they need not be, and A-ing can be intentional even when no manner it exhibits is. Suppose we were to take ⟨A-ing M-ly⟩ to represents an action, B, and that B has a description under which it is intentional. Then, if we simply describe someone as doing B, this description cannot be understood apart from grasping an element in the content of the act-type, B, that includes the manner in question – otherwise there is no point in speaking of the mannered action as itself an act-token rather than an act-token that (possibly non-intentionally) *has* a particular manner. Plainly, however, you might intend to sign a check without intending any of the manners in which you will inevitably sign it. Suppose you do it hastily but when haste is not in your intention. Must we say that because you signed hastily and you intentionally signed, your signing hastily was intentional? Surely not. The point is that manner need not enter the content of intentions and that when it does, it is secondarily to the way in which the act-type enters that content.

One could hold that ⟨A-ing M-ly⟩ represents action only when *both* A-ing simpliciter and the relevant manner, M, are intentional. If there is a manner-inclusive intention – so that its content is *to A M-ly*, say to refuse peremptorily – we might speak of its instantiation as an intentionally *mannered action*. If, however, there is an intention to A simply accompanied by a conditional intention to A M-ly, for instance to refuse peremptorily *if* offered a bribe, then, if *S A*-s *M*-ly, we might or might not have an intentional action with a related intention focused on manner. The peremptory manner could be a mere by-product of a bad mood.

Often, manner *should* enter into the content of intention, and this is one reason for its significance in ethics. The broadest point here, covering a vast range of manners as well as diverse act-types, is perhaps that in relating to others, we should act *respectfully* – a moral term to be explored in detail in Chapter 5. In morally sensitive agents this may be habitual, whereas (unfortunately) for insensitive people, acting respectfully toward others may often require that the relevant manner be an object of a thoughtfully formed intention.

4   Actions and Activities

Much discussion in ethics concentrates on actions that are roughly momentary or, if extended, not viewed segmentally. But much can change in acting over time, and, as compared with activities, many actions tend to provide both less scope for us to style them and less variation in manner for others to observe in judging them. With temporally extended acts – which may comprise a majority of morally significant acts – some of the important variables are whether (e.g.) they are performed as quickly as possible for the agent or more slowly, whether they are accented in some way or whether they are perceptibly either rapid or delayed. Pouring a drink for someone slowly may manifest reluctance; doing it rapidly may convey either enthusiasm or annoyance.

There is a way of doing things that represents a kind of manner but not in the sense in which manners of action are a kind of style. Suppose pouring a drink is accented by voluntarily loud breathing or by humming. Whether these accompanying doings are intentional or not may bear on whether the agent is pouring reluctantly or happily. Here the manner of one action, pouring, is in part *externally determined*: it is at least largely determined by a relevant accompanying action, say humming, that has its own manner. There are two "things" – simultaneous activities – here, but their connection may be described as yielding a manner, or at least a *way* (a broader term) in which one or the other action-sequence is performed. These activities are not connected to a single basic action by *either* the in-relation or the by-relation. Humming may be basic for the agent, but it is not by or in humming that one pours, and conversely. The basic acts in question are simply conjoint, though they may be intentionally connected. The humming, e.g., may be intended to imply pouring gladly. Most of the manners that will concern us will not be of this externally determined kind, but these can be significant. These same cases may be accompanied by other actions, such as using a shot-glass to measure the liquor. The humming may be done, for instance, warningly or cheerfully, and it could even be ethically more important than the rather conventional activity it may seem merely to accompany.

Cases like these illustrate that manners of action (including activities) may be determined *adjunctively* and described by indicating accompanying actions, as opposed to adding ordinary higher-order modifications of the main act-type in question, for instance 'swiftly', 'elegantly', or 'cordially'. This adjunctive determination applies especially to activities, which may involve doing such independent things as serving a drink and speaking. It also applies to activities that are sequences of related actions, as in tying a knot. Higher-order modifications directly yield a manner in which the act whose manner is in question is performed, rather than affecting its status by different act-types instantiated in relation to it, as where humming a funeral march accompanies pouring a fourth whiskey. These modifications yield higher-order properties of the action, e.g. requesting something imperiously or tentatively, or assenting to a plan reluctantly rather than enthusiastically.

For physical actions – those partly constituted by bodily movement – there must be some elapse of time. This normally makes room for perceptible manners of action, including some that are morally significant. One might object that winning a race can be instantaneous. But for accomplishments of this kind, there is referential ambiguity: between the act-type, winning, and the act-token by which one wins. Suppose there is an exact time of winning. There is still more than one manner that the winning act, say crossing the finish line, can have. External acts, for instance, can affect the manner in which someone accomplishes the winning. One could do it triumphally, upholding a victory sign, or desperately, with an outcry of pain.

Our examples confirm that *how* we do what we do – when the 'how' is manner-specific and not means-specific – often matters greatly. Where the 'how' designates instrumental action, it may obviously have moral significance in its own right. The teaching of children and even adults illustrates the importance of manner, as well as choice of means to doing something, in multiple ways. Do we correct a child's error gently or harshly? What if the child *defiantly* errs? Do we point out a better way (means) to do a task? Interpersonal relations are not a behavioral grid with fixed points representing only act-types. Even taken in short segments, those relations are usually a multicolored dynamic patchwork, sometimes with changing colors and accompanying sounds. If we tried to eliminate adverbs of manner in favor of "simpler" act-reports, this might both reduce clarity and impair normative appraisal. It is, to be sure, convenient to have 'yelling' to describe speaking too loudly. But yelling itself can be done in many ways. If it were often enough done threateningly, we might invent a term for that behavior; but this complex behavior itself can still differ in adverbial dimensions.

There is certainly reason to think that even if adverbial act-reports can be nominalized to yield a purportedly equivalent term for an act-type, the fineness of moral appraisal would be reduced by utilizing this procedure in an attempt to do all the moral work that attention to manners of action makes possible. Even if we could invent a distinct act-designating noun for every manner of doing ordinary things such as refusing a request, we would be confronted by so many terms that action-describing discourse, far from being better for moral appraisal, would be more difficult for those with the normal capacities for mastering a multitude of terms.[9]

---

9 Suppose we eliminated act-modifying adverbs. There remain special difficulties where their force varies with the terms they modify. Consider a football
player asked to tackle a recruit gently. On one rendering of '*A* tackled *B*

5   The Moral Significance of Manners of Action

It should now be apparent what kind of behavioral phenomenon manners of actions are. This does not prevent coining terms for actions performed in a certain manner. That may be desirable, but we have seen reasons to avoid the increased complexity of moral discourse that would be caused by inventing terms for the myriad mannered acts that are morally significant. Normal moral parlance encompasses the adverbial dimensions of conduct by selecting adverbs as needed. There are at least three other considerations.

First, in numerous cases it is obvious that doing what we ought makes certain manners of action wrong or undesirable and others right or obligatory. If, for instance, we must do good deeds toward others where we can, this generally precludes doing them violently and calls for doing them respectfully. If we must avoid harming others, then apart from self-defense and certain sports, this quite evidently precludes acting violently toward them.

A second consideration is this. The ethics that governs manners of action is perhaps best taught by role-modeling. Precepts are also needed, but they often cannot cover as much behavioral ground, or cover it as well, as modeling. Effective modeling of manners of action, whether by parents or other elders, may be aimed, and perceived by children as aimed, at exhibiting performance of the right act-types. But we cannot model doing morally important things without modeling some manner of action, even if the manner is not intentional. Moral sensibility grows with observing overall behavior, and

---

gently', it would follow that there is an action that is both a tackle and gentle. But the tackle is not gentle, merely gentle *for a tackle*. We can construct a predicate for *being gentle relative to tackles*, but indefinitely many such constructions are needed to reflect the complexities of the adverbial modifications, which differ in force with contextual variables. We could call a gentle tackle a *tacklette*. We would still depend, for communication, on the adverb's open-endedness. Our understanding of behavior seems better represented by the theory that adverbs "interact" with both act-reporting expressions, e.g. 'What *S* did', and contexts of ascription, to yield conceptions of the adverbially modified actions in question.

moral education depends on making good use of that developmental pattern.[10]

The third consideration is best seen through a distinction crucial for interpersonal conduct. It is between what we *do*, including what we say, and what we *communicate*. One difference is this. We can speak in positive terms to others and even serve them in some way but still communicate something negative, such as condescension. Communication to others, unlike just speaking to them, implies their *receiving some message*. Here manner can be crucial, as in the case of ordering a meal angrily. The manner of ordering may communicate at least displeasure even when the actions in giving the order are routine and, voiced differently, would convey little besides naming the selected menu items. Another instance occurs in conversational settings. Some people, especially when excited and standing before their addressee, act and speak encroachingly: they advance closer and closer. In cases like these "actions speak louder than words." This adage applies mainly to people's deeds, but it also applies to the manner in which they do their deeds – which is commonly more evident than what motivated those deeds. It plays a crucial role in what we communicate to others. If actions speak, it is often with an adverbial voice.

Might the notion of a manner of action include motivation, in which case its moral significance would be still greater? After all, doesn't 'from self-interest', which is motivational, specify a *way* – one wrong way – to keep a promise? It might, but this simply further confirms my point that *way* of acting represents a wider category than manner of action.[11] Recall that specifications of

---

10 For much description of the influence of role modeling see Zagzebski (2017), which develops an exemplarist view of moral development and role modeling. A more general and empirically informative treatment of moral education is provided by Curren and Ryan (2020).

11 Doubtless Aristotle may have intended to include manners of action in stressing the significance of ways of acting. This is to be expected in any well-developed virtue ethics. See, e.g., NE 1103a3ff, 1105b5–9, 1107a15ff, and 1108a27–30. Note the breadth of 'way' in the point that "the just and temperate person is not the one who ⟨merely⟩ does these actions, but the one who also does them in the way in which just or temperate people do them," in (Irwin 2019: 1105b7–9). Here 'manner' seems too narrow, but Aristotle

reasons for which an action is performed answer the question *why* the agent acted, not the questions of either *how* or in what manner the agent did it. To be sure, given that Kant took the moral worth of actions to depend on what motivationally explains them, one might think he could have said that doing what one ought to do is acting in the wrong *way* if the deed is done for the wrong reason. Perhaps, but in any case, merely using 'way' to encompass motivation does not commit one to calling acting for the wrong reason a case of acting in the wrong *manner*. Manner of action can itself be motivated and can be exhibited for morally good or morally bad reasons. Speaking soothingly to a frightened child may be motivated by love or by a desire to kidnap. This illustrates one manner (and way) of acting but two radically different motives.

This example brings us to another way to see how manners of action are morally important. The general point (already illustrated) is that they can be crucial in determining the kind and degree of creditworthiness of an action and thus important for appraising character. This point may be plausibly considered implicit in a broad interpretation of the positive injunction of Kant's humanity formula: we are to treat persons as ends in themselves. Whatever Kant's specific meaning, this surely implies treating them in some manner appropriate to the overall context of action, though in some cases the need regarding manner is to avoid the wrong kind, say an offensive or patronizing manner.[12] That variable in conduct is essential for acting rightly toward them and is largely independent of what motivates the interpersonal action(s) in question. This point should be common ground between Kant and many other moral philosophers, but few if any have taken adequate account of the role of the manners of action in overall moral appraisal.

would surely have held that the relevant way would restrict the appropriate manners. For a contemporary presentation of virtue ethics that exhibits an awareness of the importance of manner, see Swanton (2001), e.g. 41.

12 This is explained in detail in my (2016), but clearly one dimension of our treatment of others is that of the manner of our action(s) toward them.

Manners of action are as pervasive as actions themselves and, like actions, can be objects of intention, whether they are focally aimed at or simply presupposed as the agent looks toward the intended act. Manners of action can make a major moral difference. Telling someone innocently napping "It's time to wake up" can be something I am obligated to say, but if I say this threateningly, I act wrongly. Here the manner of my conduct is reprehensible even though I did the thing I was obligated to do and for that reason.

———

This chapter has shown much about what constitutes a manner of action and has made a case that manners of action are neither themselves actions nor fruitfully absorbed into supposed act-types that embody one or more manners. Manners of action are often under our voluntary control, commonly not just our indirect control but also our direct control, negative or positive. Manners are specifiable by adverbs; but not all adverbial modifiers of action, including 'intentionally', 'self-interestedly', and 'sincerely', are adverbs of manner. A certain manner of performing an act may also be obligatory; and where we can at will perform it in that manner, our obligation may be of the form ⟨to A M-ly⟩, e.g. to criticize tactfully. The criticisms themselves may be clear enough for listing in a letter; deciding the manner in which to deliver them may be a great challenge to judgment. By contrast, we do not have direct voluntary control of the reasons for which we act. *Causing* ourselves to act (or tend to act) for the right reasons, as by cultivating virtue, may be obligatory and under our indirect control. Such complex behavior is not something we can bring about at will. But we can at will act in a respectful manner, sometimes even in a loving manner, which may be a first step toward fulfilling the interpersonal ideal of being a loving person. Manners of action, then, are among the things a theory of obligation must account for. But they are not the central case. Without actions there would be no manners of action. Part II will introduce a morality of conduct that accommodates not only action as the core element in human conduct but also its motivation and manner.

Part II

Moral Obligation

4   Moral Principles

The Traditional Common Core

W hen we act in some morally significant way, it is often natural to call the behavior in question conduct. Conduct has three dimensions: its "matter," determined by act-type(s); its motivation, constituted by at least one desire (at least typically embodied in an intention); and its manner, an adverbially describable way it is realized. Conduct is most characteristically interpersonal, and in contexts of moral appraisal we most often refer to a person's morally appraisable behavior in terms of some salient act-type, e.g. lying, promising, requesting, and helping. The variety of such acts is enormous, and their specificity varies greatly. Shaking hands is more specific than greeting, for instance, and there are indefinitely many ways of helping, whereas greetings may normally have only the diversity allowed by custom. Despite this diversity there are moral principles that are at once simple and comprehensive. This chapter concerns some major ones.

1   Conduct and Its Vehicles

Conduct requires action: no action, no conduct. For explicitness, it is convenient to speak of the *vehicle* of conduct in referring to a salient action or activity. There is no simple rule here. If you know what *A* said to *B* and you ask what *A* did that upset *B*, someone might reply, '*A* accused *B* of lying'. But a general answer to the question what upset *B*, asked by someone with no knowledge of the upsetting occasion, could also be answered just by saying that *A* accused *B* of wrongdoing, which would also describe the action. What is cited in reporting action is context-dependent, but it commonly includes an act-type whose specificity is meant to meet the contextual need.

Is there, then, no uniquely correct answer to such questions as 'What is he *really* doing?' In many cases, this kind of question is aimed at ascertaining the intention whose object is the agent's "ultimate" aim in the context. Thus, in carrying groceries for an elderly lady, someone could "really" be preparing to steal her purse. Here the vehicle of the conduct is not the most significant act being performed. Significance of various kinds is another criterion that may guide describing what the agent is "really doing." But such descriptions are mainly guided by what motivates the agent to act. Here the action is intended as a means to theft, not (mainly) to help the woman, and the governing motive is desire to steal her purse. The aim of assisting her is also (at least morally) less significant. There may, however, be no unique answer to 'What is *S* really doing?' Agents sometimes have coequal ends, say to nurture shrubs and to prepare property for ultimate sale. One can be deeply concerned with both ends and intentionally aim at each. Moreover, different adverbs may apply depending on what act-type(s) the conduct is taken to instantiate. The carrying of groceries is done politely; the building of confidence (to prepare for pickpocketing) is done deceitfully.

Such cases of deciding how to describe an agent's "main" or "significant" action by noting its motivation should not, however, be assimilated to cases in which we ascribe trying. *Trying* is higher order. Even if you know I'm trying to nurture a plant, you don't thereby know *by* what action I'm aiming at that; and although you know one purpose I have, you may not know what I'm "really" doing, which could be using gardening to conceal spying. Here lack of specificity as to act-type combines with indication of only one end being pursued. Trying also contrasts with succeeding and has many dimensions. Its moral importance can be accounted for in the framework I'm developing, but its action-theoretic complexities need not be pursued further.[1]

2   Commonsense Moral Principles in Moral Education

This chapter concerns moral principles of a kind that indicate the matter of actions that belong to what may be the main types representing the obligations basic in ordinary life. I begin with eight that correspond to well understood virtues of character, appear in major ethical theories from Aristotle to Aquinas to Kant to leading utilitarians, and are famously formulated and defended by Ross in (1930). I often formulate them differently than Ross, and Chapter 5 describes two other obligations that seem similarly important in moral theory. It is useful to begin, however, with revised formulations of the core of commonsense principles Ross defended. These have been deservedly much discussed, and they remain among the plausible candidates for a core of intuitive, universally respected moral principles. It will suffice to clarify each sufficiently to enable it to serve (if in a revised formulation), in a comprehensive core of principles that should belong to any adequate normative ethics. There is no better starting point for appreciating them than consideration of moral education.

Often, we are at our most direct and unbuttoned in bringing up children. In the course of moral education, we may say, 'Don't hit', 'Share', 'Don't lie', 'Keep your promises', and 'Help people who need you'. When children receive gifts, we may say, 'You should say "thank-you"'; if they negligently hurt others, 'You should make it up to them'; when they watch too much TV, 'You must do your homework now'. These eight examples correspond to the principles central in this chapter. Something rather

---

1 The points made in this section apply to social action, as with the confidence trickster, and to individual action, such as watering someone's shrubs. Trying may occur in either case. For detailed theories of social action see Tuomela (1995); Bratman (2018); and Lackey (2021). Trying is considered in detail in the exchange between Fred Adams and me in Timmons, Greco, and Mele (2007).

different would be indicated by addressing not act-type but manner of action, as where we say to a child hurriedly helping a sibling to dress: 'Do it gently'. That kind of teaching is explored in the next chapter.

A skeptical response might label these teachings just enforcements of convention. I reject that description, though of course requirements of convention can largely coincide with those of morality. I have been describing genuinely moral rational agents, and their attitudes of approval and disapproval align significantly with the standards in question. A related consideration is that the conscience of such agents is apparently structured in good part by respecting these standards. Connected with both points is that descriptive and critical discourse about right and wrong is guided, in ways that will shortly be evident, by these standards. (A partial but systematic defense of the principles will be set out in Chapter 7.)

The everyday parental injunctions I have cited recall Ross's prima facie obligations of justice and non-maleficence, of veracity and fidelity (to promises), of beneficence and self-improvement, and of reparation (for wrongdoing) and gratitude.[2] Ross did not specifically address obligations of manner, and for these there are no summary formulations as natural as those derived from encapsulations of behavioral types reportable by a single term, such as 'promising', 'lying', and 'harming'. This is because *any* of the obligations can be fulfilled in better or worse ways, as also with or without creditworthy motivation.

3   Major Moral Principles: Illustrations and Clarifications

A full-scale explication and defense of these principles of obligation is not needed here. The aim is to present them clearly enough

---

2 In ch. 2 of (1930). Ross did not, however, always avoid using moral terms in specifying grounds of obligation, as where he identified the duty of reparation as "resting on a previous wrongful act" (21). The importance of avoiding them in specifying grounds is brought out in Part III (and in more detail in my 2016).

to indicate what kind of place they should have in a comprehensive ethics, how quite similar principles may be defended, and how the obligations they describe are connected with value. Given this aim, I will discuss them in relation to the obligatory act-types they specify and, so far as possible, the non-moral elements that ground those obligations.

Harm

Prohibitions of murder and other harms are common to all the major ethical theories. It is also widely recognized that these prohibitions are not absolute. The obligation not to kill, e.g., is defeasible, at least in certain cases of self-defense. In my terminology, it is *prima facie*, which I take as roughly equivalent to the agent's having a moral reason to A that is (1) grounded in some fact or circumstance(s) or state of affairs, such as promising to A; (2) strong enough to justify the action if unopposed by any at least equally strong normative consideration; and (3) defeasible by conflicting normative considerations.[3] It is not easy to explicate defeasibility, as where self-defense suffices to defeat the obligation not to harm. Having one's life lethally and directly threatened by an unprovoked attacker is a typical example, but even this description may not entail defeat. Defeasibility explains why it is reasonable to use not the imperatival language of 'must', but more moderate terms, as illustrated by the principle that

---

3 This is not Ross's sketch of prima facie duty in, e.g. (1930: 19–24), but it may capture his main uses of the term. The formulation uses 'harm' rather than 'non-maleficence' to avoid the motivational coloration of the latter. It also leaves open the difficult question of how non-moral reasons are related to, and may figure in conflicts with, moral ones. Partial answers to that question, taking account of some historically important positions, are defended in my (2001b), (2010b), and (2013b). I defend (1) and (3) in Chapter 7, but do not directly defend (2) in this book. Here I am inclined to take 'others' to include sentient non-persons and hypothetical persons (e.g. persons one may rationally expect to come into existence), but unfortunately extending the theory I am developing to population ethics is beyond the scope of this book.

We Should Not Harm Others

This *harm-avoidance principle* is meant as a rough equivalent of what Ross proposed (for human persons[4]): this obligation is prima facie, and this qualification, like 'pro tanto', entails that the obligation has variable strength and may be affected, e.g. reduced, by the normative force of conflicting obligations, but 'pro tanto' does not imply a priori grounding (to be discussed in Chapter 7).

Should we not simply say, then, that harming others, with killing them as a typically extreme case, is wrong? There is no error in saying it with the presupposition that the wrongness is prima facie. This is often presupposed; but where it is not, the speaker is usually presupposing a reprehensible case of wrongness. In philosophical ethics, unqualified uses of 'right' and 'wrong' typically presuppose prima facie status (as ordinarily in this book). The obligation not to harm others, then, though not absolute, is in many cases properly taken to be undefeated. Prima facie obligations as I understand them are not merely defeasible, i.e., yielding overall obligations *if* they are not overridden by a set of conflicting obligations. Some kind of appeal to wrong-making grounds of action is needed to capture the notion. In my view, it is even possible for overriding to come from non-moral normative considerations, but this is not something that need be argued here.[5]

In line with the idea that everyday moral principles are offered and commonly stated in language that, whatever its presuppositions, is simple, I am here stating everyday principles using 'should' and 'should not' rather than 'prima facie obligation' or

---

4 It would be more accurate to say 'for normal adult human persons', but I don't want to rule out the possibility of non-human persons. This matter of scope is complicated. What are we to say of adults with mental deficiency too great to understand moral standards? What should be said of persons who greatly differ from us in biology (e.g. not subject to physical pain)? Fortunately, much can be accomplished without answering these questions.

5 If self-preservation is not considered a moral reason for action, such overriding is plausible for certain cases; but this is not the only case. I have discussed relevant issues in (2010b).

'obligation' simpliciter. But in saying that we should not harm others we presuppose that there can be adequate reasons for doing otherwise but that, apart from these, our overall obligation is the act in question.[6] What harm comes to, however, is matter enough for a book in itself, but much of what is needed here can be brought out by examples.

Helen. Helen was hurrying on foot to pick up her son from elementary school. The shortest route between her bus stop and the school takes her to the middle of a city block with cars parked on one side. It is a long block and, after looking quickly, she began to cross the street from between two empty cars. The car on her left was tall and obscured the view of oncoming traffic from that direction. She didn't see a speeding van going too fast to avoid. Her right foot was run over and badly broken. The pain was excruciating. Screaming in pain, she clutched the car to her right to avoid falling to the pavement. Surgery saved the foot, but she would always have a slight limp. Realizing he had hit her, Kang, the driver, stopped. He was apologetic and distressed. He too had been in a hurry and exceeded the speed limit. (He was ticketed – it was a school zone indicated by a sign and flashing yellow light and had many pedestrians at that hour.)

Crushing Helen's foot was clearly a harm. Kang's hitting her was clearly a wrong. Could she have been harmed without being *injured*? Suppose the van was going slowly and simply spun her around by hitting a tray of cookies she was carrying to an after-school activity. Kang might well say 'Thank heaven she wasn't injured!' This is consistent with saying that her safety was jeopardized and that she suffered a terrible fright. On both counts, he did something wrong toward her (more formally, "wronged" her).

If being harmed in such a case is a wrong to the person harmed, it is not necessarily important that the wrong causes

---

6 On Ross's conception of his principles of prima facie duty, they are both a priori (as expectable since he considered them self-evident) and necessary (owing to the underlying metaphysical grounding relations he cites for them). I have explained this conception in detail in (2004) and defend it further in Part III. For a different but overlapping view, see Phillips (2019).

injury. Injuring may of course be a case of wronging, but neither wronging nor harming need be injuring. One might think that *every* case of injuring a person is one of wronging, even if excusably. But consider surgery for an appendectomy, which requires an incision that would be fatal if conducted unprofessionally. This procedure is not properly called injuring the patient even though it *wounds* before it cures. It does, however, require appropriate (at least hypothetical) consent. One way to view injuries to persons is to conceive them as doing damage to them that *would* be a harm, and would be wrong, apart from special circumstances, such as medical need. This is one reason why it is harms, and not injuries, that play the more important and more basic moral role.

If every injury to a person would in certain circumstances be a harm, may we say that every harm is an injury? There are psychological harms that are not properly called injuries. Some adults have caused psychological harm to children by inducing fear in them through frightening them with horror stories. In at least some of these cases, the effect may be both temporary and the act a wrong yet not properly an injury. Speaking here of an injury that quickly heals may seem acceptably metaphorical, but if it stretches 'psychological harm' to speak of injury here, we can at least see that the description makes sense regarding some children scarred by such frights. There is a way to drop the metaphor: if we may speak of the psyche as an essential element in a person, then causing a serious fright may injure it.

Killing is in most cases a clear harm (this does not entail that death itself is a harm or an "evil"). But what, then, should be said of courageous suicides of a kind that may be plausibly thought essential for fulfilling stringent obligations? One can imagine some people volunteering for important risky assignments and promising to take a fatal pill if it is the only way to fulfill the need. Consider those who can launch nuclear missiles, and imagine that it is possible for certain terrorists to get the launching code by brain manipulation from which guards cannot protect themselves. If those guarding a site are captured by them and send a message to the launch officers that terrorists are about to enter the control room, would the officers be harming themselves in taking a painless fatal pill? If the action is obligatory and courageously performed, then even if it is a harm, it seems both heroic and, as a killing, morally justified.

Many harms and even more injuries cause physical pain. But with certain harms there need be no bodily or psychological damage. Imagine that someone doing an experiment gives Helen a very brief but painful electric shock (without her consent) while she is seated in a waiting room. It hurts her arm but the pain quickly passes. Causing pain in this way is harmful even if it does not injure. Here we can imagine defenders of the experiment saying that since the shock did her no harm, imprisonment would be excessive punishment. I doubt that no harm is done, and would call the experiment harmful. Harm can be momentary and leave no trace. Pain, however, tends to *impair agency*, and causing it is typical in harms. Pain certainly tends to interfere with concentration in tasks such as tracking information, writing, and driving. Shocking people is also the kind of thing that, extended in time, rises to torture.

A more controversial case might be that of a terminal illness in which the person wants to die. Suppose I am dying of cancer and am in pain so great that I can bear consciousness only for short periods. During these I can communicate. Imagine that my children are under great strain in supporting me and that they must bear expenses that compromise the education of their own children. If, with their approval, I take a fatal pill, am I harming myself? Some would instead call it a release. But there is no question that if a self-appointed visitor administered the medication, this would be considered a wrong. Some would say the visitor harmed me ('injury' seems the wrong word); others would say this is not so, given the elimination of pain I wished for, but it is wrong at least by overstepping my rights. There are certainly cases in which what one does to oneself does not constitute a harm though someone else's doing it to one would be a harm. Consider (safely) drawing blood for donation to a patient in need – the "donor" would be harmed (though not necessarily injured) by someone's forcibly producing the same "donation." Like some of our other examples, this one shows that whatever exactly harming a person is, when it is clear that harm has been done to someone, it is also clear that there is a kind of wrong.

The notion of harm is both multi-dimensional and vague. It is vague in ways that leave room, on the positive side, for needed discretion in moral judgment and, on the negative side, for regrettably recalcitrant disagreements. Dimensions of harm include bodily, psychological, economic, and other categories. In all these realms, causing pain, including suffering and even certain kinds of discomfort, looms large in understanding what unifies harms, but deprivations of pleasure, reductions of capacities, and restrictions of liberty may also count. Here ethics (as simply moral thinking) prefers the risk of inflating the category of harms to other people over the risk of allowing acts that diminish our quality of life.

Lying

Lying to others, like physically harming them, is uncontroversially considered wrong, even if more often excused than physical harms. Here the simple *principle of veracity* is that

We Should Not Lie

Lying is prima facie wrong. Sometimes, the obligation of veracity – which I am taking as negative – is described as a duty to tell the truth. But telling the truth to someone entails communicating and one can avoid lying by simply not communicating, nor is one obligated to speak at all to some people or on some topics. The case to follow helps to understand the difference between lying and deceiving – which doesn't even require saying something.[7]

Lauren. Lauren is a middle-aged woman whose father is dying. In an attempt to be comforting she says to him that she, as

---

7 Why deceiving, even intentionally, does not entail lying, is explained in ch. 5 of my (2004), which cites wearing a hairpiece. Lying obviously does not entail deceiving but can still harm, as with ego-wounding attempts. I am not addressing the positive obligation of truth-telling, which seems both complex and derivative. Cf. the obligation to cooperate as described by Cullity (2018).

executor, will do everything the will asks. He might say, 'I know you don't agree with everything in the will, but I'm glad that you will carry it out faithfully'. The conversation ends there. Lauren, however, knows that she can and will redirect some of the bequests, especially those implicitly intended for a brother who has begun to gamble. She intends to give those funds to his children, which she thinks her father would likely approve of but is not up to discussing in the deathbed circumstances. Many would consider this a case in which the lie would be excusable, and one reason might be that it would seem to do no harm to the father. It is clear, however, that it would call for excuse.

The case also shows something else. One lie often produces another. Lauren's brother might wonder why he was bypassed in favor of his children when their other brother was not. It would be natural for her to prefer saying that she and his father agreed on this rather than saying, forthrightly, that she herself had sadly judged that the money would be lost in gambling. If the brother protests and asks about the conversation, Lauren might have to lie further to conceal the truth. She might also lie to the second brother if she judges he would disagree about the decision regarding their gambling brother. In these cases, excusability for lying to the brothers is not clear. Is the gambler wrongly deprived of a chance to make a case for escrow of the funds while he abandons gambling? Might he at least have a right to protest and argue? More abstractly, what kind of relationship is now created between Lauren and him? On her side, it will be burdened by the need for cover-up. On this brother's side, it will be fraught with doubts about why his father treated him differently (not trusting him to use the money wisely) and perhaps also with resentments toward him.

That Lauren's lies are (prima facie) wrong is both intuitively clear and confirmed by the need they generate for excuse. This is a need in the sense that if there is no excuse for the lies, then she is blameworthy and, accordingly, properly subject to disapproval. There is more to be said, of course, about the lies' effects on the relationships among the brothers. But even Lauren's first lie, coming at the end of her relationship with her father, is a blotch

on the trust that may (and certainly should) have characterized
that relationship. This is a metaphor, to be sure. We might also
say that the lie is unfitting to the relationship, but although that is
clearly true it is not a premise on which the wrongness of the lie is
based.[8]

Promising

If we bear in mind that 'should' here expresses prima facie
obligation, then it seems plain that also among commonsense
ground level moral standards is a *fidelity principle*:

We Should Keep Our Promises

Promissory obligation seems a basic kind. But suppose promising
to do something while intending not to is a case of lying – and we
might call such cases 'lying promises'. Then one might think we
should take promissory obligation in general to rest on the obligation not to lie. But such promising is not a case of lying, in part
because it is not a case of assertion – in the broad sense of saying
that something is so. It *is* misrepresentation, which is a wider
wrong than lying. Still, though we should not promise to *A*
without intending to *A*, promising to *A* is not, and does not entail,
asserting that we intend to *A*.

Is the converse view more plausible? Is the obligation not to lie
based on the obligation to keep one's promises? It may appear so
based if one thinks of what is assertively said to someone as

---

8 Lauren's lie does not harm her father but could harm her. Granted, self-
  deception, which sometimes harms the self-deceiver, has been characterized
  as lying to oneself; but if that is lying, it is not the normal kind in which one
  person says something to another while believing it false and (normally) at
  least seeking to get the other to accept it. Lying *often* harms the addressee, but
  an action can be wrong on many counts simultaneously, and here I want to
  bring out what is distinctive about various grounds of wrong or, positively, of
  obligation, by coming as close as possible to isolating cases in which just one
  kind of ground is operative. I leave open whether if, intending to deceive, *S*
  says that *p* only mistakenly believing it false, *S* lies. Some would call this
  attempt lying. It is prima facie wrong; and is deceptive and untruthful. My
  major claims about lying do not depend on whether such cases constitute
  lies proper.

implicitly in the scope of a tacit promise not to lie. It may well be in that scope where I say something like 'ok' to you in answering 'Promise to give me your unvarnished assessment of X'. If, later asked to give it, I refuse, some would complain that I "said I would." Granted, I *committed* myself to giving the assessment. But did I say that I would? This is doubtful. What I said (uttered in English) is not truth-valued. In any case, failing to do what I promised to do does not entail having made a "lying promise," as opposed to having expressed a false expectation. There is not even a misrepresentation if I had good evidence that I could keep the promise.

Take a different case suggesting that assertion does not imply some kind of promise not to be untruthful. Suppose I am your guest and, wanting you to know that my evening was good, I simply recount at breakfast my dining with you and other friends, attending a performance, and enjoying the solo in it by Soneka, a singer you admire. If the conversation is casual and you are not counting on my information and did not even request it, I could be lying about enjoying the solo (I could tell it was good but was too distracted by a worry to enjoy her singing), but not violating an implicit promise. This might be called a "white" lie, yet it is still a lie. It could be fully excusable, however, and that possibility provides some reason to think that merely lying need not violate any understanding close to a promise. Some white lies, in any case, seem a kind that counts against the promissory conception of assertion. In any case, it is important for moral theory to clarify what promising is even apart from whether its wrongness is the basis of the wrongness of lying,[9] and other

---

9 There are further difficulties for explicating promising. Can we promise to do something that we do or should see is (at least nomically) impossible? Can we promise to do something when we are coerced under threat of death? I am inclined to allow certain cases of both kinds, but both have subtleties that I cannot now address. I *am* presupposing that sincere promising to A normally entails forming an intention to A, but leave open that some promisers might only hope to A while aware of poor odds and not unqualifiedly expecting success. *Realizing* that this is one's cognitive state should, of course, lead to promising (e.g.) to *try* one's best.

differences between promissory obligations and those of veracity will emerge in considering the next case.

Peter. Imagine that it was Peter, not Lauren, who was executor of their father's will and that on his deathbed the father said to Peter, 'Will you promise to carry out the will?' Peter replies, 'I promise'. Saying 'yes' would also suffice for promising. Perhaps in this context even saying just 'I will do it' would suffice; but it is not true that *whenever* we say we will do something, where our interlocutor wants it done and may assume we intend to do it, we have promised to do it. We have, to be sure, raised a legitimate expectation, and various cases of that seem to many to be promising and certainly to generate some obligation. Peter has done more, and I want to set aside creating non-promissory obligations in this way. It is difficult enough to clarify promising and the obligations it grounds without conceiving making statements that create a legitimate expectation of one's *A*-ing to suffice for promising to *A*. It may yet be true, however, that there is a general prima facie obligation not to create legitimate expectations of us that we cannot fulfill.

Peter's case is like Lauren's in that we may suppose the wrongs they both do are not harmful to their father. She makes a lying statement but has not promised (her father did not think a promise required). Peter both makes a lying promise and breaks it. It is true that both lying and promise-breaking are failures in fidelity to one's word, which may be why Ross spoke just of the duty of fidelity here.[10] But making a promise is not stating something and, deceitful though it may be, promising to *A* while intending not to is not strictly a case of lying (though it is not inappropriately called a lying promise on at least the ground that the promisor is being deceitful and *would* tend to lie about whether the promised deed is intended). It is true that in making a lying promise one does a wrong; but this is not telling a lie, nor failing to make a genuine promise. Someone who later decided to keep it would be credited for keeping it. The characteristic wrong

---

10 In (1930), ch. 2. For a contrasting account of the fidelity account of promising, with detailed discussion of Ross's view of it, see Stroud (2017).

in cases of lying is in an assertive action and is simultaneous with the wrongdoing. The characteristic wrong in cases of promising is in non-performance of the promised act and occurs later than the promise. Lying, then, violates a contemporaneous obligation, whereas promise-breaking violates a future-directed obligation. With lying, both the obligation and its violation are grounded at the time of deceptive communication; with promise-breaking, the violation is later than the promise it breaks.

Promising, moreover, implies a kind of relationship, though possibly one that is very thin. Lying does not imply a relationship, if standing in a relationship entails more than does mere attempted communication. A related point is that lying is in general avoidable at will, by simply withholding speech or other affirmation. Promise-breaking is not generally avoidable at will and is often necessitated by circumstances utterly beyond one's control; and typically, it is avoidable only by performing non-basic actions required for keeping the promise, such as traveling to the place where the promised action is to occur. Keeping promises often requires tracking and responding to both the passage of time and changes in circumstances.

There is a further difference important for understanding both lying and promising. Promising confers a right on the part of the promisee, a moral right to have the promised deed done.[11] Assertion does not in general confer a right on the part of its addressee. Some of us – arguably all of us – *have* a right not to be lied to in ordinary situations in which we are told this or that; but this right is antecedent to the assertion and not conferred by it. Lying characteristically violates a standing general right; promise-breaking violates a conferred special right. Peter's father had a legitimate expectation that he would execute the will, but his right to expect this, assuming he had that right, had a different basis, such as Peter's agreeing to be an executor. Clearly, then, breaking a promise violates a right, whereas lying either violates

---

11 There is promising *that*, say that the vaccine will protect you; but this is a kind of solemn assurance and, though it may raise a legitimate expectation, does not confer a right to have the speaker do something specified in the assurance.

no right or is not the violation of a right necessarily conferred by the very person who violates it.[12]

Justice

It may already be apparent that moral standards are more often clarified, or often better clarified, by considering their violations than by considering adherence to them – more vivid "in the breach than in the observance," one might say. Take this commonsense ground-level *negative principle of justice* as a case in point:

We Should Not Do Injustices

This is a widely accepted moral principle. We understand injustices best in relation to various kinds of unequal treatment in distributive cases and, in retributive cases, punishments of the innocent. This is not to say that justice is strictly equivalent to a non-normatively characterizable kind of inequality or disproportion. But in clarifying moral principles, we should go as far as we can in explaining them in terms whose application does not require moral evaluation.

It is also widely agreed by moral thinkers that we should seek to rectify injustices, but whether this may be conceived as a facet of the obligation of beneficence, and whether retributive justice requires a different principle, are not easy questions. The *notion* of justice is crucial for identifying the maldistributions and wrongful punishments to be avoided in its name, but the *obligation* of justice in the negative form just expressed is not directed toward *doing* justice. Let us concentrate first on distributive justice.

Jonathan. Imagine that Jonathan is responsible for giving food supplies to starving families: one portion for each person. But he likes some groupings better than others and gives extra portions

---

12 One could of course promise to tell the truth, in which case lying would break a promise as well as violate any independent right to be told the truth. However, there are times when, as with would-be murderers of innocent people asking where they are, the questioner has no right (or only an overridden or perhaps forfeited right) to be told the truth.

to some families, placing more of the plastic bags of rice and dried fruit in some family boxes than in others even when the number of persons indicates a different allocation. This is an unjust distribution. It also seems to violate a right to equal treatment, but it would be unjust even if there were not such a general right. It would also be unfair, and some might find that the preferable word.

If every injustice is a case of unfairness, the converse is not obviously true. Suppose Jonathan brings out a tricycle to amuse a six-year-old son of friends who are visiting. The boy's brother, a sporty five-year-old, wants to try it out and is capable of that. If he receives no comparable route to amusement, would it be fair for Jonathan or the parents to deny a ride on the ground that the boy hasn't reached six? It seems unfair. A less natural term is 'unjust', though calling it unjust would perhaps be only misleadingly disapproving rather than altogether inapt. Again, however, the unequal treatment seems the ground of the wrong. To be sure, *differential* treatment is not necessarily unjust, and at least since Aristotle's *Nicomachean Ethics* (Bk 5) some kind of proportionate equality seems to be what justice requires to justify differential treatment.

A major problem of applied ethics is how to determine appropriate proportions. These are difficult enough for salaries of workers who make quantitatively measurable contributions, but it becomes far more difficult with professional compensation and, especially, executive compensation, particularly in cases of partial ownership of the paying organization. Strict quantitative proportionality is often not possible in human affairs, as with academic grading, and here some kind of ranking given approximate "measurement" is all that can be achieved. The difference between an A and a B in grading may not be equal to that between a B and a C, but surely justice requires that no record earning a C be stronger than the weakest record earning a B. In employment cases, there may often be even more dimensions of assessment than in grading, though this challenge may be offset by an agreed overall goal, such as profit, which is more readily measured than degree of academic excellence.

Quite apart from injustice as inequity, there is such a thing as making unjust demands, even when they are made equally. Requiring real excellence in the subject matter for a B on an assignment would be considered unfair. Perhaps even a B+ rather than an A- would be unfitting to generally excellent work by a conscientious student, even if not an injustice. Certainly unfittingness may apply in determining lengths of imprisonment; and with that point in mind we may say that harsh punishments for minor crimes may also be considered unjust. Such cases seem less clearly unjust than, say, unequal punishments differing only because of skin color, but some of the former cases are intuitively clear.

Justice has been widely considered an essential element in good government. Again, a kind of equal treatment is crucial: of all citizens under the law (and of non-citizens who are within the scope of the law), of religious people and institutions in relation to secular ones, of opportunities of the kinds that government can provide, including educational ones. It should be clear that *equal* treatment is not necessarily *uniform* treatment. Remuneration and taxation are common (if controversial) illustrations. A theoretical question here that this book does not pursue is whether, in framing a theory of social justice in political philosophy, the basic standards should be drawn from the realm of justice among individuals in non-political relations. I leave this open and maintain only that the individual cases are at least highly relevant to determining standards of social justice, and that they bind government officials as individuals even apart from the broad standards of justice that those officials must uphold as agents of government.

What should be said here about the obligation to rectify injustice? Surely there is a *positive principle of justice* that can be quite demanding:

We Should Rectify Injustice

This seems not only true but a moral imperative to which many admirable people have devoted their lives. Is it reducible to an obligation of beneficence, on the ground that such rectification is a good? One could conceive it that way, but clarity is better served by noting that some injustices may not be harms, that eliminating them may yield no non-moral good, and that the obligation to rectify injustice seems rooted in the distinctively moral value to be served. An example might be an employer's unfair distribution of work among people who are cooperative, uncomplaining, and mainly pleased to work together, say friends who like working together and are more interested in getting the common task accomplished than in being sure they do exactly their "fair share." We might be right to disapprove of the distribution and indeed the act of making it, yet wrong to think beneficence is what calls for rectification.

Retributive justice might also be argued to be derivative from distributive justice as applied to restrictions of liberty, or from blameworthiness, or from beneficence toward those punishment protects. But retributive justice is essentially both historical and directed toward some living person(s), whereas distributive justice might address circumstances of "inequity" that are not due to historical doings or not tied to any specific person(s). To be sure, although punishment presupposes past wrongdoing, one might even have a theory of punishment on which, as with Dostoevsky's hero in *Crime and Punishment*, the right kind of punishment might be seen as justified partly by contributing to the good of the person punished. There is some plausibility in these and other routes to deriving retributive justice from other moral standards; but it may well be that the core notion in retributive justice is overall fittingness to the wrong that calls for it. Such fittingness apparently embodies a kind of normative proportionality; but the fittingness is more likely of a kind that encompasses both distributive and retributive justice than a species of distribution.[13] In any case, there is a *retributive principle* here to the effect that

---

13 Some wrongs are so egregious that it would be at best difficult to determine a "proportionate" punishment. Even if years of torture followed by execution could befit, say, slaughtering a thousand people, what would be just for slaughtering twice that many? What punishment is proportionate to the wrong of a premeditated theft of an elderly person's life savings?

We Should Not Punish People Unfairly

There is no question that one kind of unfair punishment is punishment different in severity from other punishments imposed for the same crimes under the same conditions. Even if accidental, this is both an inequity and a kind of maldistribution, and it partly accounts for thinking of equal treatment as the heart of justice. Such inequity is sufficient for injustice; but it is not necessary. Punishments may be unfittingly – some might say disproportionately – harsh even if they are imposed with scrupulous uniformity. If the element of unfittingness cannot be eliminated here, then retributive justice seems irreducible to the other kinds, and a case can be made that the overall standard of justice embodies at least three distinct principles. One centers on distribution, another on rectification, and the third on retribution, where a kind of unfairness can be a failure in doing justice even if the term 'injustice' may be too strong. All three principles seem partly constitutive of commonsense morality.

Beneficence

The most famous story of beneficence might be that of the Good Samaritan:

> A priest happened to be going down the same road, and when he saw the man, he passed by on the other side. So too, a Levite, when he came to the place and saw him, passed by on the other side. But a Samaritan, as he traveled, came where the man was; and ... he took pity on him. He went to him and bandaged his wounds, pouring on oil and wine. Then he put the man on his own donkey, brought him to an inn and took care of him. The next day he took out two denarii and gave them to the inn-keeper. 'Look after him,' he said, 'and when I return, I will reimburse you for any extra expense you may have'.
>
> (Luke 10: 25–37)

The story is particularly significant in portraying paradigmatic circumstances that *call* for beneficence and provide for a core case exhibiting it. Presumably, contributing to a fund to fight disease in a foreign country one cannot even identify is also a beneficent deed, but even in that case we can readily imagine personal goods that the funds will do. Do we also have a prima facie obligation to contribute to the good in the abstract, no matter where or when our action takes effect and regardless of our having any sense of the beings benefited? This is not obvious.[14] Still, vivid media presentations of sentient life we cannot experience firsthand make hypothetical relationships vividly imaginable. If the obligation of beneficence is in principle limited to cases of some appropriate relationship we have or could have to potential beneficiaries, this does not eliminate the obligation's having *some* force in circumstances far from those of our "neighbor." There is no quantitative answer to how much force, and philosophers have often been cautious about suggesting the extent of our obligations of beneficence.[15]

The Samaritan story also portrays beneficence in the form of reducing the suffering and promoting well-being. These are capable of non-moral explication and thus serve as "descriptive," often perceptible, anchors of the notion of beneficence. Conceived generically, beneficence is doing good things for someone else, and a simple formulation of the moral standard in question is the *beneficence principle* that

We Should Do Good Deeds Toward Others[16]

Since pain and suffering are intrinsically bad, the fact that reducing them counts toward beneficence suggests that reduction of pain and suffering are good *in themselves*. This seems clearly so.

---

14 Cf. Ross (1930) where he endorses a "duty to produce as much good as we can" (25; cf. 21). I doubt Ross's overall view requires this strong a beneficence clause. His view implies, moreover, as points of mine do, that the well-being of sentient non-persons is morally important.

15 Kant, e.g., in explaining the obligation to treat humanity as an end, illustrates the duty of beneficence in terms of personal relationships (1785/1997: sec. 423) and speaks of beneficence as everyone's trying "as far as he can," to further the ends of others (sec. 430).

16 Beneficent deeds may be done toward animals too; but, for people living in this world as we know it, goodness to animals and none toward human beings (given suitable opportunities) would not suffice for fulfillment of the obligation of beneficence.

The point is important in that hedonism is often represented as the view that the basic intrinsic values are pleasure and pain. Yet this is clearly too narrow, at least if we do not take reduction – or spontaneous diminution – of pain as a kind of pleasure. Doing that would surely conflate pleasure with (at least) the welcome experience of relief. There clearly is intrinsic value in the welcome sense of diminishing pain, even where this experience does not embody pleasure. Some kinds of growing pleasure in doing a task may also be instances in which hedonic change is valuable in itself without being identical with pleasure or pain. In any case, some instances of a rewarding sense of accomplishment, especially where obstacles are skillfully overcome, are intrinsically good without being instances of pleasure.[17]

Given how fitting benevolence is to beneficent deeds, one might think that we could as well speak of the obligation of benevolence. But unless 'benevolence' here designates beneficent deeds, this would import into the obligation of beneficence a motivational constraint on its execution. Perhaps, as a plausible virtue ethics would suggest, the obligation of beneficence normatively calls for cultivating and nurturing a pattern of action that yields or sustains benevolent motivation, particularly as sufficiently underlying our beneficent deeds. It befits those deeds to express benevolence, but doing that is not a constraint on what constitutes them.

Barbara. Teaching is a realm with wide scope for illustration. Barbara teaches a humanities subject. Her students are generally able and do not show signs of suffering or distress of the kind that calls for remedial help. But Barbara likes to invite them to her office and her home and seeks ways to enhance their enjoyment of the subject as well as its mastery. She looks back at their writings even when they already merit a good grade and there is no question of defects; she offers ideas about readings; asks about their plans; offers to write supportive recommendations for

---

17 In some cases, a positive sense of achievement may be mixed with pain but still be overall positive. For discussion of the variety of such cases and the value of achievement see Bradford (2015).

those seeking higher degrees or employment; looks for research opportunities for them, such as conference presentations, tutoring, or translation work; and holds sessions (at her expense) for discussion over refreshments.

There is a kind of generosity prominent here, but beneficence does not entail generosity, and generosity does not entail beneficence, even when generous deeds are toward charities and aimed at helping them do good work. Would Barbara have to be generous overall to count as being beneficent in all the things mentioned? Surely beneficence as a pattern of action does not entail generosity – or indeed overall beneficence – toward *all* the kinds of people Barbara interacts with, though in a teacher like her one might expect a wider range of good deeds than is required for generosity only to those she is responsible for. Moreover, although she could not have the *trait* of beneficence if, without excuse, she were cruel to some people, she could still do beneficent deeds even if she were cruel in most aspects of her life. Beneficent deeds are of course characteristic of beneficence as a trait of persons, but the relation between these two notions is complex. It is important, however, that we consider whether beneficent deeds must be beneficently motivated – roughly, motivated by a desire to realize the relevant good *for the sake of* the intended beneficiary. This may seem so given how rare it is for a sustained pattern of beneficence to occur other than from motivation that manifests *benevolence*, conceived as good will.

Such beneficent motivation is altruistic and would be expected in a beneficent person. But let us look more closely at Barbara. Suppose she does most of the things described mainly to inspire a teaching award. In that case, the deeds are not altruistic. But may they not still be beneficent? Some would say that if the motivation for them is wholly or primarily instrumental in this way, they are not beneficent. We certainly might say that they lack moral creditworthiness. But suppose Barbara does the things some of the time in a natural way and without needing to *think* of the possible instrumental payoff. Instrumental motivation can yield good habits, and its governing end can be unobjectionable or even quite worthy. Here it may help to imagine that we observe only one or two occasions on which, well beyond the call of pedagogical duty, Barbara helps students advance their work. One sees students and teacher at a nearby table looking at essays, hears Barbara making thoughtful comments on the content, listening to the student, and suggesting other lines of inquiry. One would be likely to speak of her being good to the students, even if, on knowing of the instrumental motivation, one would not attribute to her beneficence as a trait.

My aim here is to treat beneficence as capable of realization in conduct toward others even if it is not motivated by the expected desires. One reason for this is that we need a way – and in my view commonsense ethics has a way – of describing at least most of our moral obligations behaviorally. From this point of view, we do need to presuppose that the kinds of behaviors in question will be intentional (hence in some way represent the will of the agent), but we do not need to know what the agent's underlying motivation is. Barbara must be behaving in a helpful way toward students whose papers she is discussing. Calling this beneficent presupposes that she intends to help (or has an intention in that positive range), but it does not require an ultimate basis in non-instrumental, altruistic motivation.

One more thing about motivation is pertinent here: beneficent motivation need not be moral and probably need not even be normative. Barbara may have to intend something appropriate to helping the students, but the notion of fulfilling an *obligation* to do it, or even the notion of being such that she (morally) *ought* to do it, need not come into her motivation. Perhaps she need not even conceptualize what she is doing as in some way good, though this would be normal. Here the case of teaching is too complex to make the point evident. Imagine Barbara simply observing the delight of a guest eating the apricot whip served for dessert. Offering a second portion simply to add to gustatory pleasure would suffice for beneficence in hosting. So would preparing an ice-pack to reduce the pain of an ankle that another guest twists rising too fast from a deep sofa. Other things equal, the degree of beneficence of a deed grows with the agent's difficulty in achieving it, and the obligation to do beneficent deeds is correspondingly lessened as their difficulty rises.

Reparation

If we wrong someone, we normally owe at least an apology. If we harm someone even in an excusable accident, then, if it is possible to give some comfort or help in recovery, this is normally fitting and may be obligatory. Ross spoke of the duty of reparation as arising from wrongdoing toward someone else,[18] but at least if it is a basic obligation, it seems undesirable in bringing out what the obligation is to define it in moral terms. In developing an ethical theory, we should seek, so far as possible, to explain the basic obligations recognized by the theory in language that does not require a prior understanding of moral terms, such as 'wrong'. For the obligation of reparation to be activated, there should be some sufficient condition describable non-morally, such as hitting a cyclist while driving a car. It is true that for determining overall ("final") obligations, we must appeal to or presuppose moral standards, but the basic standards should be intelligible and indeed applicable on a "descriptive" basis. The ultimate grounds of moral obligation are natural (and so non-moral) facts.[19]

It is through perceptible descriptive facts that children learn moral standards and enter into moral discourse; and we depend on such facts for both morally guiding our own actions and appraising the deeds of others. In cases like that of a driver's hitting a cyclist, failing to do something at least symbolic when one has harmed someone and can readily do it seems at least a

---

18 Ross (1930: 21).
19 My (2016) discusses this matter in detail in relation to explicating treatment of persons merely as means (versus ends). Explicating the grounds of the reparational obligation descriptively is possible so long as we can achieve sufficient clarity without invoking normative notions. This seems possible even though there are notions or harm – and important descriptions of doing it – that are (conceptually) normative. For a contrasting view on this issue, see J. Gert (2003).

slight – an indication of not caring enough about the person to acknowledge that one has done the *kind* of thing that, if intentional, would culpably violate the obligation not to harm. In broad terms, the *reparation principle* here is that

We Should Make Reparations for Our Actions that Harm Others

If the harming is accidental, it is not naturally said to be *toward* others, though it may still call for reparation; but many actions calling for reparation are non-accidental and even directed toward others. Actions that harm others do harm *to* them and must be understood in part causally, even if the harm is not intentional; whereas harm *toward* others has an essential purposive element. This reparation principle is connected with the wrongness of treating people disrespectfully; but it seems to have some degree of normative force that is independent of the other obligations I am mainly exploring and to be explicable partly in terms of harms describable in non-moral terms. Here our accident case is again instructive.

Kang and Helen. In driving too fast and hitting Helen, Kang incurs an obligation of reparation. The harm he does to her is not through an unavoidable accident, and he does a serious wrong to her. There is no doubt that for wronging others we should make reparations. This holds even for unavoidable accidents. If Helen is driving on a road cut along a slope ravaged by a forest fire, a mud slide may force her to jam her brake with the result of skidding into another car whose driver, Leo, is thereby seriously injured. Here the accident might be unavoidable (and might have been unpredictable). As compared with Kang, who, apart from speeding, could have avoided hurting someone, there is a lesser ground for Helen's having an obligation of reparation. Would it suffice to express sympathy to Leo? Suppose he explains that he has just received an eviction notice and is doubly upset because he was rushing to apply for immediate legal protection. Should she not help by recommending a good attorney for such cases if, as a close relative of one, she is in a position to? Again, her involvement in harming him suggests that even apart from beneficence she should, and that, if time permits, she would be wrong not to mention the possibility (or offer some other help).[20]

Is it always true, however, that if we do something impermissible to another, we should make reparations? This may be impossible. The victim may die. If there is no relative, friend, or descendant we can reach, even vicarious reparation may not be possible if it must be to somebody one can try to compensate in some way.[21]

In characterizing the obligation in question, particularly using 'reparation' rather than, say, 'compensation', it is natural to speak of reparations for wrongdoing. But (as already indicated in a somewhat different way) if we are to clarify morality as much as possible, we should seek to describe, in non-moral – and if possible behavioral – terms, what grounds the reparational obligation. Fortunately, harming others can be at least quite comprehensively so described. So can injury, which also grounds such obligations and can apply to certain offensive behavior or even some kinds of unintentional damage to a person's reputation. Indirect harms must of course be included, as where killing a person harms the family but (say because the wrongdoer dies simultaneously) precludes reparations toward the victim.

Such obligation as there is here might, however, come from the obligation of beneficence made prominent by the accident. If we vary the case so that Helen steers into a car to avoid damaging hers in dense but not impenetrable shrubbery, the picture changes, and the change seems to imply that her harming Leo is avoidable. Here, he apparently should receive some kind of compensatory treatment for the harm. This is an obligation of reparation. Deeds that

---

20 There is no sharp distinction between what should be done in reparation and certain obligations of beneficence. Obligations of beneficence, too, may overlap with what is called for by solidarity. For discussion of that notion as normatively significant, see, e.g., Zhao (2019) and Stuchlik (2021).

21 This leaves open that institutional wrongs such as slavery can harm people in ways that may call for compensation – which overlaps but is not equivalent to reparation – of those disadvantaged as a result, even by those who have not wronged any of them but are beneficiaries of wrongs that are at least partly responsible for the relevant disadvantages.

suffice might be of a beneficent kind, but the ground of their reparational obligatoriness is having harmed – even if not necessarily wronged – the other. That a deed might not normally count as reparational unless it is of a beneficent kind does not imply that the obligation to do such a deed is based on the grounds of beneficence. One evidence of this is that whereas the obligation of beneficence becomes stronger with a certain kind of integration of the agent's ability to do good deeds toward the other(s) with their capacity to benefit, the obligation of reparation becomes stronger with the degree of harm done to the person (s) harmed and not with their capacity to benefit from what the agent of the harm can do.

With certain unavoidable accidents, harming does not entail wronging, yet some prima facie obligation of reparation is created. Insofar as we can descriptively characterize the grounds of this obligation, it may qualify as a basic obligation (even if characteristically limited in extent by comparison with, e.g., promising). But there is a difference between requiring descriptive grounds as capable of generating the obligation and requiring that only those may figure in explicating it. An important point about reparation is that even when it rests on an unavoidable harm, doing that harm is *excusable* rather than simply a person-harming event, such as a lightning strike, which is comparably harmful. The point is that the obligation of reparation may have some conceptual dependence on other obligations (such as the obligation not to harm) in a way not all the other basic obligations do. Nonetheless, given its having distinctive descriptively sufficient grounds, it may still play a needed role in the theory of obligation.

Gratitude

Many of us have been cautioned about accepting gifts. This is in tension with the idea that giving is a good thing, since it wouldn't generally be good if accepting gifts were generally bad. How might we resolve the tension? I've heard it said that if you accept a gift, you become obligated to the giver. This caution has some plausibility. Normally it is wrong to accept gifts or services without at least expressing appreciation. This clearly holds, at least, when those are not owed to one. Like failing to make reparation for harming someone, it is a kind of slight. The principle here is that

We Should Express Gratitude to Others for Good Deeds They Do Toward Us

Expressions of gratitude are multifarious. If they are insincere, they ill-befit the person's words or gestures; but this should not be taken to show that the obligation is *to feel gratitude*. Its object is appropriate gestures, including verbal thanks. These should not be given in a manner that reveals a lack of appropriate feeling; but, if they are, that would illustrate doing the right thing in the wrong manner, not a failure to fulfill the obligation.

What kinds of acts lie in the scope of this principle? They will characteristically be intentional, but 'actions toward' allows for at least certain non-intentional actions that are foreseen. If you choose a charity in a way you see will benefit me when you could equally well have chosen another, you might have been acting toward me without aiming at benefitting me. Is a properly expressed 'thank-you', for instance, enough to fulfill whatever obligation of gratitude there is here – or in general?

Geraldine. Imagine that I lose my wallet, containing a driver's license, credit cards, and some cash. I worry about it for some hours before Geraldine comes to my home with the wallet and all its contents. I meet her at the door and thank her profusely. I think I should offer something in appreciation. I say that I'd like to express great appreciation for her time and conscientiousness and pull from the wallet all the cash (thinking that this is fitting given her trouble, and that people less conscientious than Geraldine might have kept the cash and anonymously mailed the wallet). She refuses emphatically, saying that she was happy to do it and considered it a responsibility.

I owed her an expression of gratitude, but did I fulfill it? What she did wasn't a gift, but did she owe it to me to bring my wallet, as opposed to taking it to a police station, or phoning me to pick it up, or perhaps mailing it? Suppose I initially owed more than thanks. More is certainly fitting, less is unfitting. Still, she had a right to cancel (or at least override by objection) any obligation beyond thanking her. Compare this with a case in which, at a drugstore, I drop my wallet and proceed to leave. Someone behind me who sees this does have an obligation to return (or at least identify) the wallet to me, nor is this level of beneficence normally an inconvenience. It remains a service, however, and not expressing thanks would be wrong. Offering a cash gift (if a substantial amount might be called a gift rather than a tip), might be fitting but is not obligatory.

The case of receiving gifts is different. Here I must recount an occasion of initially anonymous giving. With my wife, our school-age children, and my mother, I lunched at a large but thinly populated restaurant. We likely appeared to be having a good time. When I asked for the bill, the waiter told me it had been paid. Surprised, I asked how that could be. I recall receiving an initially evasive answer. The mystery was too much to resist, and further inquiry revealed that a man seated at the bar some twenty feet from our table had paid the bill. I approached him, thanked him, and said something like: this is very kind but we really can't let you do it. He smiled and said he was happy to. I then asked if I could at least pay his bill. He declined emphatically. I thanked him but couldn't help asking if there was some special occasion. I remember his words: "Let's just say I had a good day." What was especially unusual is that the gift came from a stranger, could not be declined, and could not be reciprocated. Was there any obligation to reciprocate, for instance pay for his lunch, though reciprocation was prevented by his refusal to allow it? I doubt it. If any such obligation was overridden, the obligation of gratitude that remained seemed to me a kind of *recognitional* obligation. I doubt that in this case non-reciprocation entailed a failure to fulfill an obligation of gratitude.[22]

---

22 Here I differ from Ross (1930: 23), who seemed to think that the duty of gratitude requires something approaching proportionality, whereas I consider this at most a prima facie desirable element in expressing gratitude. What is required must befit the deed calling for gratitude, but this does not

Granted, reciprocation can both express the appropriate appreciative recognition and fulfill the obligation of gratitude. On some occasions, gifts can, moreover, call for reciprocation and not just gratitude. This is a kind of case in which one must not accept them if reciprocation would be wrong, as may be so for candidates for public office who are given large campaign contributions. What if the gift or benefit is major and one *cannot* reciprocate? Suppose someone nominates one for a prize and, as can happen, one will never be able to reciprocate the honor, as with someone much older who would not be a candidate for anything one can give or support. There is an obligation to express appreciation here, but efforts to reciprocate might be foolish or even offensive. In this case, there is not only the element of recognition but also one of respect. One way to see this is to note an adverbial dimension of the obligation of gratitude: knowingly failing to give thanks as a minimal recognition is acting *inappreciatively*.

4   Morality and Prudence

There is a certain naturalness in thinking of reason as the ultimate standard for judging human action, of morality as the realm of optimally rational standards of social action, and of prudence as the realm of standards governing self-interest, whether in individual or social action. Much has been written on whether rationality demands morality[23] and whether, in practice, what is prudent is ultimately equivalent to what is right. My concern here is not these very broad issues but mainly whether self-improvement – which is surely called for by some normative standard – should be considered a moral standard not reducible

---

entail proportionality – even if it calls for avoiding great disproportionality – and anyway the proportionate, as with an unsuitable gift of the same cost, need not be fitting. Highly pertinent to this issue is Horgan and Timmons (2022).

23 I have discussed this in detail in (2001b) and extended the points made there in (2010b).

to interpersonal moral standards or instead a prudential one. I proceed as before by working from an example.

Self-Improvement

That failing to do things toward one's improvement as a person is "countervirtuous" seems plain. Sloth is a vice, laziness a related defect of character, self-centeredness a moral fault. By contrast, enhancing skills is a natural end in most reflective life-plans, and, even apart from this, devotion to learning is an admirable trait. That self-directed beneficence supports the desirability of self-improvement need not be denied, but the cases that follow indicate reasons to think that such beneficence is not the only basis for self-improvement. To many philosophers, it has seemed clear, even apart from the obligation of beneficence and prudence, that

We Should Seek to Improve Ourselves

This may be impossible – either from lack of ability or opportunity or – at best rarely – because one has done everything one possibly can toward self-improvement. Even then, however, the principle presupposes that we should at least sustain our capacities. But the obligation is prima facie, and impossibility in a situation may be taken to eliminate or defeat it.

Verity. Verity believes that, like all normal human beings, she is imperfect and should improve herself. She considers this possible under many conditions often realized in normal lives. Assuming she is right, is the 'should' moral? Suppose that simply because she feels like it, she spends an entire Saturday watching films she has seen and considers mediocre. She might naturally think, if she has normal vocational and family commitments, that she *should* be doing something more worthwhile; and if she does such watching often, her friends or relatives might call her lazy or undisciplined. They can regard her as, say, lazy even if they do not think of her as doing anything wrong. In contemporary English, calling failure to improve oneself wrong needs argument. It is not in any clear way immoral for me, on a free summer weekend, not to do, for instance, serious reading or musical practice or good exercise. A natural response to such facts is to say that the 'should' appropriate to self-improvement indicates a requirement of prudence, not morality.[24]

If the counsels of prudence are solely those of self-interest, then calling self-improvement a wholly prudential requirement would seem too narrow. But if prudence is a realm of choices governed by practical wisdom, as for Aristotle, then the requirements of self-improvement are plausibly thought to be supported by those of prudence and at least usually encompassed by them. If, moreover, ethics is taken to be the domain of standards central for living a good life, one might take the 'should' appropriate to self-improvement to be broadly moral as well, though it includes more, such as learning and maintaining skills. It is not obvious that ethics must be construed this broadly in order for that 'should' to be properly conceived as moral. But let me offer three significant considerations that support the view that there is a moral obligation of self-improvement that has some basis in considerations not reducible to collateral requirements of either prudence or conduciveness to a good life non-morally conceived.

5 Prudence, Conscientiousness, and Self-Directed Virtues

First, given how demanding morality is – as witnessed by the difficulty of living up to the seven principles just explored – there is a strong empirical connection between adhering to them and improving oneself. This applies, at least, to children in development and to most adults. Normal life is full of temptations to do wrong; many people have too few or too weak beneficent desires; and even those who resist serious wrongdoing often fail to achieve the beneficent deeds they can do without major sacrifice. Admittedly, if this is the only non-prudential moral basis of the 'should' of self-improvement, then that 'should' is *derivatively* moral, rather than directly so, as are the other principles we have

---

24 This has been argued by B. Gert (2007) against Ross and me, and I have replied to some of Gert's points in my reply to him in Timmons, Greco, and Mele (2007: 212–213).

considered. This need not make it less important for human flour-ishing or even for the moral status of human society. It is important: a 'should' to which morally conscientious people are attentive. Moreover, being in this way derivatively moral does not imply reducibility to any single moral obligation or even any proper subset of the seven so far considered.

My second point here is that morality may be taken to concern how persons ought to be treated, including how we should treat ourselves. There might be negative obligations toward oneself even if not positive ones; and if, as is plausibly arguable, one can wrong oneself by, say, self-degradation and false ascriptions of vice and wrongdoing, we may at least consider the way open to view some self-directed obligations as moral. The plausibility of this broad conception of morality is most easily seen in relation to mistreatment of oneself. Suppose that Davora is a bullied and sometimes depressed teenager and suffers self-hate. She gets tattoos on both arms without even admiring the designs; she buys treats for girls she dislikes but hopes to pacify; she even allows herself to be sexually used in the hope of being liked. Such a person could even take the blame for a theft by a "friend" and suffer punishment for it. Such things are wrongs toward herself and likely also degrading. If moral standards require disapproval in such cases, might they not also call for it in cases of failure to improve oneself?

A third consideration that favors viewing self-improvement as a moral standard is that the ground – or one ground – of the wrongness of self-harm is the value or importance of oneself as a person or, in any case, of much the same elements of personhood that ground beneficence. Whatever the personal factors that ground beneficence, this moral significance is a matter of what they are, not of whose they are. If something intrinsic to persons is a basis of an obligation of beneficence calling for our preventing their degrading themselves and for our contributing to the well-being of others, why should it not call for our preventing the same degradation, and, positively, promoting the same kind of well-being, in ourselves? Davora can wrong herself by doing the kinds of things to herself that she should think she ought to try to prevent being done to others. Why should she not have a related obligation to do the kinds of positive things to better her life that she ought to do for others? To be sure, one could argue that the obligation of self-improvement does not apply to persons whose level of moral uprightness is sufficiently high. But unless the level is ideally high, the kinds of considerations mentioned would still indicate that there is an obligation of self-improvement for human beings as we know them.

A further point here is implicit in the conception of ethics as concerned with conduct, which embodies the motivation and manners of action. Our moral status is largely determined by how well we treat people, and this is a matter not just of what we do toward them but also of the motivation and manner of our actions toward them. Feeling a sharp pain can cause unintention-ally speaking hurtfully to friends. Our motivation is also impor-tant. We should not treat others well just from self-interest, and, if we do, this is commonly sensed. The point here, however, is that one way we should improve ourselves is to increase the fit between acts morality requires of us and our motivation for performing them. We should seek *aretaic integration*, which includes elements of character that, in our conduct, tend to make us fittingly combine what we do with appropriate motivation and manner in our doing of it. Virtue calls for this, and it is central for moral conscientiousness. Few if any are without some room to enhance the desirable integration. Reducing our distance from the best such integration we can achieve is a kind of self-improvement that can be quite challenging. If we do the right things, this may be highly creditable in itself, but virtuous char-acter requires a tendency to do these for the right reasons and in some appropriate manner. Here some may achieve overt recti-tude by undetectable artifice; but virtue is best manifested by interpersonal relations that rise to the artistry of sensitivity and grace. Without efforts of self-improvement, at most a few achieve or maintain this level of social interaction.

One might agree on most of what has been said here and still maintain that what seems an obligation of self-improvement turns out to be one of self-directed beneficence. If beneficence is not conceptually tied to interpersonal conduct, that objection is fair. But apparently it is properly so conceived.[25] We simply do not and properly cannot ascribe it to people even in part on the basis of how they treat themselves. Indeed, Davora's bad treatment of herself is compatible with much beneficence and would not seem even to detract from its extent if we conceive its focus as toward others. Furthermore, much of the kind of behavior that counts toward beneficence does not, when self-directed, count toward fulfilling the normative requirement of self-improvement. Davora's nursing the wounds of a friend or giving pleasure to an ageing aunt are beneficent; but nursing oneself and giving oneself pleasure, do not count toward fulfilling the obligation of self-improvement.

To deny that the obligation of self-improvement is not just self-directed beneficence does not require ignoring an important connection between the two. Notice that the obligation of beneficence tends to gain strength in rough proportion to the magnitude of the good for others and the ease with which one can do that good. If we do not give to a charity we approve of when it requests a donation we can afford, this may be a wrong, but it does not compare with the gross failure of beneficence implied by walking on when someone trips on stone steps and is bleeding profusely. This is an especially serious wrong if one is medically trained, equipped to stop the bleeding, and not pressed by some competing obligation. Suppose, however, that the case is instead one of declining to learn a skill that facilitates one's work, say a fingering technique that makes one a better pianist. If the

---

25 Cf. Mill's *On Liberty*: "What are called duties to ourselves are not socially obligatory unless circumstances render them at some time duties to others. The term duty to oneself, when it means anything more than prudence, means self-improvement or self-development..." (1859: 177). Mill would doubtless give a utilitarian account of the value of self-development and self-improvement, but I simply note that he considered these conceptually important for understanding the obligation of self-improvement and may not have considered that obligation reducible to either a counsel of prudence or an obligation of beneficence.

learning is easy, as where a friend offers to teach the technique with no suggestion of burden on either party, and the gain is substantial, why should declining to learn not show a kind of disregard for one's own potentialities? It is certainly not admirable, but is it not also counter-virtuous?

It may be in part because the obligation of self-improvement (unlike other intuitive obligations of the kinds we are considering) is *self-directed* that it is easily assimilated to a counsel of prudence narrowly conceived. There is another distinctive element in it – though this also fails to distinguish it from prudence conceived broadly: it is *trait-directed*. Granted, individual deeds can be essential to self-improvement; but we do not improve ourselves, as opposed to our records, if we do not change ourselves in some constitutional respect. Trait development, of course, is not achievable at will, whereas many obligations are fulfillable at will. We might also say, at a high level of generality, that whereas the point of view of prudence is self-interest, the point of view of self-improvement is that of excellence – or at least of change in that direction. Excellence of character, moreover, include not just doing the right kinds of deeds but also an internalized tendency to do them in a morally appropriate manner and for one or more reasons that, at least morally, befit the context. Achieving this tendency is a challenge to self-mastery, and we may have secondary obligations to integrate motivation and action, which cannot be done at will and requires self-understanding.

It turns out that including the 'should' of self-improvement as broadly moral is not self-evidently correct, but defensible only on a broad conception of morality. It is perhaps clear that ordinary (non-excusable) failures to seek self-improvement *ill-befit* being a moral person, and making efforts toward self-improvement are quite fitting to that status. Related to this, failures in self-improvement are criticizable from the broad point of view of the conception of a morally sound person. This still leaves the question of whether the 'should' in question is basic. I see no way to show that, but the more important question is whether a broad conception of morality – one that takes it, as did Kant, to concern our treatment of *persons* no matter who they are – favors includ-ing the obligation in question. My provisional conclusion is that it does.

6   The Comprehensiveness of the Principles

For any set of commonsense moral principles with the breadth of those formulated so far, the question naturally arises whether more are needed or whether some reduce to combinations of others. There is no doubt that some of the principles can be understood with sufficient breadth to enable us to *derive* one or more others from some subset of the remaining ones. But deri-vation does not entail *reduction*. I take reduction of the kind in question here to require finding a set of *properties* such that having the reduced property is equivalent to having the property it reduces to, as, say being obligated to improve oneself might be taken to *be* simply being obligated to be constructively beneficent toward oneself. I doubt such reductive attempts will succeed. Suppose, however, that we could show the derivability of one commonsense obligation from one or more others[26] – or indeed from some master principle such as the categorical imperative. We still gain in both perspicuity and normative guidance by articulating and separately explicating the individual principles in question.

One might object that if a principle is derivable from others, it is not *basic*. That holds for one notion of basicality and certainly for basicality conceived as Aristotelian indemonstrability.[27] But what is self-evident does not stand in need of derivation for its knowability or justifiable believability; and this epistemic status

---

26 Here B. Gert's (2004) is an instructive unification of plausibly formulated commonsense moral principles.

27 This is described in Aristotle's *Posterior Analytics* 72b. Intuitively, what cannot be known on the basis of any epistemically prior proposition – one "better known" than it – cannot be demonstrated, as opposed to validly inferred. Such indemonstrables might be called "strongly axiomatic" (terminology explained in my 2004) and might apply to, e.g., ⟨If $A = B$, then $B = A$⟩ and to ⟨No proposition is both true and false⟩.

can give it a *systemically basic* role in guiding action. It need not be conceived as depending on or even following from one or more others to be action-guiding in its own right. This status can be plausibly claimed for the principles discussed here (a view that will be explained and defended in some detail in Chapters 7 and 9).

Note, too, that even if properties are reducible, the corresponding concepts need not be. Suppose the property of being a circle is reducible to that of being a plane figure whose circumference is pi times its diameter and that the property of being water is reducible to that of being H_2O. The concepts differ in each pair of cases, and this makes possible different roles in intention and belief, and thus in guiding behavior.[28]

There is a kind of comprehensiveness quite different from derivability of all our moral standards from a master principle. Call it *normative completeness*: A set of moral principles is normatively complete in this sense if (and only if) every true (singular) moral judgment can be accounted for by it, roughly in the sense that it is explainable by appeal to one or more of the principles.[29] This notion of completeness is significant in a qualified form in which it applies only to judgments of prima facie obligation; but I consider it plausible even with the understanding that a final judgment in a case of conflicting obligations must be explainable by a plausible argument that it is supported by the best weighting of the conflicting prima facie obligations. On the common and highly plausible assumption that normative properties are consequential on non-normative properties, this explainability hypothesis can be supported by analogies in which all the relevant non-

---

28 Whatever we take property reduction to be, it requires less than conceptual reduction, which seems the very strong kind our examples show to be needed, between act-types *A*-ing and *B*-ing, which I conceive as *property-types*, for validly inferring, from *S*'s intending to *A*, that *S* intends to *B*.

29 The notion of normative completeness is introduced and considered in some detail in my (2001b). In epistemic terms, normative completeness, at least in principle, enables the theory to take us from knowledge of an agent's overall (moral) obligation, to a plausible account (ideally to knowledge) of why the action in question is obligatory (85). A contrasting notion of *epistemic* completeness, on which a moral theory enables us to derive obligations from certain non-normative facts, is also introduced there (85–86).

moral facts are the same. If all the relevant non-moral facts regarding two drivers' hitting a cyclist are the same, then if one has an obligation of reparation, so does the other. This point suggests the possibility of formulating some universalizable principle in which the relevant variables regarding accidents figure, but in practice doing so may be difficult or impossible.

Normative completeness is difficult to show for any normative ethical theory, but the difficulty is reduced if one avoids taking the obligation of beneficence to be ubiquitous in human behavior. Utilitarianism tends to invite this view, and even pluralists such as Ross have said things inviting it, as where he affirms a prima facie obligation to bring about as much intrinsic good "as possible".[30] Similarly, Kant, in speaking of beneficence and calling on each of us to try "as far as he can, to further the ends of others," leaves the scope of the 'can' open.[31] Its scope is a challenge to explication, but there are surely many cases in which, for some good that it is *possible* for us to realize, either we have no prima facie obligation to realize it or doing that is so plainly overridden by one or more other obligations as to pose no challenge to explaining our final obligation in the context. In either case, normative completeness of the set of principles proposed in this book (here and later) is plausibly defensible.

The eight principles discussed here – ten given the threefold obligation of justice – represent a comprehensive normative ethics, and anyone who conforms to them is likely to exhibit morally commendable conduct. We have seen, however, that ethics concerns more than the things we should do – the vehicles of our conduct, which are central in the principles so far discussed. It also concerns the manner in which we should do it and the motivational elements that underlie our doing of it. Some concerns of ethics in relation to motivation and manner are implicitly accommodated in our discussion of the obligation of

30 Ross (1930: 24).   31 Kant (1785/1997: 430).

self-improvement. We should and often do care about what motives determine our actions and how we carry them out. But there are obligations, at least in the dimension of manner, that can be fulfilled at will, by contrast with the indirect and more limited control we have over why we act. There is also a dimension of action that, quite apart from manner, still needs discussion here if we are to achieve a more nearly complete account of the central standards of moral obligation. The next two chapters will develop these points.

5   Higher-Level Moral Obligations

It is often difficult to act in accordance with the moral principles we have been exploring, and there is reason to think that those who achieve it will act in manners that are morally appropriate and for reasons that make their actions creditworthy. But the manner of an action is a higher-order property, and a morally good manner of a right action is not guaranteed either by the lower-order property of its rightness or by underlying moral motivation. However, as desirable as it is that people act both in a morally permissible manner and from motives that suffice for one's doing the right thing to be creditworthy, there is something morally objectionable about *making* people act in that manner or for creditworthy reasons. Imagine brain manipulation as a possible resort. Doubtless such coercion is likely harmful in some way and might thus be impermissible under the obligation to avoid harm. But quite apart from harms, are we not in some sense entitled to a great deal of liberty regarding our conduct? What is the moral status of such liberty? Might there be obligations that, though connected with the wrongness of both manipulation and coercion, also arise from the independent moral importance of liberty? This question deserves examination.

1   Liberty as a Moral Standard

Liberty is something virtually everyone wants. Particularly when people's liberty is restricted, they tend to demand it. One question here is what liberty is. Another is whether its preservation or enhancement is in itself an object of obligation; and still another is whether that obligation is basic. Let's take these in turn, with the idea of supporting the *liberty principle* that

We Should Preserve and Enhance Liberty

The importance of liberty is most prominently represented in protests against its deprivation, but this does not imply that we do not also have positive obligations in relation to it. In pursuing this question, I do not assume that liberty and freedom are exactly equivalent but will sometimes use 'freedom' as contextually more appropriate.

The kind of liberty of concern here is a matter of a range of possible acts and manners of action for the person(s) in question. It is roughly an agent's freedom *to do* the thing(s) in question, which is roughly a matter of there being no barrier to doing such things and no compulsion not to do them. The notion of compulsion needs analysis, but it is clear enough for my purposes here.[1] It is possible, however, to be free *to* do something and still *do* it under compulsion to do it. This is a case of *overridden autonomy*. Here one is free *to* do it but not free *in* doing it. From threat of blackmail, one donates to a cause one would freely give to. Such cases can occur regardless of the kind of action in question. That partly accounts for the higher-order character of the liberty principle: it bears on what we do, the manner in which we do it, and our discretion in choosing either; it does not call for any particular kind of deed, not even for deeds in the indefinite range covered by the other obligations we have considered. In the sense I intend, the preservation and enhancement of liberty encompasses the preservation and enhancement of autonomy, but I prefer to use 'autonomy' more narrowly than 'liberty'.

---

1 In (1974) (reprinted in my [1993a]) I proposed a detailed account, extended in my (1986) and (1993a). The account is an "actual worlds" one and treats 'could not have done otherwise' in the relevant sense as *non-conditional*, by contrast with accounts of "alternative possibilities" proposed by Harry Frankfurt and others. For discussion of such accounts see, e.g., Fischer (2011).

There is a close connection between freedom *in* acting and promotion and enhancement of freedom *to* act. What we will do under compulsion, and thus will not freely do, reduces what we are free to do – including the numerous deeds precluded by the compelled one. As some kinds of compulsory national service illustrate, this does not entail that we have been done an injustice, but it does impair our autonomy. The impairment may come in degrees, at least if not all compulsion entails the impossibility, as opposed to a certain kind of high cost, of doing otherwise. Clearly, then, if we should care about the scope of our liberty, we should care about its limitation by compulsions or even lesser degrees of duress. Normally, we are averse to being compelled to do things, even to being compelled to do something that we would otherwise gladly do. There are important ethical questions about why we should not have to do under compulsion what we are free to do and like doing, but those are answered here only in part. As with other obligations, we can gain clarity about obligation regarding liberty by considering examples.

Lena. Suppose Lena is traveling and finds she is not free to enter a certain restaurant because of her color. She might be expecting this, uninterested in the restaurant, and psychologically unhurt by the prohibition. Clearly, she still should be free to enter, and those who can do something about such a restriction of liberty should oppose it. The opposition is justified because the restriction is unjust, but must considerations of justice (or harm-avoidance) fully explain why she should have the liberty in question? Suppose instead that the owner-host has a dangerous vulnerability to Covid-19 and excludes people who have not been vaccinated. This might excuse restricting access to the restaurant or at least behavior in it. Given this kind of reason for these (limited) restrictions, there might be no injustice in excluding Lena on *that* basis, but this would not alter the morally undesirable element of reduced liberty on the part of people unfortunately affected.[2]

---

2 One way to see the *moral* undesirability of limiting liberty in the required way is to associate it with the harms to persons that come from restricting their

Some quite different cases also suggest that considerations of justice do not fully explain the obligation to preserve and enhance liberty. Imagine that I am watching over a child of six, who is playing in my backyard. The child might be apparently content with playing in a sizable area equipped with outdoor toys. But there would be more room to run and use the toys if I opened a gate allowing use of a further (safe) area with more lawn space and different shrubs to explore. Even if the child does not ask to use the full yard, should I not make it available to provide more options for the child? This is certainly fitting, even if it promises no greater pleasure and is not needed to realize the situational demands of beneficence. Admittedly, the 'should' is not such as to make me criticizable if I do not open the gate. Nonetheless, someone who cares about children might wonder why I neglected to do something I should have. It is true that providing more options may enhance enjoyment, but even apart from enjoyment there is a satisfaction in simply trying out options. Liberty can enhance the scope and value of such experimentation and, more generally, satisfying curiosity.

There is another way to see that considerations of justice do not fully account for the liberty principle. Justice requires that we not abridge the liberty of others, at least not *unequally* and without a reason such as protecting personal safety. But neither the obligations of justice nor those together with obligations of beneficence require us to enhance liberty. Indeed, neither egalitarian nor retributive justice explains why the obligation of beneficence does not require much that is only supererogatory. That obligation is to do the good deeds we "can," but the scope of that 'can' is limited by the obligation to protect and enhance liberty, including our own. A utilitarian view that construes as obligatory what is properly seen as supererogatory is not too strong because (or

---

liberty, which seems wrong partly as a kind of harm. One may also see the limitation as infringing a *right* to liberty. Appealing to rights simply to clarify the wrongness of limiting liberty leaves open their relation to moral principles. That relation is explored in some detail in my (2005).

mainly because) it is unjust; it is too strong because it undervalues the liberty of those it obligates.

In relation to such cases some have spoken of the feeling of freedom as a good element in human experience. At least two cases should be considered. First, there is a feeling that is enhanced by pursuing things from sheer curiosity and sometimes even through simply finding opportunities to pursue one's desires. This feeling can even be experienced positively in the mere contemplation of options one is free to pursue. In a second case, even if, during times one is unoccupied by any project, one does not act, one may have a welcome sense of an open future. Even where this sense is leavened by an awareness of limited options, it seems valuable in itself. It need not be a means to anything valued instrumentally nor to realizing anything else of value.

More abstractly, both the exercise of agency and even opportunities for its exercise are something morality forbids us to restrict apart from special concerns. That exercise is also a dimension of life that morality calls on us to support and enhance in certain ways. One major domain that illustrates this is education. We educate children not just for survival and life-sustaining work but also for the ability to conduct their lives according to their own plans. Many of us conceive such plans as independently chosen and freely carried out – surely a reasonable parental aspiration. Our educating children in this way tends to be beneficent, but beneficence is not the only basis of the 'should' that goes with the preservation and enhancement of liberty. Even if our having options would not be good for us, say where we would make unwise choices, there remains some reason to support this liberty.

Something more should be said about why the liberty obligation is higher order. In part, this is because, unlike the obligations described in Chapter 4, its object is not necessarily to bring about a change in someone, such as a reduction of pain or enhancement of ability, nor to do a particular kind of thing, such as a promised deed. The obligation is to enhance the scope of opportunities, mainly for others. Enhancement of liberty widens the scope for self-expression. Doing that is often good in itself. This enhancement may not lead to any action by its beneficiaries.

A related element in the liberty obligation is that it bears on preservation and enhancement of autonomous action, in which ideals, commitments, and even personality are commonly expressed. Again, preservation and enhancement of liberty may not lead to action by beneficiaries; but it does contribute to the likelihood that they will be free in doing some of what they do. The liberty obligation, then, neither prescribes specific types of action on the part of those who seek to fulfill it nor calls on its beneficiaries to do any particular kind of deed.

2   Self-Expression and the Permissiveness of Liberty

A different kind of ground for the obligation to preserve and enhance liberty is connected with the reasons for wanting not only to be free to do various things but also to do them freely when one does do them. Acting freely is self-expressive. In many cases it also has a positive phenomenology. The experiential elements figuring in that have a kind of intrinsic value as part of the agent's conscious life. Think of the value of simply taking a walk, even when the weather is not inviting and the setting not lovely. We can be ourselves, go at the pace we choose, find a path that attracts us, stop to view an unusual tree. This self-expression and various feelings of freedom can occur even when the conduct in question is entirely non-verbal. It need not even be overtly behavioral, as is stopping to view the landscape. It may be a matter of the freedom of thought and conscience that many have greatly valued. Granted, it is violations of this freedom by restricting it that commonly call attention to its value; but it does not follow that there is no prima facie obligation to enhance this liberty. Without education and indeed support for liberty, mere non-interference by the state and by powerful individuals does not make it possible for children even to find the intellectual space for exercising freedom of thought and conscience.

A related point is that we have a moral right to free expression, and it is far from clear that this is derivative from some other right. There is plainly a moral obligation to protect moral rights, particularly such "natural" rights as this. Enhancing freedom in a society conduces to protecting the right to it and thereby to protecting human rights; it also tends to contribute to the degree to which people exercise freedom in expressive ways. To be sure, a right against having one's freedom restricted does not entail a right to have one's freedom enhanced. But there is an element in our liberty obligation that goes beyond this purported basis in negative rights. The playground example may be matched by others. Think of opportunities that parents should give to their children even if the children do not have a right to be given them and there is no reason to think the children will be happier or better for having them.

The moral right to self-expression is inextricably connected with a value distinctive of the kind of action expressive of our liberty – a kind of value different from the kind manifested in freely doing what, in a moral sense, we are obligated to do and not free *not* to do. Doing what you please expresses your freedom differently than acting freely though from a sense of obligation. Such morally obligatory actions are indeed free but do not exhibit a liberty of spontaneity. The obligation to protect and enhance the value of that liberty may be irreducible in a way that implies that the obligations to preserve and enhance liberty are deontically basic. The more important point here, however, is that they are a distinctive kind of obligation and ascertainable by moral reflection. In this way, protection and enhancement of liberty may be viewed as part of the structure of standards constitutive of a sound morality.

The range of the freedom that figures in the liberty principle is indefinitely wide. We have seen that this range is unrestricted as to the types of acts that can manifest it. The liberty obligation is also higher order in applying not only to protection and enhancement of freedom *to* choose what deeds one will do, but also freedom to do them in a certain range of manners. Not only is there something missing in being free to do something that one cannot freely do; it is also true that obligations not to harm should be understood to preclude introducing coercive elements, such as brain manipulations, in anyone's motivational system. This might be taken to indicate that the liberty obligation as applied to autonomy is derivative from the obligation of harm-avoidance, but this does not follow. The obligation to protect people from such coercive elements is partly positive; it goes well beyond reducing and avoiding limitations of the scope of liberty or of autonomy, and it is not reducible to obligations of beneficence or harm-avoidance.

3   Permissibility and the Scope of Liberty

In the light of the liberty obligation, the related notion of moral permissibility should be explored further. Permissibility regarding an act *A* may be simply the absence of an obligation to do otherwise. There may indeed be an equivalence between an act's being morally permissible and the absence of any obligation to do otherwise, but this equivalence does not by itself provide positive insight. One might also think that *A*-ing is permissible when no one has a right against one's *A*-ing. That view, however, seems not only unhelpfully negative but mistaken. There are times when withholding charity or, especially, failing to do an easy beneficent deed toward an accident victim would be wrong and is in a clear way not permissible, yet does not violate any rights. There is a right to *complain* about the (intentional) omission. Indeed, that confirms that there is a kind of wrong that explains the sort of impermissibility just indicated; it does not show that the victim has a right to a passerby's beneficence. Granted, if the injury is serious and assistance is easy and achievable only by me, then my omission is not consistent with moral virtue. But this shows not that there is a violated right but that virtue goes beyond according others what they have a right to. This is an important point. Some may say that there is an excusably over-ridden right; but clarity seems better served by avoiding positing rights so easily outweighed as to undermine the moral urgency that normally goes with properly claiming them.

By contrast, on my view the obligation to preserve and pro-mote liberty does not entail a general right to have this done for us, but it does indicate why we should think there is reason to recognize an immense range of permissible acts. On this weaker, *non-rights-violating* notion of permissibility – call that *rights-protected permissibility* – it is permissible not to do beneficent deeds unless the potential beneficiaries have rights to them (which is arguably only in benefactor-beneficiary relationships). On the wider, *non-obligation-violating* notion of permissible action – call it *deontically discretionary permissibility* – there is an immense range of permissible options. It includes all those whose realization violates no obligation. One might deny that no obligation is violated by discretionary limitations in beneficence if, as some utilitarians should, one takes the obligation of beneficence to require, in a world with all the suffering of this one, a life dominated by beneficence. But on my view liberty obligations and the associated rights do limit the strength of the obligation of beneficence. Beneficence should not be taken to require the level of beneficent activity apparently implicit in the injunction to maximize the good.[3]

On the deontically discretionary notion of permissibility, morality has a stronger claim on us than on the more common conception of the permissible as simply what avoids rights-violations. The former view represents our permissible options as fewer than those that merely do not entail some rights viola-tion. A hermetic hoarder might go a long way in a self-serving life

---

3 My (2004) approached this "beneficence problem" partly by appeal to an interpretation (defended in detail in [2016]) of the negative injunction of Kant's humanity formula. The idea – in rough outline – is that if one considers the obligation of beneficence to be as strong as under a maximizing utilitar-ianism, one will be obligated to go too far toward treating oneself "merely as a means" to enhancing the general good. Even non-utilitarians have described the obligation of beneficence with insufficient qualifications, as with Ross, e.g. (1930: 25, 27). Price, however, proposing a plausible qualification compatible with my approach, said, "if a man endeavors to do all the good *which is suitable to his station and abilities*, we never condemn him for not doing it in a particular way, or for rejecting particular objects that are offered to him; except these objects are such, that it is right he should *prefer* them" (1787/1973: 121, initial italics added).

without violating others' rights. But, in one important sense it is not permissible (even if it should not be punishable) for the prosperous to make no charitable contributions. Even in these deontically discretionary cases, however, there is normally a vast territory fit for the exercise of liberty, and that includes abstention from doing all the good one "can." This is a narrower territory than the rights-protected range of options that merely do not entail some rights-violation. In either case, however, there may be strong conditional obligations. If, for instance, it is permissible to support neither charity *A* nor charity *B* when approached by both, it could still be in some way wrong not to give to *A* as the clearly better charity *if* one gives to either.

Perhaps we may say that insofar as permissible acts are not morally wrong and are fully eligible as options – deontically discretionary and not just rights-protected – choosing among them often represents potential expressions of liberty. The liberty may include kinds, or indeed manners, of acts some people might disapprove of. The acts and manners of action are nonetheless optional in a way that can make them positive elements in a normal life. We should preserve and promote opportunities within this wide range. Enhancing this range of discretionary options, as well as protecting the more prominent rights-protected liberties, is a concern of morality even apart from con-tributing to fulfilling obligations of beneficence.

It is not unnatural to think that some acts are the kind often thought to go with "free time" – when we simply do as we like. Here not even beneficence or self-improvement imposes a moral obligation. For utilitarians and many others, in a world like this we are never utterly free and the third category of permissibility – that of the *purely discretionary* – is empty. I am inclined to doubt that it is. One reason is that if free autonomous action is good in itself, then there *is* reason to pursue it on occasions where one can foresee it as good (a thesis to be defended in Chapter 10). As I understand beneficence and self-improvement, moreover, there are some lives – at least some possible lives – in which these obligations do not prohibit doing as one pleases for some (perhaps quite limited) period of time. That may be fully compatible with virtue.

Doing as one pleases is not a duty, not even one of liberty. The point is that the *value* of liberty, like other non-moral values, can provide non-moral reasons of sufficient weight to make it both reasonable and consistent with morality to do as one pleases on certain occasions. This is still another reason to take the liberty principle as a distinctive element in ethics. It is as if ethics makes room for the prevalence of non-moral reasons of the right kind to justify actions of certain sorts in deontically undetermined circumstances. In the realm of the purely discretionary, there is also room to do the supererogatory, using one's freedom to do, for the good of someone else, more than obligation requires.

4   Respectfulness in Conduct

Anyone who reflects on interpersonal relations will easily see that the manner in which we do what we do toward others can in some cases be morally as important as the deeds we do. This is illustrated in Chapter 3, but an extended example like the termination case described in the Introduction will further clarify the general (prima facie) obligation of respectfulness. The *respectfulness principle* here is that

We Should Treat People Respectfully in the Manner of What We Do

The term 'respectfully' also has a sense broad enough to capture much (though not all) of what is required by Kant's positive injunction to treat persons as ends, as well as the kinds of actions obligatory under at least the positive (non-prohibitional) principles among the eight described in Chapter 4. But treating others respectfully also applies to the manners of our actions toward them. This adverbial aspect of respectfulness is the focus of the respectfulness principle in question here.

Is there a ground of this obligation describable in non-moral terms? I have elsewhere argued that there is and that the central notion is that of treating persons in a way that expresses caring about their good intrinsically ("for its own sake").[4] This notion is

---

4 What it is to treat persons in a way that expresses caring about their good for
  its own sake and how this can be understood descriptively is explored in detail

sufficiently broad to capture restrictions of act-types. We must rule out, e.g., harming, lying, and promise-breaking. But, given the comprehensive principles described in Chapter 4, which govern mainly act-types, my formula here, though centered on manners of action, is readily integrated with moral principles positing obligations to do the indicated deeds. Here, too, the good of the person toward whom we act is a basis for understanding respectfulness. It is particularly the vulnerability of persons to being subject to depreciatory manners of treatment, say being treated degradingly, hurtfully, condescendingly, dismissively, or the like that are the focus of the respectfulness principle. One might argue, of course, that this amounts to the adverbial side of beneficence. If so, the principle is no less important. In any case, it addresses the manner of actions specifically and in a way that deserves systematic treatment in ethics. Here is another illustration.

Rudolfo. Rudolfo must give a year-end performance report to a junior member of his sales team. The company procedures call for rating work as excellent, good, fair, poor, or unacceptable. Rudolfo realizes that he must communicate a rating of *fair*. He has flexibility as to how to do this. He can build up to it by citing the weak sales figures with or without comparisons with those of others. He can speak in a matter-of-fact way or with a tone of disappointment or with empathic distress. Here are three contexts of communicating a rating of "fair." With a salesman who is irresponsible and self-satisfied, one range of ways to communicate the rating is appropriate; with a young person selling for the first time, another range is appropriate; and with a saleswoman who had a difficult pregnancy ending in miscarriage, still another range is preferable. In the first case, communicating the rating disappointedly and disapprovingly might be appropriate. In the second, doing so sympathetically and (assuming no termination is required) with an optimistic tone might be appropriate. In the

in my (2016), esp. chs. 5 and 6. Even the obligation to treat others as ends is prima facie. There may be ways of treating others as ends that are paternalistic and wrong, for reasons provided in ch. 9 of Cullity (2018). This confirms the force of the liberty principle.

third, one would expect a communication of the rating that is done sensitively and might be combined with such terms as 'given the circumstances'.

Conceiving the obligation of respectfulness, as I am here – as an obligation of *manner* rather than of *matter* – does not require us to deny that exhibiting *attitudinal* respect can sometimes be full-bloodedly realized, by what one does – what act-type one instantiates – toward whoever is in question. One might thus speak of an *ethics of respectfulness* as encompassing all or virtually all our moral obligations. My respectfulness principle has narrower scope, as illustrated by the case of Rudolfo. That case also accommodates another use of 'manner'. It shows that the manner in which we do something – especially if it is as complex and temporally extended as communicating an evaluation can be – may be partly determined by what actions we perform in communicating it, as well as partly determined by the manners of some of these actions. The manner of our treatment of others in extended social activity toward them is affected by both the individual actions the treatment embodies and the manner of their performance.

My main concern here (as in Chapter 3) is with the manner of individual actions (act-tokens), not the manner of overall treatment of others, which encompasses all three dimensions of conduct and may be long-term and partly constituted by many disparate actions. What the manners of actions and activities will be in our treatment of others is often causally connected with the current state of the agent(s) and may reveal an agent's current state or overall character. Given psychological discomfort or resentment toward a dinner companion, one might loudly ask for a simple thing, such as passing the salt, in a way that evokes an impression of being annoyed. Saying 'Would you *deign* to pass me the salt?', given normal conventions, counts as requesting this rudely. For any act-type that is not by its nature limited to few manners of instantiation, there is more than one way to do the thing in question, and this can make a normative difference. Consider simply saying 'no'. Even this can be done decisively, hesitantly, painfully, reproachfully, and in many other ways.

It may be true that, for any act-type considered as instantiated in a given manner, an act-name can be given. Propelling oneself in a certain way is running; speaking very loudly is (in some cases) yelling. But even these mannered acts can be done (e.g.) threateningly or indignantly. It should not be assumed that differences of those sorts are never morally important. The need here is not to decide what to do but to determine in what manner to act. As explained in Chapter 3, to absorb the manner of an action into an act-reporting expression would reduce the richness of moral evaluation. We could call refusing decisively "mega-refusing," but we would have to explain that for clarity, and there might still be questions about how to do *that* in terms of intonation, facial expression, explanatory gestures, and more. The peremptory 'No!' on being offered a bribe is different from the descriptive 'I *can't*' that goes with inability or moral prohibition.

These points do not require downplaying the points that *fulfilling* obligations of manner is often achieved spontaneously by our actions in simply doing the right thing, and that determining what this is implicitly comes under the eleven moral principles so far described. Rudolfo cannot communicate his rating to the inexperienced salesman sympathetically without such actions as using words that express the relevant rating, explaining the evidential facts, and mentioning the possibility of improvement. These actions might be required by the obligation of beneficence or indeed by fidelity to the manager's contractual promises. They can be done admirably in manner or in some reprehensible way. If, by contrast, one's obligation is only to sign a document, obligations of manner may be minimal or effectively absent.

The obligation of respectfulness, then, is closely related to the other obligations I have described as basic in normative ethics, but it does not reduce to any single one and indeed is not eliminable unless adverbial act-types themselves may always be reduced to doing-types. That reduction seems at best unlikely, but there is no need to try to achieve it. In the most general sense, what ethics concerns is above all what is under the control of the will; and we can will, and intend, to do a thing in a certain manner. An obligatory act-type, however, can be willed or intended apart from being intended as having a given manner. But as the case of Rudolfo shows, it can be morally bad to allow oneself to intend to do something or, especially, to form a *plan* to do it, *without* forming intentions about the manner in which one should do it. A decision to communicate a rating to an employee illustrates this, particularly if the rating is so low as to require terminating employment.

My final point regarding the obligation of respectfulness – construed adverbially as an overarching obligation of manner – is quite simple: how we do what we do is significantly *expressive* – of our mood, thinking, desires, or even character. Self-expression is central for self-realization as a major part of human flourishing. Here again we can see the importance of liberty, which we exercise both in what we do and in how we do it. Indeed, often the burdensomeness of having to do something we dislike doing is reduced by our freedom in the manner in which we do it. Ethics makes demands on us in both these dimensions of conduct, and in both we should protect and enhance freedom. Think of waiters and waitresses in a formal restaurant; salespeople in a closely held proud family business; students in disciplined classrooms. Here ethics calls for a certain range of manners in acting and protects latitude for the myriad individual styles they can represent.

5   The Scope and Unity of the Principles

For any set of commonsense moral principles with the breadth of those formulated so far, the question naturally arises whether more are needed or whether some reduce to combinations of others. Doubtless both Kant and Mill, as the kinds of master principle theorists they are, would take the categorical imperative or the principle of utility to allow derivation of all the less general moral principles we have been exploring. But suppose, as I consider likely, the most that is achievable is not reduction of one commonsense obligation to one or more others, but only its derivability from one or more others. We still enhance both perspicuity and normative guidance by articulating and separately explicating the individual principles in question. This point may indeed hold even where some reductions are possible.[5]

Even property identity, which is a strong ontic relation, does not preclude conceptual distinctness of the equivalent elements. To see how difference in concepts bears on guiding conduct, suppose that the property of preserving and promoting liberty *is* reducible to, say, that of preserving and promoting some combination of justice and utility. The concepts corresponding to these properties (in a sense entailing that their instances must have the properties) would still differ, and there would be a corresponding difference in the desire (or intention) to preserve and promote liberty and the desire (or intention) to preserve and promote the relevant combination of justice and utility. This could make a considerable difference – even apart from the relatively greater theoretical complexity of the combinatory concept – in the actions of a person guided by one concept versus those of an otherwise similar person guided by the other.

It should help here to recall the notion of normative completeness introduced in Chapter 4: a set of moral principles is normatively complete in this sense if (and only if) every true (singular) moral judgment can be accounted for by it, roughly in the sense that it is explainable by appeal to it. Even the principles described there might be plausibly considered normatively complete, but given the addition of the liberty and respectfulness principles – which explicitly take account of obligations of manner – the normative framework now before us may be refined and developed in a way that makes it a strong candidate for normative completeness. Beyond that, it has a

---

5 The normative scope and power of the principles receives some confirmation from their role in justifying both policies and individual actions. Particularly where one of the principles is violated to our disadvantage, we have a right to a justification, as argued in detail in many works by Först (e.g., 2012 and "Justice; Procedural and Substantive," forthcoming) that show the pivotal role of this right in political philosophy. In my view, the commonsense principles are essential in determining what elements are crucial for a sound justification. In both individual actions and policy decisions by institutions, considerations of liberty, harm, and justice (among others) may always play a role, whatever the difficulties of weighting them.

perspicuity and fit with commonsense moral thinking that is surely desirable in ethics.[6] Some philosophers may prefer to identify an even longer, more diverse group of moral principles as basic; others will attempt to reduce some of the principles to one or more others. I have suggested that the twelve described here are good candidates for a group that combines diversity, perspicuity, and comprehensiveness; but if the principles are as important as they seem in moral thinking, they should suffice for the normative element in moral theory developed in this book.

———

Apart from the obligation of respectfulness, all of the obligations I have described are prominently among the most common kinds of obligation associated with ethics as usually conceived: as directing us to do things that are right and avoid doing things that are wrong. These commonly recognized obligations are each broad, but nonetheless are obligations of matter. If the idea that ethics is directed toward what we *do*, especially toward our overt interpersonal acts, were not so pervasive and so powerful, there would likely be less inclination to think that motivation, such as motives of duty, and manner, such as speaking to others respectfully, can be encompassed by expanding the category of act-types. Chapter 3 explains why such expansion, which absorbs motivation into act-type, is misguided, but we have not underestimated the great importance of motivation, and in some ways of manner as well, for the creditworthiness of actions and indeed of agents. Important as motivation is, there is much to be said for the view that, morally, it is usually even more important that one do the right thing than that one's doing the right thing be for a morally appropriate reason. Sometimes, indeed, it is more important that one do the right thing in a morally appropriate manner than for a

6 A contemporary comparison worth pursuing in relation to these aims is Cullity (2018). I believe that the framework proposed here captures the most plausible normative standards implicit in his categories of concern, respect, and cooperation, but showing that would be a major undertaking.

morally appropriate reason. These points partly explain the great importance of stressing act-types in moral education, in teaching ethics as a subject, and in describing and upholding moral commitments. Calling act-types of a certain kind the vehicles of moral conduct reflects this point. But the other dimensions of conduct – its motivation, including action-guiding intentions, and manner – are central for a life that, overall, is moral. The next chapter will explore what kind of life that is.

6   Living Morally

Suppose one accepted the moral principles presented so far. Intellectual acceptance, even with conviction, would not suffice to yield moral conduct. For that, the principles must be internalized. But even internalization of a kind implying strong conviction does not entail what would be required: a normally predominant tendency to do the right deeds, for morally appropriate reasons, and in the right manners. This is in part because, in much of life, an enlightened but ultimately egoistic beneficence easily passes for altruism and can guide both action and acceptable manners of action. Self-interested motives may also be disguised to pass as kinds appropriate to moral conduct and may sometimes deceive even the agent. Yet motivation is crucial for understanding what it is to live a moral life. Actions that conform to moral standards but are motivated wholly by selfish desires are neither morally creditworthy nor manifestations of morally good conduct.

A central concern of ethics is how one should live, where the 'should' is that of practical reason conceived as encompassing, but not exhausted by, moral considerations. I am not arguing for the view that practical reason supports the moral life over the life of enlightened egoism, but I believe that that view is plausible only in the light of a good understanding of what constitutes the moral life. A major point to keep in mind is that the interpersonal realm is morally primary. As I conceive ethics, what it most urgently calls on us to do is lead a moral life in the interpersonal realm, which is the main territory that ethics governs, though it also concerns solitary conduct.

The moral life, however, need be neither moralistic nor self-consciously morally motivated at every turn.[1] Indeed, the 'should' and 'ought' that govern a reflective occasion on which one asks 'How should I live?' or 'How ought I to live?' are, for many, those of practical reason. It is possible, however, to live morally without explicitly structuring one's life in moral categories or being morally motivated in the pervasive way that the moral life, as sometimes understood, demands. The moral life does not require a highly intellectual conception of one's conduct or regular subsumption of one's actions under rules. But it does require a strong preponderance of good conduct: doing morally right things, for morally appropriate reasons, and in morally desirable ways.

1   Thick and Thin Moral Questions

To see what constitutes living morally, we can do no better initially than to explore the range of answers to major moral questions. Living morally is roughly constituted by living up to a certain proportion of sound answers to self-referential versions of these questions. Some answers come from taking appropriate account of the intuitive commonsense moral principles sketched in Chapters 4 and 5. There are of course subsidiary principles, say those that concern avoiding certain special kinds of harms, or giving particular attention to the needs of certain people, for instance friends and relatives. There are also higher-level principles, such as the categorical imperative, utilitarianism, or the second love commandment, from which one might think the intuitive commonsense principles are derivable.[2]

---

1 Kant is easily read as taking ethics to govern rational action overall – to call for the moral life in a strong sense of that phrase – at least if all our important deeds should conform to the categorical imperative in being based on maxims and in respecting human dignity in the way his humanity formula is easily taken to suggest. My (2016) indicates how Kantian ethics may be conceived as more permissive.

2 As noted earlier, this view is implicit in Kant's *Groundwork* (1786/1997), sec. 421 and also sec. 429, which describes rational nature as the ground of

I call 'What should I do?' a *thin* moral question because, in deciding among alternatives, it is aimed at selecting the right act-type and not at appraising conduct conceived three-dimensionally. Being thin does not make the question unimportant or narrow in scope. In some cases, however, one might see that manners of action will be important and ask oneself '*How* should I do it?' A less thin moral question, being double-barrelled, is 'What should I do and in what manner should I do it?'

There is a still thicker moral question, already illustrated: 'What should my conduct be?' This may seem a misleading question because of the difficulty of controlling the motivational element in conduct. Given the clear limitations of normal human agents, we cannot determine at will for what reason we will act, and indeed, when we have two or more motivational reasons, say one of duty and one of profit, we cannot determine at will – if at all – which reason(s) will actually motivate us. These are limitations in positive self-control. We can, however (often at will) abstain from acting at all in a matter in which we believe we will act for the wrong reason. Our negative self-control in such cases is morally significant, particularly from a deontological point of view. Asked to judge in a competition in which you know you are biased toward one contestant, you may be quite sure that you would make the right judgment, but also realize that you would be aware that your selecting the person you favor could still be motivated by a personal preference. Even if you doubt that this preference would affect your judgment, you may believe that it could and that it is a bad ground to stand on even if your weight is primarily on the objective criteria. Fortunately, good grounds may readily engender motivation to act accordingly; but they do not always prevail, either in yielding predominant motivation or in producing action.

A related case would be one in which you already know what to do, thus what should be the vehicle of the appropriate conduct,

the humanity formula, from which "it must be possible to derive all the laws of the will."

but may still be concerned with how and why you would do the thing you should do. The act might be chiding an arrogantly errant teenager. You might or might not think you can chide calmly rather than angrily, but you might worry about whether a desire to deflate the headstrong ego would move you. If it could move you, it could also produce a wrongful manner of action you had not intended. The two worries are distinct. One worry concerns manner, which may be under direct voluntary control; the other concerns motivation, which is not. The conduct question, as triply thick, is appropriate in either case.

2   The Principle of Double Effect as Applied to Conduct

One other illustration of the moral importance of the notion of conduct comes from its bearing on principles of double effect. A rough and strong but not unintuitive formulation might be the principle that if an action, such as bombing a weapons depot, has two effects, one good and one bad, you may perform it only if (a) your intention in acting is to bring about the good effect, (b) you do not intend to bring about the bad effect (whether as a means or as an end), and (c) the value (or at least the overall moral merit) of the good effect suffices in the circumstances to outweigh the disvalue (or at least the moral demerit) of the bad effect. There are many other formulations, but the major common element – and the one crucial here – is that the difference between what we do intentionally and what we do only fore-sightfully is morally important.[3]

Let me illustrate how the three-dimensional notion of conduct can clarify the principle. Take two pilots. One would bomb an ammo dump knowing but regretting that civilians will be killed. The other would do the same deed, causing exactly the same

---

3 For FitzPatrick (2012: 97), the principle is: "It is sometimes permissible to bring about as a foreseen but unintended side-effect of one's action some harm it would have been impermissible to aim at as a means or as an end, all else being equal." Cf. Stuchlik (2021, ch. 1).

damages and deaths, but would be happy to kill civilians and would even have this as an additional and also motivationally sufficient end in bombing. On the principle, even if the bombing is warranted by a sound just war theory, the second pilot, in an important way, acts wrongly. Many critics would deny this but grant that one motivating *reason* for this bombing *would* be morally bad.

I believe the issue has not in general been adequately analyzed and that, in any case, the conduct theory developed here is a good framework for appraisal. The action-type – the *deed* to be done – *could*, for some agent, be right, even obligatory. This answers the *thin* ethical question, 'What should be done in this crucial military situation?' But *conduct* that, on the part of any particular agent, realizes the option may be morally criticizable, at least for its motivation and manner. Both the militarily justified deed and the conduct in which it is the vehicle are morally important. Suppose I am in charge and assign the first pilot. I do not produce conduct that blotches character. But if I assign the second pilot, I would produce that – and I should avoid facilitating such malicious conduct. Imagine, however, that I myself am the *only* pilot who can do the bombing, am ordered to, and act in the light of the thick moral question of what my conduct would be. I would see that if I obey and proceed to *doing* the bombing – actual conduct – I also have a good moral reason to eliminate or at least "bracket" any desire to kill civilians, thereby preventing the desire's discoloring my conduct. If I have this desire, however, can I count on eliminating its motivational and emotional influence? Suppose I can. Is it a moral (prima facie) obligation to try? If so, might a *substantial* effort be supererogatory? I might see this possible influence as a liability; it might lead to doing the deed with thoughts and feelings I regard as shameful, even in a shameful manner, say gleefully. If perhaps I do have an obligation to try, how I might fortify my motivational posture to avoid acting for the wrong reason, or in the wrong manner, is a problem in moral psychology. The needed self-control raises questions with both conceptual and empirical dimensions.

A great deal has been written on formulations that take account of double effect, but for the most part the controversy has concerned whether the formulations bear on the permissibility of the act-types in question.[4] It should be evident that I am not defending any formulation so conceived: i.e., in my terms, as bearing on answering the thin moral question 'What should be done?', raised where the options in question are expected to have double effects. This thin question may be raised either by me in self-directed deliberation, or with some particular person in mind (say someone acting for me), or even independently of who might do the thing. But the principle does bear on the thick question 'What should my conduct be?' So viewed, the principle may be revised and given a defensible formulation in which it at least provides a reason to prefer one foreseeable kind of conduct over another.

A first-approximation of a revised principle may be formulated by imagining an agent who considers prospective conduct and not just the thin question, 'What should I do?' We can sometimes foresee what would be our motivation and manner in doing something. Here one guiding principle for prospective deliberation might go as follows. Suppose S is choosing between two kinds of conduct, C and C', having two effects, one good and one bad, where in A-ing (doing the deed that is the vehicle of both C and C', say bombing a particular depot), S would satisfy the earlier double effect formulation by C but not by C' –owing to S's A-ing, in realizing C', on the basis of a motivating desire in a way that makes the bad effect S's means or end (thus intended). Then conduct C would be, for S, prima facie morally preferable to C'. This does not entail that A-ing (say bombing a Nazi depot with collateral killing of civilians) would be *overall* wrong, even if S A-s for a morally reprehensible reason; but the principle does bear on whether one should abstain. It entails, for instance, that if S

---

4 For references to much recent literature critical of the principle of double effect so interpreted, integrated with a qualified defense of the principle, see Stuchlik (2021). Less recent noteworthy essays include Thomson (1973), Russell (1977), and Quinn (1989).

cannot act in accord with the double effect principle as first formulated, then, other things equal, if (a) someone else can A in
accordance with the principle, then (other things equal) it is morally better that the other person A rather than S, and (b) S should A
only if no one else will and A-ing is morally more important than
S's avoiding the reprehensible conduct in question at the cost of no
one's A-ing. Suppose, for instance, that I am a pilot considering
volunteering to bomb the depot, and I want to do it both to
advance a just cause yet also, and far more, to kill as many civilians
as I can. Suppose I know that anger and hatred will be my main
motivation for the bombing and I consider this kind of conduct –
which is killing from hatred – morally bad. Do I not have a reason
to abstain and seek another pilot to fly the mission? Or suppose
I have just lost innocent family members to enemy fire, am full of
hatred, and want revenge. The principle might at least lead to my
preferring to cool off before my mission. Might one not be
ashamed of killing innocent people out of hatred, as opposed to
doing this wholly as a result of acting for a morally adequate
reason, with regret, and wishing it could be avoided?

Admittedly, destroying the depot could be so important that, if
I were the only pilot who could do it, or anyway do it with fewer
collateral deaths, it might be overall better for me to do it in this
shameful way rather than not at all. It might be overall important
that someone A, and I might have a final obligation to A even
though my conduct in doing so would be like a blotched painting
that is overall aesthetically good despite the blemish. The general
point, then, is that in moral deliberation it may be morally important to ask the triple-barreled conduct question and not just
thinner moral questions. The same triple-barreled question is
relevant at the level of the officer who chooses a pilot to fly the
mission. Even if the targeting need is clear, one should prefer to
send someone whose conduct will be fully moral than someone
who will do the same bombing but will kill noncombatants with a
kind of happy satisfaction that a morally upright person would be
ashamed to experience. This is a morally bad kind of satisfaction,
and it might strengthen motivation to do comparably satisfying
deeds that are in no way justifiable.

The case of double effect illustrates the importance of distinguishing act-types from conduct-types. The latter, as three-dimensional behavior-types that embody motivational behavior-types, are even broader than two-dimensional behavior-types such as action for reasons. Much of the plausible criticism of the principle of double effect is based on taking it to concern thin questions such as 'Should I *A*?' But the answer to the thick moral question here has no simple connection to what the agent considering whether to *A* would intend or foresee. It depends on the answer to 'What should my conduct be?' This is clearer than the (related) omnibus question 'How may I *act morally* in the anticipated circumstances?' and it gives due weight to intention and foresight without allowing them to have the absolute veto power suggested by some principles of double effect. The omnibus question can indeed be ambiguous, since 'act morally', construed narrowly, may designate just a morally permissible act-type or, construed broadly, may designate conduct, which has two other morally significant dimensions. The answer to either question may depend in part on intention or foresight. Perhaps the underlying idea that explains this kind of dependence is that we have a prima facie obligation not to do at all what we would be doing for a morally bad reason. There is apparently a similar prima facie obligation not to do what we would do in a morally bad *manner*. We should not stain our character. As the only pilot who can do the important mission, I might readily see that I should do it, but I ought to realize that I should try to avoid doing it from hatred or, for instance, *frighteningly* by buzzing the area beforehand, rather than simply targeting the depot.

3   Living Morally and Living Well

A moral question can be even thicker than the three-dimensional conduct question. 'How should I live?' is indefinitely thick. It encompasses conduct conceived morally, but it also ranges over (among other matters) vocational, aesthetic, and pragmatic considerations, such as self-interest. Here we should consider the question with moral standards central in our deliberations. In the most general form, the question raises the problem of what reason demands of us where there is a conflict between rational self-interest and moral obligation. I have addressed that problem elsewhere and here focus only on the moral life.[5]

I assume here that a pluralistic ethical framework such as that provided by the commonsense moral principles discussed in Chapters 4 and 5, particularly given its inclusion of an obligation of self-improvement, is at least quite hospitable to the idea that the demands of the moral life do not ordinarily conflict with the aims of the overall good life. If one is thinking of how demanding ethics can be, 'How should I live?' might evoke a battery of projected actions and activities, perhaps as part of an overall pattern of living. I might think of following good moral rules and of doing it in the right spirit; I might think more abstractly of being morally virtuous; and I might think of treating others as morality requires. If conduct does not appropriately figure in my deliberations, they are too thin to make it likely that my resulting answer will significantly facilitate living morally or, quite arguably, in living well. This can be seen in many examples provided so far. But here Kant's framework is instructive, at least in his emphasis on our treatment of persons, including oneself. Let me develop this idea.

I have elsewhere argued that treatment of persons is a conduct-type and here I add just three points.[6] First, as earlier indicated regarding self-improvement (in Chapter 4), 'treatment' can apply to how one acts toward oneself. Second, the notion of appropriate treatment of persons encompasses the motivational dimension of morally significant behavior by incorporating a prohibition of "merely" instrumental treatment. This treatment can have as its vehicle a permissible act-type whose instantiation in the conduct in question is aimed at, say, gaining someone's confidence for purposes of later exploitation. This act is thus

---

5 Sidgwick's "dualism of practical reason" comes to mind here (1907: 506–509). I have pursued this issue in detail in (2001b) among other works. For a clear presentation of options for answering the question, see Nagel (1986).
6 I refer to my (2016) detailed account of treatment of persons.

immorally motivated. Negative control enables us to *abstain* from such conduct even when we lack positive control of reasons for which we would be acting if we should proceed. Third, the notion of treatment makes it very natural to count doing the right thing toward someone in certain manners, say offensively, as morally bad, either in some significant way or even in an overall way such that it would have been better not to do the deed at all. Even justly criticizing someone for the right reason constitutes immoral treatment if done so witheringly that the person is deeply hurt. Harsh criticism, like surgery, can be given without anesthetic.

4   Thick Moral Injunctions

To understand how comprehensive a moral principle can be and, more broadly, how living morally can be conceived in quite general terms, think of the Kantian injunction to treat persons as ends in themselves and of the second love commandment (of which it may have been intended as in good part a secular version).[7] Both raise questions about how, given the complexity of conduct and our limited control of motivation and even of the manner in which we act, these wide-ranging imperatives can figure in our intentions and plans in a way that can guide living morally. For virtue ethics (though also for some other positions), one should think of the virtue of beneficence as fully realized only by virtuously motivated actions performed in an appropriate manner. If there is any rule here, it might be a "*V*-rule", such as "Be kind."[8]

To see how such broad injunctions should be understood, consider the commandment (which is in both the Hebrew and Christian Bibles) to love our neighbors as ourselves (Leviticus 19: 18; Matthew 22: 37–39; cf. Mark 12: 29–31). Love is not an

---

7 See, e.g., Kant's *Critique of Practical Reason*, secs. 82–85 (1788/1996) and the *Groundwork* (1785/1997), sec. 399.

8 *V*-rules (virtue-rules), which we might also call be-rules, are discussed in detail by Hursthouse (1999) and by Swanton (2003), e.g. 215–216 and 242, and are implicit in Aristotle.

action, though it underlies much action. Moreover, even if there were a manageable list of loving deeds, they could be done in a manner that fails to be loving and would prevent their being an adequate response to the commandment. How, then, is such a command – which implicitly includes the injunction to treat persons as ends, which is conduct – to be accepted and behaviorally fulfilled in the way ethics requires?

To understand commands and moral principles, we must understand both what it is to accept them and what it is to act on them. Accepting commands to obey principles (other than by merely verbal assent) normally yields both beliefs expressing cognitive embrace of the enjoined principles and motivation to comply with them. This twofold condition may, however, fall short of internalizing them. That normally requires strong intentions to fulfill them, and we should take the contents of these intentions to be act-types, in the broad sense that includes activity-types. Suppose, then, that we take the commandable to be by its very nature intendable. This is not a restriction on imperative *utterances* – someone could "command" us to levitate. The point (in rough terms) is that commands are subject to a norm requiring that their acceptance conceived *as* embodying intention-formation is intelligible for the kinds of beings in their scope. Related to this working assumption, suppose we take promising to do something as requiring intendability. We can then ask what one must intend in order to promise to abide by the Kantian injunction or the second love commandment. Compare promising to love in a marriage ceremony. This provides a microcosm of *vowing* to abide by such injunctions.

Any conscientious mature agent who makes such a vow, or a promise with the same content, will have some range of actions in mind and may have a sense of how the things envisaged should be performed and for what kinds of reasons. For instance, many who marry will have observed marriage ceremonies and perhaps marriages; some will have thought of their spousal responsibilities; others will have pictured what kinds of things they will do in marriage. In some cases, such as those of a second marriage following a happy one, a person might plan to reproduce the pattern of enjoyable actions prevalent in the previous marriage. This plan could be as indefinite as intending to be good to the other, or as specific as might go into a detailed script.

Even a detailed script, however, need not be formulable by the agent. Consider intending to hum a melody one knows well. This intention can lead to humming the whole melody even if one cannot write down the score, except perhaps by first singing and then writing the notes as one sings. Similarly, one might intend to treat a second spouse as one treated the first. The details of the intention's content might be confirmable by one's noticing deviations from the familiar pattern even though one is unable to list all that the intention encompasses. Some of what is intended is *penumbral* rather than *focal*, and even what is focal may not be formulable by the agent. Granted, some scripts are formulable: one normally can write down a perfectly memorized poem. But the content of intention is far more closely tied to being able to aim at the object, follow an anticipated route to it, and correct deviations from approaching it than to verbal capacities for expressing it. Intention is, in that sense, functional.

5   Three Patterns of Moral Intention

Intentions to abide by principles such as the second love commandment may have at least three patterns. These may also be manifested by intentions to treat others as ends, but given the semi-technical element in that notion and certain distracting Kantian associations, I prefer to focus here on the second love commandment, narrowed to include either an individual "neighbor" or a determinate group of individuals rather than all "neighbors." Let's begin with a different case involving marriage.

Imagine a mischievous cleric addressing an eager young man: 'You'll be promising to love "until death us do part." What do you actually intend to *do* toward her?' One answer might be, 'I'll make sure to be loving toward her day after day'. Finding this too indefinite, the cleric might respond: 'Good, but say more'. An answer could cite acts that may have been only implicit in the young man's thinking but, with some reflection, he replies: 'I'd support her career, care for her if she's sick, do fun things with her, interact with her family and friends, and all that sort of thing'. Call this an *altruistic pattern construal* of the object of intentions to love. It has a high level of generality.

In such *umbrella intentions*, whose content in this case is an open-ended altruistic pattern, the behavioral focus is acts the agent sees as vehicles of the loving or end-regarding treatment, acts like joining in projects and, on the negative side, pointing out ways to rectify errors and avoid omissions. But there is also an accompanying *penumbral aim* that differs among persons in a way *focal aims* (aims to do specific things) need not. The penumbral aim contains acts that one might call *presuppositionally intended*, as opposed to being just foreseen, and it may include what one takes to belong to or support the motivational and manner requirements of conduct. Arguably, some voluntary acts that are not intentional but foreseen may also be presuppositionally intended beforehand. If we believe we should move our feet on long flights, we may focally intend this yet carry out the intention without each foot movement's being focally intentional, as where we move a foot to tie a shoe.

The notion of what is presuppositionally intended is unlike that of the content of an intention as usually understood, i.e., as an envisaged act-type. What is presuppositionally intended is at least doubly relative: to both agent and circumstances. One element in what is presuppositionally intended is a kind of expectation, possibly based on habit, of accompanying deeds or of some manner of performance of these or indeed of the intended act or acts. If I focally intend to lock a car, I may, from a cautious habit never consciously acquired, do it with an extra push of the button. Must the second push be intentional? It is surely voluntary; but what is presuppositionally intended and actualized, though it cannot be *un*intentional, is not envisaged in the way the focally intentional commonly is.

Presuppositionally intended acts are in most cases and in some way part of a plan one is carrying out at the time (or, for familiar behavior, are even included in a script), but they do not express a central "point" of the intended act. For me, supporting penumbral elements in intending to teach my students might include reminding them of both some constructive aims of the course, say by recounting some main points, and putting out of mind annoying deadlines that might sour my mood. Other penumbral elements might be more a matter of bearing in mind students' needs and vulnerability, which most teachers know will strengthen their tendency to act toward students for the right kinds of reasons – the end-regarding kinds of reasons that "aim" at their good.[9]

On the altruistic pattern construction, then, the content of the intention to treat someone as an end (or, more strongly, to act lovingly toward the other) is roughly the higher-order aim to bring about some pattern that characteristically manifests such end-regarding treatment. The aim may also be to sustain an existing pattern of end-regarding treatment, and one might have a disjunctive intention or both these intentions. Since bringing about is action (though often not basic action, if it ever is), this interpretation accommodates the idea that the objects of intention are acts or activities. This altruistic pattern (umbrella) interpretation leaves open what is in the penumbral area of the intention and thereby helps in accommodating individual differences among agents.

A different kind of intention that might be formed in accepting the commandment to treat others lovingly might have a compound object. On this *conjunctive interpretation* of the intention to treat others as ends would indicate not a single wide-scope higher-order act-type but an open-ended conjunction of first-order actions and activities of a beneficent kind (open-ended because it might embody an element such as *and the like*).[10]

---

9 Kant is inexplicit and sometimes even negative concerning treating others as ends; e.g., he says, "[R]ational beings are called *persons* because their nature already marks them out as an end in itself, *that is*, as something that may not be used merely as a means..." (1785/1997: 37); second set of italics added. But clearly, he takes the duty of beneficence to require some positive conception of the good for persons.

10 A conjunction of intentions might also fit the agent's psychology, and in different situations one or the other case may fit better. If what is, say, resolved, is a course of action constituted by dozens of discrete things the

Imagine someone who is doubtful about marrying but resolves to make a go of it. After discussion and reflection, such a person might have in mind, as part of the content of the marital promise to love, a list of the main things to be done. The list may be long and detailed; this depends on the concerns (perhaps including anxieties) of the person. The difference from the altruistic pattern interpretation is that whereas in that case a behavioral umbrella notion like *bringing about* expresses the content of the intention, on the conjunctive interpretation 'to treat others lovingly' is conceived more concretely as a shorthand for a list of specific kinds of deeds. The list, however, is unlikely to yield scripted intentional content: the scope of the intention to love (or even more broadly, to treat persons as ends) is too wide to admit of scripting in normal agents.

In the narrowest case of a conjunctive intention to love (or treat lovingly), we can imagine a prenuptual listing of major planned acts. *Doing* such a listing would normally miss the spirit of the commandment, but with suitable wording it might be possible for a certain kind of scrupulous but not unloving person. In the much more common, open-ended case, although the umbrella notion need not figure as a wide-ranging element in the conjunctive content, it likely will if the intention reflects the full content of treating lovingly or, more broadly, as an end. No specific vocabulary is required; but, with wise deliberation about the future, an emerging intention should include deeds aimed at causing, or making likely, doing the intended things *for* the right kind of reason. Moral agents often do, and arguably should, have a sense of the appropriate range of preparatory actions here. Think of the intention *to be* a better friend. This could bear an altruistic pattern or conjunctive interpretation, depending on circumstances.

agent in some sense foresees, it may be more plausible to attribute intentions to A, and to B, and to C, etc., as opposed to a single intention to A *and* B *and* C, etc. We might expect the same behavior given *either* of the corresponding ascriptions.

These two understandings of the intention to love or to treat another as an end may each apply in cases in which the other does not. If we consider promises as raising similar questions about the scope of intentions formed in promising, then the second, conjunctive interpretation may accord better with the psychology of many who promise to love. For a complex illustration, think of sincerely promising to love a child adopted from among homeless refugees. One would describe oneself as intending to do nurturing deeds, provide resources, comfort during illness, and so forth, but many more acts would likely be penumbrally intended in such promises.

There is a third kind of intention, of a sort not commonly considered, that can play the kind of role needed for understanding such broad injunctions as the second love commandment. Consider a *subjunctive intention*, say that one act more lovingly. Such broad intentions – quite akin to umbrella intentions – can be fulfilled by actions realizing either of the first two kinds of intention. They allow for indefinitely rich penumbral content, and they provide for interpretations of acting lovingly, and of treating persons as ends, with advantages over the other two interpretations taken by themselves. Intentions *that*, despite indefinitely wide content, characteristically imply the agent's having some intentions *to do*. These would usually include open-ended intentions *to bring about something*, yet they do not require as detailed a conception of the acts in their scope. They are *act-directed* but not *act-specific*, and they are instrumentally unified by their goal.[11] There are countless ways agents can take their goals to be achievable.

We can, then, take injunctions to act lovingly toward others and to treat persons as ends to require for their fulfillment *that* one be, in a certain way, altruistic toward the people in question

---

11 Intending *that* seems irreducible to intending *to*, but this leaves open a supervenience relation such that no two cases in which people fully alike in intentions, and dispositions to form intentions, *to do* can differ in their intentions *that*, their subjunctive intentions. Such supervenience may also hold for intentions *to be*.

and *that* one achieve treating persons as ends, where these construals are understood open-endedly concerning act-type, motivation, and manner of action. Given their indefinitely broad content and the range of penumbrally intended acts that this breadth may imply, intentions *that* may embody the behavioral content indicated on either of the first two construals of intentions formed in accepting the second love commandment. In the light of these three options, we can retain the idea that genuinely accepting a command requires intention, provided we clarify this by indicating the kind of intention and the elements and range of its content.

It should be clear that none of these options for understanding an ethics emphasizing acting on principles implies that acting-for-a-particular-reason is itself an act-type or that *only* treatment-types (such as treating someone as an end) are genuinely objects of moral obligation. The assumption that, for Kant, they are the only genuine objects of obligation – perhaps a natural assumption given his taking his various formulations of the categorical imperative to be equivalent – may be one reason why he is sometimes viewed as committed to conceiving acting for a particular reason to be an act-type.[12] But (for reasons indicated in Chapter 2) doing justice to Kant's overall view does not require so interpreting him.

6   Intention and Conduct

I have so far explained how, in rough terms, on the assumption that the commandable is (in some possibly indirect way) intendable, the content of the intention formed in accepting a love commandment is constituted by intended act-types (including higher-order types such as bringing about being a more loving person.) We can thus still give a reasonably clear interpretation of imperatives that may play a major role in clarifying what it is to live morally. On one plausible counterpart of the second love

---

12 Chapter 2 explains why Ross in, e.g. (1930: 5–6) and (1954), as well as Korsgaard (2008), apparently so interpreted Kant.

commandment, to live morally is to treat persons lovingly and as ends, to keep promises to love, and the like. But since simply doing deeds one intends to do does not entail doing them for some appropriate reason, complete fulfillment of such injunctions and the love commandments requires more than mere behavioral conformity with them. It is achieved only by the relevant deeds being based on end-regarding motivation *and* being done in an appropriate way: by conduct. Conduct is not constituted by action alone, though action is its most salient element: its vehicle. Conduct, including the loving kind intended in 'Love thy neighbor as oneself', can, however, be commanded. If we can readily perform the relevant action(s), and especially if we have considerable control of the manner of our performance, we can at least *begin* to fulfill the requirement the command imposes. Some of the actions required for this fulfillment are aimed at indirectly influencing our own motivational constitution. Moreover, we apparently can, at will, sometimes extinguish certain anti-social feelings, such as resentment or, at will, do things for others which, beforehand, we have good reason to believe we will in fact do for their sake.

I have been taking it as clear that if, throughout life, and in accord with the principles discussed in Chapters 4 and 5, one treats others as ends, then, assuming one leads a life among others, one will achieve at least a minimally moral life. If, in addition, one loves one's neighbor as oneself and is regularly motivated by that love in interpersonal conduct, one will have achieved far more than that. The moral life need not be suffused by love, but its being so is an enrichment.

If living morally requires good conduct, which we should aim to cultivate as normal in human relations, can we at least rank in importance the dimensions of conduct for purposes of cultivating the relevant dispositions toward others? Surely not. By and large, it is better to do the right deed for the wrong reason rather than do something wrong. But this is not always so. Similarly, for adverbial contents: we should not hold that a wrong in the manner of doing something right is never morally as bad as doing a wrong deed instead. An angry nurse might bandage a superficial

wound hastily and roughly. The motivation for bandaging simpliciter need not be in question. It is done from professional obligation. In some cases, however, it could be less a departure from duty
for the nurse to abstain and let the patient deal with the wound
unaided than to give the rough treatment the anger causes. But in
other cases, as where a rushed surgeon, motivated only by the
prospective high fee, angrily stanches profuse bleeding, the patient
might best try to ignore the resentful mumbling and be glad of the
competent treatment.

———

So far, this book has developed a normative theory – a pluralistic theory of ethical conduct ranging over obligation, moral
creditworthiness, and manners of action. The theory has been
developed in the context of a moral psychology that fits the
everyday behavior of ordinary moral agents. I have sought to
avoid commitment to an intellectualist account of such behavior.
Living morally does not require governance by moral motivation
in all our actions, nor even taking morality to bless all we do as a
fulfillment of one or another obligation. Living morally may
require generally treating persons as ends and avoiding treating
them merely as means. These treatment standards are morally
important elements in any ethics that suits the moral life, and
I consider them elements in the normative account of conduct
I am proposing.[13] Such broad conduct requirements are, under
conditions common in normal lives, realizable without constant
self-prodding and do not require moral motivation suffusing all
our conduct. Nonetheless, despite the latitude that the notion of
living morally allows in pursuit of private ends, morality does call
on us to achieve more than simply doing only deontically permissible deeds. Here the cultivation of altruistic desires and, ideally, a kind of love of others, are compelling ethical ideals. So is a
pervasive sensitivity in the manners of what we do. Nothing less

13 My (2016) indicates much about their content, their apparent departure from
    Kant, and how they can be non-morally grounded in the way I've indicated
    for the "ground-level" moral principles presented in Chapter 4.

is required for acting morally in the fullest way in adhering to the everyday moral principles that appear partly constitutive of any sound ethics.

An overall moral theory – encompassing both normative standards and a philosophical account of them – should have an epistemology appropriate to defending, interconnecting, and applying those standards. Can the moral principles sketched and illustrated in Chapters 4 and 5 be known or at least justifiedly believed? I maintain that they can be. Arguing for this in the way I will should clarify their content and application, particularly in cases of conflicting prima facie obligations – cases Mill called the "knotty points" in ethics.[14] The epistemology and ontology most appropriate to the intuitive commonsense normative framework presented so far will be the topic of Part III.

14 See the closing paragraph of ch. 2 of Mill (1859), in which he says, of "cases of conflicting obligation," "These are the real difficulties, the knotty points, both in the theory of ethics and in the conscientious guidance of personal conduct."

Part III

Moral Knowledge and Normative Realism

7   The Epistemology of
        Moral Principles

Rationalism has been a minority view in recent decades, though never without appreciation on the part of many who, though stating or presupposing major elements in it, have not affirmed it. Naturalism is a factor. Certain versions of it are compatible with rationalism, but most of its proponents seem more inclined toward empiricism and, in any case, to think that only analytic propositions are candidates for apriority. In ethics, rationalism has suffered both from epistemological errors by proponents and misrepresentation by critics. Moore, Ross, and other intuitionists have not only claimed self-evidence for their central moral principles but also regarded self-evident propositions as unprovable. Kant's moral rationalism, moreover, is part of a package of doctrines that, individually and collectively, are a challenge to interpretation. But in my view, all of these rationalistic philosophers had in mind the idea that at least basic moral principles are a priori in a way that makes them synthetic, yet knowable on the basis of reflection. Clarifying this idea is one central concern in this chapter.

1   Intuitionist Moral Rationalism

At least since Ross (1930), rationalism in moral epistemology has been regarded by many philosophers as epistemologically naïve. Moreover, claiming self-evidence for the moral principles described in Chapters 4 and 5 may easily seem dogmatic. If, however, we understand self-evidence as the term itself suggests we should, we can see how those principles might qualify. The intuitive idea is that some propositions are evident "in themselves" – discernibly true without the need for premises – even if the discernment requires considerable reflection on the proposition itself. On my view, self-evident propositions are truths meeting two conditions: (a) an adequate understanding of them – of the propositions "in themselves" – is a ground for justification for believing them (which does not entail that everyone who adequately understands them *does* believe them) and (b) believing them on the basis of adequately understanding them entails knowing them.[1]

This conception allows for provability of self-evident propositions but does not imply ability to give a proof. It also allows for complexity that precludes obviousness; for rational disagreement; for the vagueness appropriate to moral language; and for experience to play a role in both discovery and application of self-evident principles. Without being endorsed and certainly without being obvious, they can be in certain ways basic in everyday life. They can have a governing role in moral discourse, in inferences regarding behavior, and in critical practices concerning rightness and wrongness. This chapter illustrates and explains these points.

The intuitive commonsense moral principles in question are so widely presupposed, and so often invoked as evident to mature moral agents, that it should not be surprising that there is a case for their self-evidence. That high status, however, is compatible with the kind of double life they lead. We invoke them as high authorities when we defend our actions or try to influence others; but, especially under skeptical influences, we may doubt their authority

---

1 This account derives from work of mine in the 1980s but first published in some detail in my "Intuitionism, Pluralism, and the Foundations of Ethics," in Sinnott-Armstrong and Timmons (1996) and later in my (1999) and (2010a). Condition (b) contrasts with believing self-evident propositions on external evidence, such as premises that provide epistemically independent evidence for them. Chs. 7–9 of (2020a) describe how adequate understanding is to be conceived and how self-evidence may be conceived as the basic case of the a priori. I take a ground for justification as understood here to be such that, in virtue of having it, one is justified.

when we try to understand them philosophically. Nonetheless, for nearly everyone, the moral principles and moral terms we've explored are apparently quite well understood when it comes to bringing up children – an activity in which our true colors surely show – but deeply puzzling as targets of analysis.

In this, to be sure, moral language is much like many other kinds. We master moral terms, much as we do psychological and other "descriptive" terms, and in that crucial way we know what they mean. Yet even moral philosophers find it at best hard to capture their meaning. This plainly applies, moreover, to action-explaining psychological language and to at least a great many physical terms. These analogies between moral and descriptive language are one among many reasons to explore the moral domain on the assumption of realism. I begin by clarifying moral properties in relation to normativity in general.

2   Moral Properties and Their Grounds

One thing that many philosophers are inclined to say about moral and other normative properties (and the corresponding terms and concepts) is that they are not *descriptive* but rather, say, prescriptive, evaluative, or expressive. Descriptive properties of the most familiar sorts are in some way observable. In more complex cases, 'descriptive' designates properties that, whether observable or not, are (a) causal, (b) of a kind appropriate to constituting subjects of (empirical) scientific investigation, and (c) capable of figuring directly in predicting and explaining events. This threefold claim, though widely accepted, is nevertheless controversial, and I will rest no major contention on it.[2]

What is probably not controversial is that things possess normative properties in virtue of possessing other properties – those

---

2 Moore, in (1903) is plausibly thought to have held that natural properties meet these or similar conditions. This view might be denied by "Cornell Realists," e.g. Boyd (1988), Sturgeon (1985), and Brink (1989). They might grant that normative *concepts* are non-natural but hold that normative properties are natural.

constituting the base of the former properties – that seem descriptive in the sense sketched. Even anti-realists in ethics may grant the linguistic counterpart of the point: that normative *ascriptions* meet a parallel condition, namely, applicability to actions, persons, or other bearers of normative properties on the basis of their having such descriptive properties. Thus, even if calling a person honest expresses a certain attitude as opposed to a proposition, if two people are *exactly* alike, the term applies to both or neither.

This grounding condition on moral properties, then, leaves open whether normative properties (or terms) are themselves ultimately descriptive. But the consequentiality – *in virtue of* – relation is not only common ground between non-naturalists and (cognitivistic) naturalists; it is also a basis for anchoring moral judgments in intersubjectively accessible facts. Whether the relation is a priori, as rationalists commonly hold for normative cases, or empirical, as empiricists would likely consider it to be in all cases, is a matter of continuing disagreement.[3] The conception of self-evidence employed here, together with the points to follow in this chapter, provide reason to think that it is a priori. If so, then the counterpart moral principles, such as those considered in Chapter 4, are also a priori.

3   Two Kinds of Normativity

The semi-technical term 'normative' is used quite variously and is not uncontroversially definable. Two kinds of normativity should be distinguished: *normativity in content* – which could also be called normativity in (conceptual) constitution – and *normativity in upshot*.[4] Consider first the concept of pain, which exhibits the latter. Taken generically, the concept is psychological: pain is (as

3 For early references to the notion of grounding, mainly under different terms – including 'resultant' and 'consequential' – that (for these authors) designate the converse relation, see Moore (1903) and Ross (1930). A short contemporary account is provided by P. Audi (2012).
4 The distinction between these two kinds of normativity is one I have long made and have discussed epistemologically in (2013a). The present discussion is based on my (2020b). I should add that normativity in content is apparently

a matter of conceptual truth) a psychological phenomenon with both phenomenal properties and tendencies to produce observable behavior. Yet instances of pain – of the property of being pained – also cry out for a palliative response. A creature's being in pain makes such a response fitting and often strongly justifies it. Pain is central for understanding the obligation of beneficence. Beneficence, as normally understood in describing persons, is partly constituted by a tendency to want to relieve pain in others. In the language of fittingness, benevolence befits beneficence, and beneficent deeds that are not benevolently motivated commonly bespeak motivation unbefitting to them.

That pain has the property of normatively supporting a palliative response is also, on my view, a conceptual a priori truth. In providing, a priori, a reason for action, pain is normative in upshot.[5] Cooling a burning hand, for instance, is, typically, fully justified. We need no empirical evidence to see this. Those inclined to deny it should be able to show that they have not misunderstood it. Someone *could* both understand and deny it. But skeptical or other pertinent objections, such as some deriving from a strong particularism about moral obligation, will surely come from a priori reflection on the concepts in question.[6] If pain is normative in upshot in the way just noted, then so is the principle that there is prima facie reason to reduce pain. This principle is central to the moral principles that we should do good deeds toward others.

Certain normative attributions, e.g. being an intrinsically good experience, can also provide a priori reasons for action, but where a normative consideration is, like this one, normative in constitution – as an attribution of a normative property such as

---

not equivalent to normativity in *ontic* constitution. I leave open its exact relation to normativity in conceptual constitution.

5 The apriority of the reason-giving relation is controversial. I have defended it in some detail, e.g. in (2004) and will extend the case here. It is most plausible for the kinds of pains that are suffered, and (as Garrett Cullity has stressed to me) is most plausible with suffering included under pain broadly conceived.

6 See, e.g., Dancy (1993) and my reply to his particularism in (2004) and (2006a).

goodness, badness, or wrongness – I do not call the attribution normative in upshot. The two kinds of normativity are of course connected. If a property, such as being pained, is normative in upshot, then attributions of it entail the existence of a normative reason, for instance a reason to relieve the sufferer. The proposition that you are in pain entails that there is reason to relieve it, and this proposition, in turn, is both important and normative in content. It does not, however, entail anyone's being motivated to relieve the pain (except possibly the sufferer). As normally understood, however, that there *is* a reason to *A* presupposes that it is possible for someone to *have* reason to *A*. The property, *being supported by a reason* – in the sense of 'support' that goes with counting toward the moral justification or at least the rationality of an action – is a paradigmatically normative property.

The reason-giving power of pain has great normative significance – enough to warrant speaking of what I call normativity in upshot as a kind of normativity. But, in content, the concept of pain is not deontic, axiological, or otherwise normative. A person brought up amorally could fully understand what pain is, and even be averse to it, without acquiring normative concepts or seeing that pain entails reasons for action. A partial explanation of this fact is that a wound is not painful in virtue of providing a reason to help the wounded; it is painful in virtue of the kinds of phenomenal properties that ground pain – and indeed also ground that reason. This grounding role is consistent with the concept of pain's being fundamentally psychological and descriptive. But because the fact that some being is in pain provides – and a priori entails (indeed, arguably self-evidently entails) – that there *is* a reason to do something that would eliminate it, that fact bears an important relation to the normative "proper" – to what is normative in content.

One might wonder whether normativity in upshot is equivalent to what is expressed by terms for phenomena said to have "thick" normativity as opposed to the thin kind characteristic of 'right' and 'good'. It is not equivalent. Consider 'cruel', 'kind', 'just', and 'unjust' as clear cases of what are widely considered thick moral terms.[7] The first two can be given non-normative descriptive accounts, such as (in part) 'characteristically causing or seeking to cause pain for its own sake'. But 'just' cannot be described in precisely this non-normative way. It must be explained in terms of, e.g., appropriateness, fittingness, or merit, say rewarding people in one's power in terms of their merit. The point is not that these thick terms are not complex. Rather, recognizing the two kinds of normativity described here helps to distinguish among different sorts of "thick" kinds of agential characteristics and other properties important in ethics.

What is normative in upshot is reason-grounding, but not conceptually normative.[8] By contrast, the entailment of the grounding phenomenal properties by the existence of pain is partly constitutive of what pain is. An analogue on the side of theoretical reason might be such basic sensory states as visual experience of a snow-capped peak. We have reason to believe there is something white before us (partly) in virtue of such visual experience, but although that experience entails a reason for believing there is something white before us, this property is psychological in nature, and it is normative in upshot but not in conceptual constitution.

---

7 Anscombe's (1958), which influentially argued for advantages of virtue ethics as against a "law conception" of ethics, is a source of the idea that 'right', 'wrong', and other general ethical terms are thin. My distinction between what is normative in upshot and what is normative in constitution cuts across the thick-thin distinction and is meant to clarify it.

8 In my terminology, what is normative in upshot is not also normative in content, though both are reason-entailing. Other conceptions of normativity allow for my distinction. Wedgwood views intentional phenomena as normative; e.g., "(i) It is essential to *beliefs* that they are causally regulated by standards of rational or justified belief and (ii) the ultimate purpose ... of conforming to those standards is not just to have rational or justified beliefs for their own sake but to ensure that one believes the proposition in question if and only if that proposition is true" (2007: 154). See 155–173 for defense of the view. This apparently yields a broad notion of normativity – call it *essential teleological appraisability*. Stones lack it; pain apparently does not: it might be "regulated" by standards of rational behavior, since pain tends to signal potential harm and motivate avoiding it. (If the regulating factors are *grounds* that the standards appeal to – as where we do not ascribe beliefs that fail to cohere with overall behavior conceived as minimally rational – a reading of (i) that makes good sense – then that part of the view is perhaps compatible with mine.)

4   Grounds of Normative Reasons

One response to the distinction between normativity in upshot and in content is to say that pain (for instance) is normative in upshot *because* it is normative in content. I grant that if a normative attribution – say that something is intrinsically bad – is true, then, connected with it, there *is* a reason for action. But being intrinsically bad is – as a matter of conceptual truth – not a brute property. Indeed, if one did not have a sense of why the things that are intrinsically bad are so, one would not understand why something's being intrinsically bad entails there being a reason for action to avoid it. By contrast, pain directly provides a reason for action; and someone's being in pain *explains* why palliative action is called for. The kind of explanation in question, moreover, is not causal or nomic, but conceptual and a priori. The statement ⟨Jan is in pain, but that implies no reason to do anything to relieve it⟩ is at best conceptually puzzling.

As these points suggest, an attribution of obligation or intrinsic value is an exercise of a normative concept and, more specifically, cannot be adequately understood apart from having some concept of a reason and a related, if "implicit," concept of the appropriateness of criticism for denying that the attribution entails there being a reason. By contrast, attribution of a property normative in upshot does not meet this condition. One could attribute pain fully comprehendingly without having – and certainly without exercising – the concept of a reason or any equivalent. It is only when one *also* has such a concept that one should find deviant (say) attributing pain to someone together with denying that there is any reason for action. The speaker would apparently be using both concepts; and here, denying the grounding relation between being in pain and reason for action can be attributed to a failure to see an a priori and necessary connection between the former and the latter. This connection is also important for understanding the normative content of the concept of a reason and seems conceptual and a priori. Imagine that someone who understands what pain is sincerely denied that pain provides any reason for action. This would be strong evidence of a lack of full understanding of the concept of a reason for action.

Given the wide range of things that are good or bad in themselves – commonly taken to include a great diversity of entities, from people to seascapes to artworks to elegant proofs – one might wonder whether anything whatever, say a rock, can be normative in upshot. I have not implied that. Only what a priori entails the presence of a property normative in content (and, in my terminology, is not itself such a property) is normative in upshot. Being a rock does not a priori entail any reason for action, though *in* an appropriate context – say one in which we are pledged to save rocks from being pulverized to make a desired powder – a normative consequence may be derived. This, however, requires a connective premise that entails the normative significance of rocks, as where they are needed to fulfill promissory obligations. It shows only that what is normative in upshot, such as promising, can endow anything with what might be called *derivative normative importance*. If Sarah has promised to paint a stone, it has the derivatively normative property of being essential to fulfillment of an obligation.

We have so far seen in outline how moral properties *ontically depend* on (non-moral) descriptive properties. This dependence is implicit in the grounding relation. We have also seen why it is plausible to consider the former *epistemically dependent* on the latter as well. Roughly, this is to say that (1) our *knowledge* that something has a moral property depends on our knowledge of its having, or at least on our possessing an adequate basis for knowing it to have, an appropriate descriptive property and (2) our *justification* for ascribing a moral property to something, depends on our justification for ascribing to it an appropriate descriptive property.[9]

There are philosophical differences over whether the knowledge and justification in question – knowledge of, and justification for

---

9 There is a possible exception: our having "natural knowledge" – roughly, knowledge without a justifying ground – of something's having a moral property, such as might be implanted in us by an omnipotent being. For discussion of such knowledge, which, since the knower lacks a ground for it, does not require justification, see ch. 10 of my (2010a) and ch. 6 of my (2020a).

believing, certain moral generalizations – are empirical. Moreover, there can be agreement on the necessity of a relation or principle without agreement on its apriority. My view in this matter is a moderate rationalist intuitionism, on which knowledge of certain moral principles has both properties: being a priori and being of necessary truths.

5   The Epistemic Status of the Commonsense Moral Principles

Let me sketch a case (I don't say a proof) for the apriority of the grounding relations for moral properties, with a focus mainly on obligatoriness and everyday principles expressing prima facie obligation. The obligatory – understood as the *obligation-making* – is representative of such properties. The underlying idea (which is arguably self-evident) is that if a grounding relation for a moral property is a priori and necessary, then so is the corresponding principle. If being promised grounds (necessarily and a priori) a prima facie obligation to do the promised thing, then the principle that if one promises to A, one has a prima facie obligation to A is a priori and necessary. I leave the relevant axiology aside until Part IV; but a similar strategy applies to goodness.

My case will not depend on providing an analysis of obligatoriness. I do not believe my overall view requires analysis of that concept.[10] My strategy here is to support the apriority of the propositions in question by showing that they play certain pivotal roles – roles that, taken together, are not played by empirical propositions – in the language and thought of relevantly sophisticated people, especially their descriptive, classificatory, explanatory, and inferential discourse. The evidences to be described support – though I do not claim they clearly entail – the conclusion that relations expressed by the propositions are conceptual, necessary, and a priori ascertainable by adequate reflection. A background assumption I make is that one way the apriority

---

10 I have argued that the self-evident is a priori and need not be analytic in ch. 5 (2010a).

of a proposition is evidenced is by governing inferences and critical discourse. Both are major segments of thought and action.

The Evidence from Moral Education

It is instructive to reflect on how people commonly educate children about right and wrong (I do not exclude even tribal or deeply sectarian people, though at least the former may educate narrowly, for in-group life, and are less representative regarding moral education). Consider as a plausible set of grounds the kinds that go with the commonsense principles so far discussed: obligations of justice and harm-avoidance, veracity and promissory fidelity, beneficence and self-improvement, reparation and gratitude, and liberty and respectfulness.[11] Moral education surely cannot be described in essential content without giving a special place – a constitutive place – to at least several of these. I refer to moral education that is jointly conceptual and ethical – aimed at both explaining the relevant moral terms and teaching the commonsense principles in which they are central. For ease of exposition, I will consider mainly fidelity, veracity, and beneficence – understood (for present purposes) in a way that is not fully comprehensive: in terms of reducing pain or suffering or, on the positive side, enhancing pleasure. These are descriptively understandable and sufficiently representative for our purposes.

Begin with veracity. Even parents who are not morally upright are likely to explain what lying is by citing such grounds as trying to deceive by saying something one knows is not true. Such actions are characteristically treated as largely constitutive of what it *is* to lie and that is treated as prima facie wrong, though no explicitly moral term need be used. The concept of lying is also commonly taught by treating certain kinds of actions as providing a reason for disapproval or even punishment. Parents who simply

11 See ch. 2 of Ross's (1930) and ch. 5 of my (2004), which explains how to understand the grounds of these obligations descriptively. I should add that I consider it obvious that what qualifies as *moral education*, as distinct from mores education, embodies teaching the commonsense principles in question. What I hope will become clear is that the way these are judiciously taught is best explained by viewing them as a priori.

punish children for lying but make no normative response to it may succeed only in eliciting self-protective prudence. Such training does not constitute moral education. Regimes of punishment of this sort might teach the empirical generalization that attempts to deceive tend to evoke resentment or retaliation; but learning this does not entail even learning what a lie is, much less that it grounds reasons for action.

Both giving and receiving moral education seem to presuppose grasping this grounding relation in some way. A common way is to explain why what someone said was a lie is calling it a case of telling somebody a falsehood while aware that it is false and wanting to get a favor, prevent punishment, or the like. This is teaching what constitutes lying. On the normative side, the principle of obligation implicit in the teaching contexts is not conceived as prudential or otherwise empirical, but as anchoring practices of praising and blaming based on agents' responsiveness to reasons for action. Good parents will both observe the difference between lies and mistaken statements and treat the former as generally wrong.

A related point is this: where we can properly speak of moral education at all, we expect some range of prohibitions of lying to be instilled. Where people regularly employ the concepts of (moral) right and wrong, we expect them to tend to apply an equivalent of 'wrong' to their children (as to certain others) when they find the latter lying to them. The case with promise-breaking is quite similar. These points indeed partly "define" what constitutes moral education and in a way no empirical propositions do.

When it comes to beneficence, we expect parents to teach their children that they should, or even *must*, act in the relevant positive ways toward at least some people in some situations, say the family, the tribe, or some wider community. The moral force of the 'should' is evidenced by its being applied on pain of the kind of principled criticism that bespeaks moral judgment. The *scope* of the requirement and the modes of its enforcement are highly variable (the kernel of truth in some versions of ethical relativism). But moral education is partly centered on instilling the behavioral standards in question as applying in certain types of situations.

Moral education usually teaches more than the kind of a priori sufficiency relation so far illustrated between the presence of a ground and that of a moral obligation. Once this relation is grasped, children are in a position to learn that the relation is not unqualifiedly sufficient for *overall*, as opposed to prima facie, obligation. Suppose a child leaves toys strewn around the living room. A mother might critically complain: "You promised to put those away." If the child replies, "I had to help Daddy," a normal response would be, "Oh, then I'll excuse you, but next time, you tell me why you couldn't do what I asked!" The excuse shows the defeasibility of the initial overall obligation. Here a child may learn both that a promissory ground need not suffice for overall obligation and that breaking promises may demand explanation.

That no particular ground (an element normative in upshot) is *necessary* for overall obligation is also commonly taught. Suppose a ten-year-old is asked to help a cousin with yardwork and declines, saying "I never promised to help." A parent may say, "I know that, but you should help anyway – she's your cousin and there is nothing else you have to do." This would be readily understood as indicating both that promising is not necessary for an obligation to someone else and that another obligation, such as that of beneficence, can suffice to make some deed obligatory. The example also indicates how the plurality of obligations may be gradually introduced to children.

One might object that there is no clear distinction between this kind of education and education in certain empirical matters. But note the kind of criticism children encounter when they do certain wrongs and the link between explaining what promising *is* and how it obligates one so as to call for negative reactions if one breaks a promise. Promissory obligations are not discovered by empirical inquiry; they are taught by good parents – moral necessitarians that they often are – as consequences of making the appropriate commitments – from the bottom up: from grounds to upshots.

Moreover, when promises are unfulfilled, this is not like a counterinstance to an empirical generalization. It is the agent who is shown wrong, not some generality expressing too high a frequency of promise-keepings. The case may be either one of overriding by a stronger, contrary obligation or an unjustified violation that, by its very failure to conform to the required pattern, implicitly reveals the necessary connection between promising and obligation to act. Learning when promissory obligation is overridden clarifies the concept of it and of overriding in a way learning when exposure to poison ivy produces a rash does not clarify the concepts of exposure or a rash. If the promissory connection (the grounding relation of promising to prima facie obligation) is a priori as well as non-contingent, as is confirmed by its role in moral education, then so is the promissory principle itself. These and other points relevant to the difference between a priori and empirical generalizations will be clearer as further evidences are sketched.

The Evidence from Partial Analysis

Whether or not we agree with Moore about the indefinability of *good*, we should recognize that the history of ethics since Moore has confirmed that our basic normative terms do not admit of any simple philosophical analysis, if they admit of analysis at all. It does not follow, however, that we cannot give partial analyses, which may be taken to indicate partial conceptual constitution. Indeed, do we not know some of the elements that must go into *any* analysis with a plausible claim to capture the concept of the morally obligatory?

One way to begin is to say that, in reference to acts, what is obligatory is what it is wrong not to do. This may be correct, but wrongness needs explication as much as obligatoriness. We could say that what is wrong is equivalent to what we are blameworthy for doing (at least if we have no excuse), but the same point applies. We have enlarged the circle but not broken out. To break out of it, we most naturally turn to paradigms. Keeping our promises is (prima facie) obligatory; not harming those around us is also; doing some good deeds toward at least those relevantly close to us is; avoiding lying is. Each of these points – which are abbreviated formulations of commonsense moral principles – indicates part of what would go into any illuminating account of obligatoriness. If one sought an "inductive" definition, propositions of these kinds would be base clauses.

To see the point differently, consider what other ways there are to bring out the content of the concept of the obligatory or, correspondingly though not equivalently, the nature of the property of obligatoriness. One possibility is to ask what must go into the "complete" thought of obligatoriness, the kind of thought that would contain all the concepts constituent in that of obligatoriness. Suppose we cannot capture with any precision *all* of the basic constituents. Nevertheless, can we think of what, at the most basic level, conceptually constitutes obligation to do something without thinking of it as promised *or* as doing something beneficent, *or* as avoiding harms to others, *or* as abstaining from lying, and so forth for the grounds of obligation that go with the intuitive moral principles we have been considering? It seems not, and our best practices of moral education reflect the point.

The same point about the constitution of obligatoriness seems implicit in any attempt to list paradigms. Indeed, can we decide what principles belong on such a list apart from seeking a reflective equilibrium between our overall sense of what cases are paradigms and our conception of obligation? I think not. A good way to see the point is to ask how one would explain to an inquiring young child what an obligation is. Here we cannot presuppose an understanding of other normative terms, but we would have no difficulty citing examples and telling illustrative mini-stories. Illustrations would likely cite grounds of obligation (e.g. promising, being in pain, and receiving gifts) and appropriate responses to such grounds. Examples like these indicate the work that the notion of obligation does, and they commonly teach children how to understand that notion and others, for instance *right* and *should*. It should be no surprise that there is this kind of correspondence between the requirements of moral education and the demands of partial analysis of moral concepts. If the grounds of obligation that anchor the commonsense moral principles each figure as indicated here in a correct partial analysis of obligatoriness, then those principles are a priori.

The Evidence from Norms Based on Grounds that Govern Moral Inferences

This is a good place to identify related evidence that proceeds from facts about our critical practices. Positively, in many kinds of case we expect people to draw inferences from propositions ascribing grounds of obligation to judgments of obligation. If, on a railway platform, you tell me that a small child has fallen onto the train tracks, I will quickly judge that someone (including me if I'm able) must get the child to safety. If, when I firmly shake your hand, you cry out and tell me that you have a bruised finger, I will see that I should apologize and say I didn't know about the bruise. Hurting your finger is prima facie wrong, and I cite an excusing factor. I draw inferences as expected given the a priori relation between the grounds of obligation and the normative properties consequential on them.

If conceptual connections are indicated by certain valid inferences, they can also be manifested by rejections of such inferences. Negatively, consider how we would react to denials of such judgments made on the kinds of descriptive grounds in question. It is hard to imagine anyone's saying that the potential harm to the child on the railroad track is *no* reason to help, or that no one nearby and able has *any* obligation to help. If someone who knows English said this, we would need a special explanation to avoid concluding that this person misunderstands reasons or obligation or both. And does anyone who apparently understands moral discourse at all ever affirm such things as 'I know you promised to *A*, but that is no reason to do it' or 'Driving through the crowd to get quickly to your destination would injure a few people, but that doesn't make it wrong'?

The emphasis here on inferential discourse is not meant to suggest that descriptive discourse does not also confirm the a priori status of the commonsense principles described in Chapters 4 and 5. Critical practices are also indicated by rejecting misdescriptions. Suppose a friend takes my describing what

I plan to do tomorrow, such as rake the friend's yard, as *promising* to do it. I might have properly said 'I intend to' or 'I'm going to'. If I don't do it, and my friend says I broke a promise, this would bespeak an inadequate understanding of promising. To be sure, in some such cases inference may play a role. This case could be interpreted either as one in which my friend drew an invalid inference or as an instance of simply applying the wrong concept, say that of informing, foretelling, or even assuring, rather than that of promising.

The Aretaic Evidence

Consider the concept of a morally virtuous person. Is being virtuous not largely a matter of a sufficiently stable pattern of appropriately motivated responses to the kinds of descriptive grounds we are exploring? The very names commonly used for basic obligations suggest this – for instance, 'fidelity', 'justice', and 'beneficence'. Much as we can identify right and wrong actions in terms of, say, lying, on the negative side, and, on the positive side, helping the wounded, we can identify morally virtuous people – as well as people with moral vices – in terms of *patterns* of such behavior, provided we may assume the normal range of underlying motivational explanations (a range also characterizable in descriptive terms). Someone who often lies (with mendacious motivation) has the *vice* of being a liar; someone who regularly (and without an "agenda") does good turns for people (and nothing significant of a contrary kind) has the virtue of beneficence; and so on. The epistemological relevance of these points is partly this. What best explains the partially definatory role that the commonsense principles and their grounds play in explicating virtue is that they are a priori resources conceptually central for understanding the right, the wrong, the obligatory, and the discretionary, all of which are crucial for understanding virtue. Indeed, although there are empirical propositions, e.g. about human psychology, that virtuous people must know in order to act from virtue, these are not the kind in question. Their rejection would be differently treated and none is such as to play the same constitutive role in explaining what virtue is.

My emphasis on motivation calls for explanation, given the distinction I have stressed between the theory of obligation and the theory of moral creditworthiness and my concern here with the apriority of the commonsense principles. The notion of virtue, unlike the notions of right, wrong, and obligation as applied to action, *is* partly motivational. Moral creditworthiness, which actions have only if they are morally motivated, is essential for morally virtuous actions. This does not reduce the importance of deontic concepts in accounting for the concept and constitution of virtue. Virtue is, after all, not just a matter of motivation but also of action (or at least action tendencies) characteristic of it.

My points here suggest a further reason to consider the kinds of commonsense moral principles we have been discussing a priori. Virtue is explicable as a kind of steadfast internalization of sound moral principles, where internalization is understood to require appropriate motivation. That virtue may be explicable in that way supports the view that the commonsense principles play the a priori role I've sketched – being justifiably believable on the basis of reflection in a way that enables them to play the conceptual role they do in explicating moral virtue. They are important for understanding what virtue is, and that is confirmed by the plausibility of conceiving it as partly constituted by their internalization. The concept of virtue cannot be accounted for apart from – or at least is best accounted for by appeal to – an agent's adherence to the commonsense moral principles for the right kinds of reasons. A full account of virtue requires conceiving virtuous action, as opposed to merely right action, as a kind of conduct, but the behavioral vehicles of virtuous conduct are indicated by the kinds of acts central in these principles.

Do these points imply that deontic concepts are more basic than aretaic concepts, such as those of veracity and benevolence? I find this plausibly arguable, but do not claim to show it here.[12] My point concerns only the close relations among them that indicate how the relevant descriptive grounding properties figure

---

12 This is argued in my (2017b). See also the papers in Birondo and Braun (2017), particularly Cullity (2017). For discussion of how what is usually considered virtue ethics is best conceived as a deontology see Crisp (2015b).

conceptually in explicating virtue and constitutively in the nature of moral properties, including certain virtues (or vices) of character. Certain moral virtues are partly constituted by action tendencies whose manifestations in action are responses to normative grounds – those basic for commonsense moral principles – whatever else may constitute these virtues. Other moral virtues, such as the higher-order virtue of moral leadership, may be seen as largely derivative from these basic virtues.

The Evidence from Conceptual Discernment

Virtue is not just a matter of behavioral tendencies; it also requires a discriminative responsiveness that at least normally has emotional elements. These lie particularly in the normative territory of approval and disapproval that go with a sense of adherence to the commonsense moral principles stressed in Part II. Approval and disapproval are not just a matter of liking and disliking. If we stub our toe, we dislike it; but if an abuser tramps on the toe, we are indignant. Similarly, if we forage in search of strawberries and don't find them, we are disappointed; but if we are lied to about their location, can't find them, and conclude we were lied to, we resent that act. A broken promise may leave us disapproving or even indignant. This applies to discovery of promises broken to others, not just to us. I refer, of course, to responses by someone of moral sensibility: the kind of person appropriately responsive to the properties that ground moral obligation. The responsiveness in question is a matter of both behavior and receptiveness to moral sentiments. Indignation, resentment, and the relevant kind of disapproval are moral sentiments, and the use of moral terms is conceptually tied to the fittingness of these sentiments in certain cases.[13]

---

13 For an indication of the importance of resentment in understanding reasons and in explaining (and I would say also grounding) obligation, see Stratton-Lake (2011); and for accounts of fittingness pertinent to the theory underlying this paper see Maguire (2018) and Cullity, "Reasons and Fit" (2023). They both may be seen as indicating how fittingness can play the kind of role reasons do, but neither undermines the view that, like obligation, fittingness is a similarly grounded property.

One way to put the overall point here is to say that lacking a tendency to have moral sentiments that befit the moral judgments justified by what one learns or experiences is akin to tending to disbelieve well-grounded moral judgments. Being a moral person has an attitudinal-affective side as well as a related cognitive side. The concept of a moral person is partly constituted by a responsiveness that is structured largely by internalization of the commonsense moral principles.

The significance of these normative responses to moral phenomena, most conspicuously wrongdoing, is apparent in the contrast already drawn in relation to moral education. The grounding, partially constitutive, relation between (say) promise-making and reasons for action is not one of empirically discoverable correlation, and one's understanding of it is not internalized in a person of moral sensibility by knowledge of any such correlation. Failure to grasp, at some level of understanding (possibly short of believing), that one *should* keep promises is not a deviation from an expected pattern but a deficiency in moral sensibility best explained by failure to internalize – or perhaps even adequately understand – the grounding relation between promising and (prima facie) obligation. This is a conceptual connection essential in explaining both the constitution of moral sensibility and our basis for ascribing it. The moral principles presented in Chapters 4 and 5 play a role in grounding internal responses to morally significant behavior analogous to their guidance of discourse concerning such behavior. This constitutive role is one among other indications of the a priori status of the principles.

Nothing said here implies that *only* the conceptually sophisticated can have moral sentiments; but their responses of this attitudinal-emotional kind support the a priori character of the moral principles in question. For instance, suppose that, without special explanation, someone with a mastery of ordinary English did not tend to have such sentiments in the kinds of situations that call for them or – especially – took them as inappropriate to those situations. This would tend to manifest a lack of understanding or (as in the case of a comprehending amoralist) a failure to internalize moral standards. Such people would not be players in the moral game, even if they might know how the game is played. The tendencies I note here are inhibited under certain conditions; but their role in describing the constitution of moral sensibility seems best explainable on the assumption that they are a priori.

The Evidence from Confirmational Roles

Still another route to seeing the a priori importance of the descriptive grounds we are considering is to inquire into the testability of singular moral judgments. This may seem odd given that we are exploring evidence for apriority and that the a priori principles in question are not testable in the sense relevant here. But those principles are general, whereas the corresponding moral judgments considered here are singular and empirical. The point, however, is that a priori conditions for the application of the concepts figuring in singular judgments are crucial for testing those judgments, and in that way principles governing those judgments play a major confirmational role. If we don't know a priori what sort of thing constitutes beneficence, we are in no position to test whether accepting an obligation of beneficence is, for instance, motivating. But we cannot test for that apart from criteria of confirmation, both for accepting the obligation and for acting accordingly.

Quite apart from whether we take moral judgments to be ultimately ascriptions of natural properties, we can likely agree that instantiating some such properties is either necessary or sufficient (or both) for their truth (or, for noncognitivists, their appropriate affirmability). Suppose someone explaining why a woman is divorcing her husband says that he often wronged her and never made amends. We consider this explanation testable; and if sustainable, it surely must cite such confirmatory indications of wrongdoing as injuries, lies, and broken promises. These are the kinds of factors necessary for justifying the judgment of wrongful treatment, and they can readily explain the distress that would lead to seeking divorce. The explanatory connection between marital distress and seeking a divorce is empirical; the constitutive connection between, e.g., lying and wrongdoing is not. The specified grounds of wrongdoing are not just empirically discovered causes or effects of wrongdoing. It might be discovered empirically, however, that women wronged by their husbands have more anxiety than before their marriages and more than women who report being happily married. This could even become an indicator of wrongdoing by husbands, but clearly it would have to be validated as an indicator by correlation with the grounding elements I have been describing. Contingent indicators of this kind gain their epistemic status through connections with constitutive indicators.

The mention of wrongdoing by not making amends, moreover, indicates recognition of the obligation of reparation. Descriptively understood, making amends, which may entail compensation of some kind, is in good part doing something to enhance happiness or reduce suffering. This may be in response to having done a harm, but it could come from having violated some obligation other than the obligation to avoid harming others, such as failure to do something that was either promised or is an obligation of beneficence. The idea is that a partly constitutive ground of obligation is doing someone a certain kind of (non-self-defensive) harm. That certain actions meet this description is commonly verifiable. In the divorce example, we can acquire, through information about the husband's behavior, descriptive factual grounds to justify the woman's moral condemnations. Given these grounds or motivational factors they tend to produce, we have a psychological explanation of her deciding to divorce.

We can also see the implications of testability from the point of view of descriptive sufficient conditions. Suppose a moral psychologist hypothesizes that wrongdoing adversely affects psychological health. Is there any plausible way to ascertain instances of the independent variable here, wrongdoing, apart from relying on the descriptive grounds we have been exploring? One would surely be dependent on establishing at least a high correlation with such grounds. One implication of this point is that the philosophical work of identifying constitutive grounds of moral properties can facilitate the scientific work of testing empirical generalizations important for understanding ethical behavior. In this respect, moral philosophy and moral psychology make good partners.

The Evidence from Criterial Autonomy

The kind of evidence to be described here is best understood as a way of responding to an objection. In both the philosophy of language and the philosophy of science there has long been a recognition of the way in which certain lawlike generalities can be in some way constitutive of certain concepts that figure in them.[14] Consider the notion of being magnetic. There are laws describing the mutual attraction and repulsion of magnetic objects having polarity, the attraction of iron filings by a magnetic object, and, more theoretically, the induction of an electric current by passing a magnet in a certain way through a copper coil. It is plausible to say that "part of what it is" to be magnetic (and arguably, part of what we mean by 'magnetic') is expressed by subsumability under these nomic generalities. Yet none of these, at least construed scientifically, is a priori. Why, then, may we not say that part of what it is to be obligatory is to be subsumable under a commonsense moral principle, and that all these principles are, though not causal, nomic or quasi-nomic rather than a priori? To be obligatory, then, would be, overall, to be subsumable under the nomic or quasi-nomic generalizations that promising yields a commitment to do the promised thing, that harming someone yields an obligation of reparation, and so forth.[15]

It is true, as the moral education argument brings out, that part of what it is to *teach* the concept of obligation is to get across

---

14 This idea has been developed in the philosophy of science by Hempel, e.g. in (1965), by Brandt and Kim (1963) in relation to psychological concepts, and, in a Sellarsian mode with application to an even wider range of concepts, by Brandom (1998).

15 An interesting question here is the extent to which cluster concepts might be instances of normative concepts as understood by Cornell Realism, which is briefly considered in Chapter 9.

the obligation-making character of promising. But the partial constitution role of each a priori grounding element in the concept of
obligation creates no presumption that the other grounding elements will be present in each case of obligation, whereas the presence of one of the criterially sufficient conditions for being magnetic
is expected to be accompanied by the others. This is largely why that
concept is plausibly considered a "cluster concept." Being obligatory
is different. It is a *multiply grounded property* (we might say something
similar about the *concept* of obligation but I am speaking mainly of
properties, which I take to be intimately related to concepts but not
identical with them). There are multiple criterial grounds of obligation, but each has a kind of autonomy: first, each alone a priori
suffices for yielding obligation of a full-blooded kind; second, none
is expected to suffice for the presence of the other grounding
elements, which would then constrain it by yielding necessary
conditions for its obtaining.

Might there be only a family resemblance between the phenomena we call obligations? Thus, promissory obligation would
be like the obligation of beneficence, but the two would not
instantiate the same deontic property. This negative point is not
plausible. One reason is a high degree of overlap in the critical
terms appropriate to violated obligations of any sort: 'wrong',
'blameworthy', and 'immoral', for instance, often apply to the
same action. Another reason is the way in which one obligation
can conflict with another of a different kind with no implication
of incomparability, as with, say, comparisons of artworks that
(somewhat like "apples and oranges") have family resemblances
but are in different media, as are poetry and representational
painting. In some respects, these are uncomparable.

This second contrast – here between family resemblance
concepts and multiple-criterion concepts – also indicates a difference between the latter and cluster properties, say being magnetic: if the criterial sufficient conditions, such as inducing a
current in a coil, do not yield the normal manifestations, e.g.
attracting iron filings, we have an anomaly and may doubt that
the object is magnetic, whereas the case with obligation is different. Consider conflicting prima facie obligations, say an obligation

to keep a promise of confidentiality and an obligation to avoid lying. The grounds of the obligation to avoid lying – which are criterial sufficient conditions of obligation – may apply in a situation simultaneously with criterial sufficient conditions for an obligation to keep a promise whose fulfillment entails lying. Such conflicts are normal, by contrast with the anomaly that might occur when an object magnetic by one criterion is non-magnetic by another. The presence of conflict between obligations also has no implication of incomparability, as is appropriate to the unity of the concept of obligation. Indeed, each obligation in question has some level of deontic stringency and is a candidate for deontic dominance in the same decisional framework.

A third difference between obligatoriness and nomic cluster concepts is that whereas, with nomically embedded concepts it is always appropriate – and often desirable – to seek an explanation of why the properties normally are coinstantiated, this does not hold for obligation. Indeed, we very often do not and should not expect more than one of the obligation-making grounds to be what yields a case of overall obligation. It is true that speaking to someone always "activates" an obligation not to lie and that some regard the obligation of beneficence as always with us given the ubiquitous possibility of enhancing goodness in some way. But the obligation of veracity does not apply in non-communicative contexts, and the obligation of beneficence, even if taken to be always in some way incumbent on us, is not in general overriding in the sense of producing a sufficient condition for overall obligation, whereas normally satisfaction of any of the criterial conditions for being magnetic suffices for its being "overall" magnetic.

Still another difference is connected more directly with the matter of apriority. The property of being magnetic, like that of being acidic and like other theoretical properties, is normally known to be present by *manifestations* rather than by grounds (if there are non-manifestational bases for attribution, they are empirical). Attracting iron filings manifests magnetism, but does not ground it. Promising to A grounds an obligation to A but, though sufficient for obligation, is not necessarily a manifestation of any obligation. Moreover, the relation between promising and being obligated is not causal; it is conceptually, though partially, constitutive. True, we may say, e.g., that politicians' accepting large gifts from supporters can cause them to be obligated; but, where this applies, 'cause' has the force of 'make' applicable to grounding. Indeed, if the claim is true – and is not a way of saying one would be caused to *feel* obligated – then the situation is one in which we may equivalently say that accepting large gifts *obligates* one. By contrast, it is not true that attracting iron filings makes the object that does this magnetic.

These considerations support, though none of them strictly proves, the view that the commonsense principles of obligation we have been considering are a priori and, arguably, a priori in the basic way the self-evident is, thus such that an adequate understanding of them suffices for justification for believing them. The data forming the basis of the considerations are not only best understood on that view; the view can also explain, and apparently best explains, the necessity of the moral principles in question. The evidences of apriority bring out that the principles figure in governing discourse and inference in the way one would expect on this apriorist view of them. They represent *criteria*, in a conceptual sense of the term, for obligatoriness. We apparently know a priori that a kind of act is (morally) obligatory if it satisfies any one of them; this is *criterial sufficiency*. We also apparently know a priori that an act is obligatory only if it satisfies the disjunction of them – or of them and certain similar conditions. This is *criterial necessity*. I describe it open-endedly because I do not assume that the set of grounds I consider criterial is a priori closed.

An intermediate position is that the principles of obligation are simply conceptually and ontically constitutive: they need not be considered a priori to play this role, but can still be part of what it is to be obligatory by satisfying one of the descriptive conditions in question. We can even say that obligation is apparently constituted by the criterial set as a whole. One could take the constitution relation to be, as ontological, necessary, but deny its apriorty. I do not accept this view, but it is not without some explanatory power.

The broadest conclusion here is that, as illustrated by the property of being magnetic – the closest kind of descriptive property to which one might assimilate obligatoriness – whereas for properties expressed by cluster concepts, our criteria (or at least our primary criteria) for ascribing the properties are manifestational, say attracting iron filings, for obligation our (primary) criteria for ascription are grounding elements. The manifestations in question causally (or anyway nomically) depend on their basis (being magnetic) and are explainable by positing that basis. Grounds of obligation, by contrast, are not manifestations of it, and they do not depend on, and are not explainable by appeal to, the obligations they ground. Promising, for instance, is neither ontically nor epistemically dependent on the obligation it grounds (which is not to imply that it is ungrounded); rather, the obligation it grounds depends on and is (non-causally) explainable by it. The several criteria for obligation are, then, epistemically autonomous with respect to that property. They are ascertainable independently of presupposing it. An obligation may exist without the presence of any particular one of the criteria. By contrast, the manifestations – in this case, manifestational criteria – of being magnetic depend on that property: they are consequences of it (of its instantiation) and indeed nomically explainable by appeal to it. What the two kinds of criteria prominently share is broadly epistemic: roughly, being evidential. But the evidence is empirical and abductive in one case and a priori and conceptual in the other.

6   Particularity, Defeasibility, and Holism

To maintain that the connection between the grounds of (prima facie) obligation and what, morally, one ought to do is a priori does not commit one to considering the obligation indefeasible. But the view does entail that the existence of such a ground entails that of a moral reason – roughly, an ought-making consideration – supporting the agent's doing the thing in question. From our exploration of the evidence from norms of inferential discourse, it should be clear that even if we may, in some cases, deny that we ought, overall, to do some promised deed, e.g. preserve confidential medical information, it does not follow that we have *no* reason to do the deed. We do have some reason to do it. Such grounds as promising indefeasibly entail defeasible reasons. This holds even where we have a clearly overriding contrary obligation, say to prevent a death, e.g. where revealing a cancer diagnosis to a patient would produce an ill-considered suicide. Suppose breaking the promise also requires, as in this case, lying. There we would have an overrider of two reasons for keeping the promise on being asked the diagnosis. An overrider of such double obligations might also be complex. An obligation of reparation owed to a lost child's mother might join that of beneficence, with both obligations calling for breaking a promise in order to find the child. The overridingness of the paired grounds may be quite clear, but numbers of grounds of the relevant obligations are not as such crucial. Moral reasons for a given act combine *non-additively*. Overall reason is organic (more will be said about organicity in Chapter 11).

The organic view of obligation entails a kind of holism: many factors may together determine overall obligation, where (as is usual) the determination is a strong sufficiency relation though not necessarily a self-evident entailment, and in some cases perhaps not entailment at all. One might also call the organic view a kind of particularism about *overall* moral judgment: such judgment is justifiable only in the light of the particular situation of action or prospective action, which may crucially involve a plurality of grounds that combine only organically. The view is not a strong particularism on which the *valence* – the positive or negative thrust – of the constitutive grounds of obligation changes from one situation to the other. On the view in question, the constitutive criteria for what we might call the basic moral properties (perhaps above all the property of being supported by a moral reason) are invariant, objective, and knowable, and this gives a kind of stability and clarity to the institution of morality. But the criteria for the non-basic property of overall obligatoriness are variable and open to rational disagreement. This accounts for a reasonable pluralism in matters calling for moral judgment.

It is natural to wonder whether holism about overall obligation implies that not all moral properties are consequential on descriptive properties after all. That does not follow from the holism sketched here. That it does not is suggested by the fact that even for overall obligation, supervenience holds: if two cases of moral choice are exactly alike except for the identity of the agents, who are perfect duplicates, what is overall obligatory for one must be so for the other. If such strong supervenience could hold for overall obligation only if the corresponding consequentiality thesis also holds for overall obligation, we could conclude that overall obligation, even holistically conceived, is a consequential property. That entailment is perhaps not self-evident. But recall that moral properties are not brute. This applies to overall obligation as much as to prima facie obligation. The overall obligation to break a promise in order to search for a lost child is based (in part) on the potentially great loss of the child and the suffering of others if the child permanently disappears or dies; and the judgment of overall obligation here is not acceptable without some such explanation citing natural facts. Nonetheless, there still may be no non-normative description – at least discoverable by us – such that *any* act satisfying it is necessarily obligatory overall. We might be able to frame such a description in some cases like this, as where the promissory obligation is simply to meet for a daily walk after class. But there could be a complicated pattern of relevant variables that prevents such a simple comparative weighting of them. The complexity might even foil our best attempts to identify precisely what grounds the overall obligation we intuitively take to be present.

The organic holism just outlined complicates moral theory. But the view accounts better than its alternatives for both moral practice and the major elements in ethical theory that command wide agreement. In practice, we normally think we can, with care, cite the variables relevant to our decision, and we can often intuitively see what obligation is overriding in a conflict case. But we are often aware of fallibility here and of lacking the quantitative precision that might sometimes be needed to formulate an unqualifiedly universal principle. Arguably, an organic holism also opens the way for skepticism about at least singular moral judgments. But skepticism is possible even for simple virtually universally accepted moral judgments.[16] Here I can only say that humility about justifying overall moral judgment is often desirable. It reduces dogmatism and facilitates rational discussion. It need not undermine a fallibilist objectivism.

The main work of this chapter is to show the plausibility of taking intuitive commonsense moral principles of the kind described in earlier chapters to be a priori. Once stereotypes about the self-evident – the basic case of the a priori – are dispelled, that term can be seen to be appropriate. The term itself, however, is not essential for my purposes. What is essential is that moral knowledge and moral justification be seen as accessible to reflection in the ways illustrated so far, and thus at least broadly a priori. This does not preclude either vagueness or, especially, rational disputability, but it nonetheless allows for a kind of testability. Singular moral judgments have testable implications in several ways we have illustrated, and the a priori framework of principles that subsumes them has numerous connections with the natural world, above all by virtue of the empirically accessible grounds of the moral properties that are the substantive constituents of the moral principles. To be sure, a priori propositions, including even self-evident ones, need not be beyond dispute.[17] But even if,

16 Sinnott-Armstrong's (2006b) makes clear why this is so, but in a way that may be compatible with my view. As to the Kantian aspiration to find rationally universalizable maxims for every right action, as in the lost child case, final obligation may, on some interpretations of Kant, be based on the kinds of elements that ground the commonsense obligations, e.g. promising. In principle, where a conflict of prima facie obligations is resolvable in favor of a particular act, such as searching for a child at the cost of breaking a promise, the agent can, at least with adequate reflection, appeal to the relevant grounds to frame a rationally universalizable maxim that cites those grounds.

17 This is explained in my (2015a), which – in part by distinguishing rationality from justification – addresses how rational disagreement is possible even for self-evident propositions, including the moral principles discussed in Chapter 4. The view is supported further in chs. 8 and 9 of my (2020b).

as rationalists grant, perceptual experience is developmentally required for a priori knowledge in human life as we know it, the moral principles in question are not empirical generalizations. Some moral knowledge is empirical, however. Some is indeed perceptual. That kind in particular must be clarified by any comprehensive moral epistemology and is the subject of the next chapter.

8 Moral Perception and Singular Moral Judgment

Chapter 7 provided examples of conflicts of prima facie obligation that raise the question whether it is a priori true that if two cases in which a singular moral judgment is to be made are exactly alike "descriptively," then the same overall moral judgments hold in both. An affirmative answer is confirmed by hypothetical cases that differ only in what seem to be morally irrelevant respects such as skin color. But even if this supervenience view expresses an a priori constraint on the justifiability of singular moral judgments, it does nothing to reduce the significance of the point that the singular moral judgments we may reasonably arrive at are empirical. One factor explaining this is that evidence for singular moral judgments usually requires perceptual knowledge, which clearly is empirical. If, however, some moral judgments themselves are perceptual, then surely some moral knowledge is also perceptual. It may embody strong justification conferred by empirically accessible facts of a quite familiar kind and correspondingly "objective." The view that some moral knowledge is genuinely perceptual is both important for ethics and quite controversial. This chapter explores it.[1]

---

1 My (2013b) develops a theory of moral perception that explains this view. What is said here will both reflect (in part) and extend the view proposed there. For a variety of different views of moral perception see Bergqvist and Cowan (2018), and for extensive discussion of the empirical aspects of moral knowledge, McGrath (2019).

1   Moral Perception and Physical Behavior

Moral philosophers have not doubted that we can perceive – say, see or hear – moral phenomena, such as a fatal choking of a handcuffed man. But seeing a deed that *is* wrong – and so *has* a moral property – does not entail seeing its wrongness. Can we, however, perceive, as such, the wrong that such a choking entails? We can. Consider some natural locutions that each appear to presuppose visual perception of moral properties: 'Have you ever seen him do wrong?'; 'I have seen her do justice in difficult situations'; and 'Several witnesses attest to seeing the accused's moral uprightness in situations of great temptation'. One objection to taking such seeing as moral perception is that we do not see or in any visual sense perceive moral properties, but only non-moral properties or events that evidence their presence. Skeptics might say that at best we perceive natural properties that cause us to ascribe moral properties (or apply moral predicates).

This skeptical view is arguable, partly because there is apparently no sharp distinction between seeing a property and tacitly inferring that the visible thing in question has that property. Suppose the inferential hypothesis in question is true and that we do indeed tend to ascribe moral perception – for instance to say we see outrageous wrongs – in various cases of perceiving certain non-moral properties. Philosophers are properly concerned with what relations hold between the two sorts of properties[2] and between non-moral judgments and moral judgments. Do these relations differ importantly from relations common outside the moral realm? Moreover, if they do, does the difference show that we do not acquire moral knowledge or moral justification through perceptions of the kinds I've illustrated?

To begin with, we should set aside certain unwarranted assumptions that may seem plausible. Above all, we should not

---

2 I assume here that there are moral properties. If my position on moral perception is plausible, that in itself provides reason to favor cognitivism and indeed realism in ethics. Perceptual beliefs are paradigms of cognition.

expect moral perception to be *exactly* parallel to physical perception, say just like perceiving everyday visible objects in normal light. Moral properties are not easily conceived as "observable": no sensory phenomenal representation is possible for them, as with color or shape. There is of course *intellective representation* – as in apprehensionally seeing – say, seeing that highly disproportionate distributions of foodstuffs to the needy are wrong. Such non-sensory seeing is possible even in mathematics and other abstract realms and is not the kind in question. There one conceptualizes the phenomenon in a general way. On that basis, we may concretely image an instance, e.g. of right triangles as formed by putting a diagonal between opposite corners of a square, or of wrongness in a case of one person's hitting another. Abstract reflection on moral wrongs may (though it need not) embody detailed representational content, and it also need not be supported or accompanied by images. Moral perception, by contrast, is concrete. In it, sensory representations produced by seeing actions are often integrated with phenomenal elements distinctive of moral experience. Seeing a face-slapping may create a phenomenal sense of shock. That sense itself may be an element in indignation as a moral emotion. This is not simply physical seeing. A cat could take the same purely visual experience with unruffled equanimity.

Even the perceptible properties on which the possession of certain moral properties is based may not be strictly speaking observable, at least in the elementary way face-slapping is. You can see one person, *A*, wrong another, *B*, by, for example, witnessing *A* slashing the tires of *B*'s car. What is indisputably observable here is the slashing. This, in isolation, could be morally neutral. Nonetheless, what we may be properly said to observe here may be partly a matter of what we visually perceive *given* what we already know. We observe that the tires of the car we know to belong to *B* are slashed by *A*. Our background beliefs enable us to see the wrongness of this action. But our background beliefs and, more broadly, our moral sensibility may also affect our phenomenal responses to perceiving such non-moral properties (including relations as kinds of properties) and may facilitate our experiencing a sense of wrongdoing. It must be granted, however, that even though we can visually observe the basis of the wrongdoing, our seeing the wrongdoing depends on our understanding the significance of acts like damaging someone else's property. Moral perception presupposes both non-moral perception *and* a certain background understanding that enables the moral character of what is perceived to affect the perceiver's sensibility in a distinctively moral way. The phenomenology of that way is a subtle matter whose character is suggested by a number of our examples but need not be described in detail here.[3]

2   The Higher-Level Character of Moral Perception

The analogy between perception and action is a good focus for clarifying the higher-level character of moral perception. Just as we do not do anything at all without doing something *basically*, i.e., other than *by* doing something else (as explained in Chapter 1), we do not *perceive* anything other than by perceiving something basically, say by simply seeing its colors and shapes, as with visual perception of trees. Consider a counterpart case of action: my greeting you. I cannot do this without, for instance, raising a hand. I greet you *by* raising a hand. For me, that is a basic act: I do not do it by doing anything else. *Someone* might be able to move the hand-raising muscles at will; I cannot. I can move them only by moving my hand. A movement I make as an action is one thing; a movement in my body necessary for it is quite another. Similarly, I see a bridge by seeing the colors and shapes of its pylons, cables, and span, but I do not see these colors and shapes by seeing anything else. Granted, I cannot see them without my visual system's conveying light to my brain, but *that* set of events is not my basic perception.

We can now see how basic perceptions reveal *the perceptible*, something we can be perceptually aware of by (say) seeing, even

---

3 I described them in detail in my (2022).

if it is not perceived basically but only by perceiving something else. We see the bridge by seeing its perceptible properties, and we perceive a subset of those by seeing their colors and shapes. Seeing the colors and shapes – which are distinct from the bridge though intimately related to it – is a case of perception, much in the way raising a hand, though distinct from greeting, can be intimately related to greeting. Moreover, just as we can see a greeting without inference from the hand movements by which we perceive it, we can see a wrong without inference from the stabbing by which we see it.

To see this point more clearly, consider whether the kind of perceptibility in question is a matter of being, for us, *observable*, where the object's surface is constituted roughly by what is, for us, perceivable basically. The 'for us' reveals a species-relativity, not the subjectivism implied by taking the 'for' to be doxastic, say entailing that what we see depends on what we believe in the situation. The idea is that, for a given species or subspecies, there will be a basic level of perception; the idea is not that the concept of perception requires positing an absolutely basic level across all species capable of perception. For any perceiving being and any time, there is a perceptually basic level for that perceiver at that time; but it does not follow, and I believe is false, that there is some "ultimate" perceptual level that is basic for every perceiver at every time and in every perceiving species.

Now consider injustice as a major moral phenomenon. Is it in some cases observable in the most basic sense, which apparently goes with *perceptual properties*, by which I mean here roughly the kind of sensory property basic for us human beings? Is seeing injustice, for example, observational in the sense corresponding to the perceptual properties of color, shape, and movement that go with observing a disproportionate handout of supplies to the needy? Or is such moral perception simply seeing – in a percep-tual way – a set of constitutive "base properties" for injustice, i.e., properties on which injustice is consequential in a way that indicates to us, upon seeing them, the doing of an injustice? As explained in Chapter 7, actions and other bearers of moral prop-erties do not have those properties *brutely* but on the basis of (consequentially on) having "descriptive" properties. An action is not simply wrong, in the way in which a doing can be simply moving one's hand.[4] It is conceptually essential to such acts that they are wrong *on the basis of* being lies, or *because* they are promise-breakings, or *as* stabbings, and so forth. Similarly, a person is not simply good, but good *on the basis of*, or *because of*, or *as having*, good governing motives together with beliefs appropriate to guiding one toward constructive ends.

One might think that the phenomenal elements in perception properly so called must be sensory in the representational way that characterizes paradigms of (basic) seeing and some of the exercises of the other four ordinary senses. But why should we expect perceptions of injustice, which are not basic for us and have normative phenomena as objects, to be just like perceptions of color, shape, flavor, or sound, which are physical or in any case sensory, are non-normative, and, in typical cases, basic for us? Normative phenomena such as injustice may be perceived in seeing overt behavior, but we should not expect the phenomenology of the sense of injustice to be "pictorial" in the way exemplified by visual impressions of trees. From those impressions, even in retrospect, some people can draw good arboreal likenesses. Injustice cannot be drawn in that sense.

When a moral perception is auditory, as with hearing a lie, or tactual, as with feeling a back-stabbing, we are not tempted to expect the perception to be pictorial, at least in the way visual experience seems to be. But wrongdoing and, positively, justice and fidelity, do not admit of being drawn, even when they can be *seen* in, say, a picturable distribution of boxes, as where the medical supplies for protecting healthcare workers are placed on tables for equal distribution among those workers. What we see must be perceptible; but even if *perceptible properties*, which include cases of being wrong or unjust, must be seen by seeing *perceptual properties*, such as bodily movements, not all perceptible properties are

---

4 This is not to imply that moving one's hand is not grounded at all, but it may lack the kind of conceptual connection to a ground that holds between wrongness and its grounds.

perceptual. The latter are "directly" accessible to the senses, which yield the perceptual base by which we see certain perceptible properties. The latter, including moral properties, need not be on the same level of the perceptual properties pictured or mapped by the senses.

3   Moral Perception as Embodying a Cognitive-Attitudinal Response

Given what we have seen so far, we may reject the demand that a theory of moral perception must provide a *phenomenal* representation of, say, injustice. This applies particularly to a pictorial representation the kind normally yielded by seeing a sunlit bridge. From a good memory impression, many could draw the bridge. A different and more plausible demand calls for representation constituted by a rich kind of perceptual response to injustice. What might serve as the distinctive experiential element in moral perception is the sense of injustice, understood as a kind of impression of it that is based on, and phenomenally integrated with, a suitable ordinary perception of the properties that ground the injustice. Recall the unfair distribution of relief supplies. There is the sight of a disproportion of food packages to the number of the needy awaiting them, the sense of the distributor's deliberately choosing whom to prefer, and, likely, disapprobative feeling toward that person. These are a manifestation of moral sensibility as shaping a response to what is in some way seen to be injustice. In certain cases, there might be a felt inclination to intervene. Such a motivational element is not entailed, but would commonly occur and might affect the phenomenology of the perception.

An important constituent in this phenomenal integration is the perceiver's felt sense of connection between, on the one hand, the impression of, say, injustice or (on the positive side) beneficence and, on the other hand, the properties that ground the moral property in question. This felt sense of connection is at least akin to what moral sensibility, as described in Chapter 7, may represent as fittingness, for instance of package sizes to the sizes of the awaiting families. The proportionality might be felt to be admirable. On occasions of moral perception, the sense of connection – which might be embodied in a related emotion – normally produces a non-inferential disposition to attribute the moral property of the action (or other phenomenon in question) on the basis of the property or set of properties (of that action) on which the moral property is grounded. I assume here that perception does not entail inference and that perceptual beliefs are non-inferential; but there is no need to deny that beliefs having the same propositional content as perceptual beliefs are not *intrinsically* non-inferential. Particularly in a complex matter such as conflict of interest, what mature moral observers directly see is wrong a novice in the matter may have to infer is wrong by applying a rule.[5]

Moral perception is like physical perception not only in the ways so far indicated but also in having an imaginational counterpart. Moral attributions may also occur in purely hypothetical cases of perceptible behavior, as where one is envisaging alternatives from which to choose. These imagined cases might feature projections of different distributions of foods to needy families one is assisting after a storm. Even without actual perception, imagined scenarios may be quite vivid. Here we might have one kind of intuition: a non-inferential sense of the truth of a judgment regarding an imagined case, say that fairness favors priority in distribution to large families with children over smaller ones consisting only of adults.

Moral perception is not the only kind of moral experience with a representational phenomenology. In normal rational persons capable of moral perception, phenomenal states related to moral perception but deriving from hypothetical cases may exhibit elements similar to those in perceptual states. If we can see the

---

5 That perception and perceptual belief are non-inferential is argued in my (2013b) for moral perception and (2020a) for perception in general; these explain why such non-conscious brain processes as may bear information are not inferential in the sense in question here. Various locutions may indicate the breadth of discourse in which grounding figures, but the most important English locution whose main use indicates grounding is 'in virtue of'.

wrong in a face-slapping, we can recall it retrospectively and can imagine similar cases if, for instance, we want to say why such violence is wrong. Given such moral perceptions or even vivid hypothetical representations of what they present to us, moral agents tend to be motivated by the moral experience of wrongness in question. The same may hold for a sense of obligatoriness. Just think as vividly as possible of a small panicky child one can rescue from a closed car parked in hot sunlight. Does it not evoke a moral sense that one should rescue the child? This, in turn, increases the likelihood that actions on a moral judgment evoked by the experience will lead to morally creditworthy conduct.

Our moral sensibility may operate at least as readily in a situation of moral perception as in one imagined in order to form a moral judgment. In some cases, however, imagination may be a better, or certainly wider, source of empirical moral knowledge than perception. Imagine seeing injustice in a distribution, say giving better protective masks to men than to women with the same medical needs. Is the appropriate moral judgment in such a hypothetical case necessarily different from the one we would form in a like case in which we have as input perceptually seeing the maldistribution? My sense of injustice in either case normally yields a disposition to believe that the distribution is wrong *because* it is (on the ground that it is) giving better masks to men than to women in the same vulnerable position. The perceptual attribution of injustice, moreover, is non-inferential. So also may be the judgment formed in imagining the same case. The perceptual judgment is not based on any premise and is a direct response to what I see. Intuitive responses to counterpart imagined cases may be similarly direct. The directness is, of course, epistemic and not causal – philosophical analysis places no restrictions on what causal processes may occur en route to the mind.

4   Phenomenal Elements in Moral Perception

Any kind of perception, on my view, is experiential in having *some* appearance in consciousness – though (apart from self-perception) not entailing *self*-consciousness or any internally directed attitude.

Moral perception in some way embodies a phenomenal sense – which may be significantly emotional – of the moral character of the act. This sense may, for instance, be or at least embody felt disapproval, or even a kind of revulsion. Imagine seeing an angry man deliberately step on his wife's foot when she says something that annoys him. The felt disapproval need not be highly specific; it may, for instance, be a felt unfittingness between the deed and the context. Compare seeing male and female children treated unequally in a distribution of recreational equipment. Positively, a felt fittingness may play a similar phenomenal role in moral perception, and both the sense of moral unfittingness that goes with perceptions of wrongdoing and the positive sense of moral fittingness that may go with perceiving fulfillments of obligation can have significant motivational power. Think of the sense of moral rebalancing if one sees an unequal distribution of equipment or medicine rectified by someone who takes over the previously mishandled case. The equality of the treatment befits the equality of need.

In each instance, the moral sense of wrongness, injustice or, in the positive case, welcome reparation is essentially connected to perception of non-moral properties on which the moral properties are grounded. In cases like these, we might be said to *sense morally*, rather as someone who hears a melody in a wind blowing through open drainpipes might be said to sense musically. This point holds not because moral properties are sensory properties – they are not – nor because there is a special moral faculty dedicated to the ethical realm.[6] It holds because there is a kind of perceptual experience that manifests a moral sensibility which

6 Here faculties are conceived not merely as capacities but as distinct dimensions of experience and behavior analogous to the perceptual modes such as seeing and hearing. Normal perceptual, conceptual, and emotional-attitudinal human capacities suffice for the possibility of moral perception. Thomas Reid's view of "the moral sense" as a perceptual faculty overlaps my conception. For explication of his view see Copenhaver (2014). As she understands him, moral judgment arises from "acquired perception" and is (as on my view) non-inferential, responsive to perceptible properties of its object, and akin to aesthetic perception.

facilitates a response to the properties that ground the moral property perceived. Perceptibility of moral properties is wider than, though it depends on, perceptuality at the level of the grounding properties.

The perceptibility of a property need not occur through that of the more basic perception of its grounds. Consider ripeness in a pear. In some cases, viewing a pear enables one to see, and certainly to perceive, its ripeness. Sight alone might justify judging that it is ripe, but the visible properties do not include the grounds (the determiners) of ripeness. Sight makes ripeness visible by its manifestations. Anger provides a still better foil for such moral properties as wrongness and obligatoriness. Whereas anger is seen by its manifestations, moral wrongs are seen by their grounds. Wrongs may also be known (often inferentially) by their manifestations, but in both cases there are a priori constitutive relations between the moral properties in question and certain evidences of them. The concept of anger is, in part, that of a state that tends to *result in* certain behavior, whereas the concept of wrongness is in part that of a status that *results from* lying. Wrongness may also be grounded even more readily in perceptible actions: wounding, killing, and many other harmful deeds. Moral perception, then, should not be conceived as limited to responses to effects rather than grounds. Such higher-order perception depends in both cases on responsiveness to constitutive relations; but it does not depend specifically on manifestational relations.

Aesthetic perception also provides analogies. One may, for instance, see the gracefulness of a sculptured dancer by perceptible properties that present it, as one may see wrongdoing by violent actions that ground it. The analogy is easily missed because we are much more easily able to formulate a prohibitive moral principle that articulates the relation than to formulate aesthetic principles connecting perceptible non-aesthetic properties with gracefulness. If this difference indicates that ethics is a more "rule-governed" realm than aesthetics, it does not show a difference between perceptibility in the latter but not in the former. Indeed, once the ethics of manners of action is seen as morally important, ethics may be seen as calling for perceptual sensitivity and behavioral responsiveness that are in some cases no more easily codified than criteria for ascribing aesthetic properties.

More broadly, why should perception not be possible as a response to a great variety of reliable indicators or determinants of the perceived phenomenon? Suppose we think of perception as – in part – a kind of reception and processing of information by a causal path from an information source to the mind, where the processing is not limited to events in consciousness.[7] This conception certainly comports well with the role perception plays in providing everyday empirical knowledge of the natural world. On this conception, it should not matter whether the information impinging on the senses is determined by what is perceived or, instead, by determiners or evidences of the perceived thing. We can know a thing either by effects that mark it or by elements that guarantee it. But there is an important difference. Where the determinants are not causal grounds but a priori grounds, the determination necessarily guarantees truth.

5   Perceptual Sources of Singular Moral Judgment

It should be clear that the sketch of moral perception just given does not presuppose that seeing or otherwise perceiving a moral phenomenon entails believing or judging that it is, say, wrong. Someone might see a wrongful assault and take it to be part of consensual sparring. But suppose I see this and judge that the hard stomach blow was wrong. Is this a judgment of prima facie or of overall wrongness? It need not be specifically either, particularly in a cautious observer. In both cases, wrongness is grounded; but prima facie wrongness is often grounded in something readily perceptible, whereas overall wrongness, as with

---

7 For discussion of the sense in which perception is information processing, Dretske (1981) remains a good source. Processing information is more than its mere reception; see Burge (2010), e.g. 299–301, for discussion of both notions and points concerning Dretske's view in (1981).

many aesthetic properties, is usually grounded in a pattern that may call for holistic judgment. Moreover, apart from being asked Socratic questions, some people might simply think of wrongness in terms of violating certain standards – say, by injuring someone. In some cases, although we may presuppose the possibility of a full excuse, we may not judge specifically that the action is (e.g.) wrong-unless-fully-excusable or that it is, overall, wrong.

This is not to deny that perception can give one enough information to yield knowledge that an act is overall wrong, and someone who uses the concept of what is overall wrong might judge certain actions to be so. In any case, if one observes two people quarreling, sees their hostile gestures and then a stabbing followed by one of them running off with a laptop, then it is almost certain that the stabbing is wrong overall. This is not, however, absolutely certain; one could have seen only a rehearsed scene from a play complete with a retracting knife blade and tomato ketchup visible in just the right pattern. But it is perhaps also not self-evidently *absolutely* certain that I am not hallucinating the window that is before my eyes, yet I think I know that there is window before me. Moral judgments, too, may in some cases represent knowledge not only of prima facie wrongs but of overall wrong.

Just how good one's grounds must be for moral knowledge of overall wrongness or overall obligation – which is harder to achieve than knowledge of prima facie wrongness – is not a question with easy answers. Moreover, where we are aware of having conflicting of obligations, and must ascertain our overall obligation, the case is often more difficult than where we observe someone else's action and can make an overall judgment guided by information provided in the context. If my obligation of beneficence calls for protecting someone, but this requires lying to a friend, it may be very difficult to determine the morally best thing to do. It is also possible that two permissible deeds are equally desirable or undesirable from the moral point of view. If, in some conflict cases, we can know what to do, we may be unable to say why, beyond indicating roughly how we see the matter. This is the kind of thing one might do if, at dusk, one cannot tell how one apparently knows that a figure on the horizon is a dog and not a wolf. In any of these cases, however, the difficulty of gaining good evidence does not give us reason to doubt that, if the perceiver does acquire moral knowledge, it is empirical. Where perception is crucial for the justification of the judgment or belief in question, the judgment depends on some causal impact from the physical world in which the action in question occurs.

Where our judgment or belief concerns what we ought (morally) to do, the prospect we consider is one of act-types (or conduct-types) competing for approval. Either way, the moral status of an abstract type one may instantiate (whether at will or by doing some instrumental deed), may be an a priori matter. A closely related kind of question is whether, if asked, say, to save someone from a fire, one should rush in and try, despite a high risk of burns. Suppose the question is about me and implicitly about the act-token that would represent my acting on my judgment. Even if I may know that any saving I achieve will be a good deed viewed abstractly, it is an empirical question whether I will in fact achieve the saving (token that type) and what my action will be like in detail, including its motivation and manner. The judgment that *anyone* who is in a situation of just the *kind* I am in (described in appropriately general terms) should A, may be a priori, and if I see this, it should be a major factor in guiding me. But that *I* should A in the situation of the kind I am in is empirical. I may see that I would A both clumsily and for the wrong reason and that you are both willing to A and more likely to do it in a morally creditworthy way. I then defer to you.

———

Moral epistemology must provide accounts of both general moral knowledge and justification and also knowledge and justification of certain singular moral judgments. The previous chapter argued for a qualified moral rationalism regarding certain general principles. This chapter has argued for the possibility of empirical knowledge of singular moral judgments. Some such judgments are subsumptive, inferential, and non-perceptual, but singular moral judgments may also be perceptual. These judgments may embody the concept of what should or should not be done. In so judging, some moral agents may have in mind prima facie rightness or wrongness, while others presuppose overall rightness or wrongness unless they have reason to consider excusability or mitigation. The fineness of moral cognitions varies with the sophistication of the person judging and the complexity of the circumstances of judgment. But we should not conclude that the kind of wrongness or obligatoriness perceived cannot be more than prima facie. Seeing the massacre of defenseless villagers in a genocidal conflict can surely yield knowledge of overall wrong. It remains, however, to explore whether the moral realism so far largely presupposed in this book can survive some significant doubts. Some philosophers, whether or not they countenance moral perception, would agree that there is empirical moral knowledge and indeed that its existence is best understood on the moral realist view that there are genuine moral properties. But at least some who hold these views would argue that moral realism is sustainable only if moral properties are natural. There is much to be learned by considering this issue. That will be the main work of the next chapter.

9 Moral Explanation and Moral Realism

The notion of explanation is central for both epistemology and metaphysics. It is widely and plausibly held that knowledge depends on a kind of explanation relation that connects what is known with beliefs constituting knowledge of it. It is also plausibly held that what has explanatory power, or anyway is essential in explaining something, is real. Causal properties such as burning, for instance, could not figure as they do in explaining other elements, such as glowing, if they were illusory. Non-causal, mathematical properties can play a similar role in explaining other abstract elements. Moreover, like the geometrical property of being a right triangle, mathematical properties and facts, even if they describe ideal, non-physical entities, can also play a role in explaining such physical facts as the area of a garden.

A major question here is whether moral properties – at least if non-natural – can play *any* role in explaining empirical facts. Can they (or something's having them) even explain non-empirical *moral* facts, assuming there are such facts? Call such cases *intra-domain explanations*. I begin with those explanations, but we must also consider the related questions of what else may be required by a moral realism worthy of the name and how the explanatory roles of apparent moral facts might support moral realism. Beyond this, we should also compare that kind of explanatory role with the explanatory role of certain mathematical facts. In making that comparison, this chapter explores the explanatory role of particular facts such as that one person lied to another, as well as such a priori facts as that lying is (prima facie) wrong. The explanatory roles to be examined range from (1) the heuristic role of leading to discovery of explanations, to (2) the explanatorily central role of being *what* explains – an explainer of – something, to (3) the subsidiary role of being essential in a fact that explains certain empirical phenomena, to (4) the auxiliary role of supplying, as does mathematics, concepts or propositions whose empirical interpretations have explanatory power, to (5) the theoretical role of providing a unifying explanatory account of a group of related phenomena. If presumptive moral facts can play all of these roles, this would constitute good reason to consider them genuine facts that entail the reality of moral properties.

1   Intra-Domain Explanation

It is useful to begin with a mathematical case. We can show, and explain, diagrammatically why the Pythagorean Theorem holds for right triangles with sides of, say, 3, 4, and 5 units by drawing squares with sides equal in length to those of the arbitrarily chosen right triangle. This also provides an informal (though valid) proof and, in a certain way, explains the theorem; but explanations, whether or not they constitute a kind of proof, need not have a formal structure.

Might ethics include similar informal, intra-domain explanations? Consider how someone's justifiably resenting an inexcusable lie can be explained (and indeed also justified). Imagine a physician's inexcusably lying to a patient about the seriousness of an illness (any physician and any patient). Then, even if well-intentioned, this action explains (and also morally justifies) the patient's resenting the act. Since 'inexcusably lying', like 'morally justifies resentment', is broadly moral, this is a kind of moral explanation, and the arbitrary choice of a physician as exemplar parallels choosing an arbitrarily sized right triangle to explain the length of the hypotenuse from that of the sides. The moral explanation is not, however, empirical, since (for one thing) it is hypothetical and does not presuppose anyone's existence, much less any actual lies usable in providing empirical evidence. Actual lies provide illustrations of this explanatory generalization but are not essential evidence, any more than physical triangles are essential evidence needed to prove the Pythagorean Theorem. The relevant kind of evidence for it is of the intuitive sort appropriate to the moral generalization just framed and indeed to the principles formulated in Chapter 4, whose internalization partly constitutes the moral sensibility that is manifested by the resentment just described.

A different intra-domain case illustrates an element that directly explains, in the sense of constituting *what* explains,[1] a kind of a wrong: one person's incarcerating another for a crime that the other did not commit violates the other's right to be free, and that fact explains its being wrong. If, as I assume, prima facie wrong is intended, this explanatory connection has as good a claim to be a priori as the justificatory connection in the previous example. But although apriority is desirable for staying close to the mathematical case, it is not presupposed in simply maintaining that the two moral examples represent intra-domain explanation.

Moral realists will hold that these explanatory statements, in part because they can provide *understanding* of the propositions explained, constitute genuine explanations. Providing under-standing is a prima facie indication that the fact providing it has explanatory power. This holds at least in hypothetical situations and in part because the explanatory statements in question *inter-connect* various important notions, e.g. those valuable for describing aspects of human life – wronging and resentment, promising and obligation, freedom and rights, and many other notions. The underlying idea is perhaps that if a thing's having a property explains its having another property (or something else's having a property) – in neutral terminology, explains why it is true that a predication applies to some object – this provides some reason to

---

1 If there are two or more sufficient explainers, each may explain the phenom-enon in question. With this kind of overdetermination it would be misleading to speak of either factor as what explains the phenomenon. Unless otherwise indicated, the cases to be discussed will not embody overdetermination.

think the explained predication ascribes a real property. If one takes it that properties are obviously real in some sense, one could say instead that if ascribing a predicate 'F', e.g. 'lying', explains the applicability of another predicate, say 'justified resentment', to some real phenomenon, this counts in favor of both predicates' expressing genuine properties.

These considerations do not prove that there are (real) moral properties, but they need not be taken in isolation. Each case cited, like the mathematical examples given, may be associated with empirical explanations. Consider the generalization that inexcusably lying to someone can explain and justify the person's resenting the act. With this proposition in mind, imagine this statement: "I don't see why Mae is justified (as you claimed) in resenting what Carson did." One answer would be, "Because she discovered that he inexcusably lied to her." These propositions, in addition to apparently positing moral properties, are empirical (in part because they are existential), and Mae's discovery entails instantiation of the antecedent of the a priori generality in question, while her having a justifying reason for disapproval instantiates its consequent. Thus, although the explanation succeeds in telling us *why* Mae is justified by virtue of an a priori connection between being lied to and being justified in resentment, it is empirical in also concerning a relation between existing individuals.

Anti-realists will object that 'Mae's discovering Carson's inexcusably lying to her' should not, without further argument, be taken to express a moral fact. Suppose we accept this. We might even grant the anti-realist that *discovering* something (regardless of its content) is a psychological property and, as a natural property, is what explains the fact in question. Indeed, it should not escape notice that discovering an inexcusable lie (a discovery that may be based on moral perception) can explain not only justification for resentment – a normative fact – but being resentful itself, a psychological fact. One broad conclusion here is that a natural phenomenon that embodies a normative fact can have normative explanatory power without losing the explanatory power it has qua natural phenomenon. A different conclusion, more pertinent to the notion of intra-domain explanation, is that an a priori, intra-domain relation, such as the relation between being inexcusably lied to and being justified in resenting that action, may play a role in explaining related empirical phenomena that are outside the abstract realm in question. The empirical explanation succeeds in part because of its close relation with the a priori, intra-domain normative connection.

Might we also grant something that can easily seem to serve anti-realism in ethics – that if the apparent discovery is not genuine because there is no actual lie discovered, the *belief* which Mae takes to come from discovering a lie might have equal explanatory power regarding empirical facts? Suppose we grant this. Realists may respond by appealing to a distinction between explaining, in the sense of being *what explains*, a phenomenon and the weaker notion of *playing a role in explaining*. Consider, for example, explaining the collapse of a wooden bridge by citing a heavy battle tank's attempting to cross it. Here the slenderness of supporting timbers may play a role in explaining the collapse, but if their condition is such as to allow normal traffic, this constitutional factor is not by itself what causes (or explains) the collapse, nor would it be properly cited as causing it. What causes and explains it is the tank's exceeding the bridge's weight capacity. In the light of this distinction, the modified realist claim would be that even intra-domain explanations may be connected in a certain way with empirical explanations in which moral facts (or properties) play a role, and that connection supports moral realism.

This claim is not arbitrary, and there may be an appropriate analogy to the mathematical case. Take the Pythagorean Theorem as a priori and analogous to the normative principle expressing the sufficiency of inexcusable lies for justification for resentment. Imagine a corner lot with the shape of a right triangle. The empirical facts about its border lengths can explain why a square lot with a side on the diagonal has the area it does. (Perhaps this area cannot be measured easily and the buyer wants to know its cost per square yard.) We measure the triangular lot's shorter sides and are satisfied that we know their lengths. We can then explain to the buyer why the area being sold has the area we say it has. Our calculations involve physical measurements that provide (approximate) physical values to the sides of the square. Suppose the north and west sides are 30 and 40 meters long respectively and that we appeal to these facts to explain why we are billing for 2,500 square meters (50 squared). We are appealing to numerical empirical propositions to explain another such proposition, not to mathematical propositions that a priori explain another mathematical proposition, as in an ideal Euclidean area calculation. Strictly speaking, even though we would not give the explanation we do if we did not believe the Pythagorean Theorem, that mathematical truth – as opposed to an empirical numerical truth – is not what explains the acreage we cite. But the theorem *is* essential in guiding our empirical assumptions about lengths and areas (though we also test those empirically). Still, the property of having (e.g.) a 30-meter length is essential in explaining the empirical proposition indicating area, as is the theorem that leads us to square the hypotenuse to determine that area.

The case in a way parallels the one in which the moral property of being an inexcusable lie plays a role in explaining an empirical proposition (that the patient is resentful). The a priori principle here is that *discovering* an inexcusable lie can explain (and justify) a response of *having* resentment. This explanatory and justificatory relation connects an act-type and a response-type, in a way analogous to the way the Pythagorean Theorem connects measurements of the sides of any right triangle to the measurement of its hypotenuse. By giving the a priori theorem a role in measurement and calculation in an empirical instance, we can explain empirical facts about distances. Similarly, by giving the parallel a priori normative resentment principle a role in understanding behavior, we can both justify the patient's having resentment upon discovering an inexcusable lie and explain at least why the resentment is expectable given the discovery. The normative principle here plays a role in explaining how the empirical fact that a physician lied to Mae accounts for her resentment. Granted, the normative property of inexcusability does not automatically give discovering the inexcusable lie predictive power that it would otherwise lack, but it does render Mae's resentment unsurprising and even quite understandable. In the mathematical as well as the normative case, the principle is abstract; but in both cases there is an application, via empirical counterparts of the principles, to concrete instances in the causal order. In the way illustrated, the normative principle plays a role in explaining concrete empirical phenomena.

2   Hard and Soft Moral Realism

The moral realism so far defended is not reductive and in that sense is "soft." For our purposes, let us take hard moral realism to be the view that moral properties are reducible to natural ones and the soft variety as non-reductive and (unless otherwise specified) non-naturalistic.[2] The reason 'soft' is an appropriate metaphor is the apparent plausibility of requiring that for a property to have any claim to the ontological status of reality, it must be able to do more than explain facts in its own realm.[3] One may well think that a real property should be such that something's having it can make a difference "in the world," and on some views this requires that the property be in the causal order. That, in turn, is commonly taken to entail being natural as opposed not only to being supernatural but to being irreducibly normative. If a version of moral realism

---

2 For Zhong (2019), soft moral realism says: "(1) There are knowable moral facts [the realist element] and (2) they cannot play explanatory roles in non-moral domains [the soft element]," whereas, for hard moral realism, knowable moral facts "can play explanatory roles in non-moral domains" (555). Zhong allows for a non-causal realism about mathematical entities (which would arguably be a non-naturalist realism), but in any case a naturalistic moral realism could be neutral toward reduction, as possibly for Sturgeon (2006). Zhong thus distinguishes explanatory efficacy from causal power (557). His explanatory condition for soft moral realism is correspondingly broad: "We can have moral knowledge only if moral facts play explanatory roles in non-moral domains (such as ... explaining moral beliefs)" (558).

3 The plausibility of this criterion is perhaps reduced if one applies it to natural properties, since one then faces the problem of how they can figure in explaining facts that, like theorems of pure mathematics, are non-natural and outside their domain. This far-reaching metaphysical issue cannot be pursued here.

requires that moral facts can explain empirical facts, then even if moral facts – which include any true moral principles – satisfy the explanatory requirements for moral realism by explaining *other* moral facts, this does not suffice for the truth of moral realism. Thus, even if the propositions that (1) lying to people wrongs them, together with (2) being wronged morally justifies resentment, can explain why (3) if one person lies to another, the second has moral justification for resenting the first, this explanation lacks the kind of explanatory efficacy some philosophers consider necessary for defending moral realism.

If, for the sake of argument, we accept this restriction on moral realism, we should explore how mathematical facts may explain facts in other domains and whether, if they can, a parallel point holds for moral facts. Here is an example suggesting how some mathematical facts play explanatory roles in certain empirical cases:

> Honeybees use hexagonal cells to build their honeycombs ... The dominant explanation among biologists is that natural selection would choose those bees that made their honeycombs in the most efficient manner with the minimal amount of wax. This explanation in fact appeals to a mathematical truth, the so-called "honeycomb theorem": A hexagonal grid is the most efficient way to divide a Euclidean plane into regions of equal area with the least total perimeter.[4]

Presumably the claim that the evolutionary explanation appeals to a mathematical truth is intended to show that this truth plays a role in the explanation of the empirical fact that bees use hexagonal cells in nesting. Can moral facts play such a role? Let me suggest how.

3   Explanatory Roles

Consider again of the ontological significance of explanatory power. Is there just one kind of explanatory power such that a

---

4 Zhong (2019: 568); he considers this a case in which a theorem of mathematics plays an essential and sufficiently strong role in empirical explanation to support realism in mathematics.

property's having it supports countenancing that property as real? There is a considerable difference between a fact's simply playing an explanatory role in explaining some non-moral phenomenon and its being what explains (what it is that explains) that fact. As will be illustrated, the latter entails the former, but the converse is false. Regarding the importance of explanatory roles, we may assume at least this: that if a fact is essential in a correct explanation of some other fact, then it plays a role in explaining that fact. This point is quite general and, whatever its significance for moral realism, it holds not just for extra-domain explanations but also for intra-domain explanations, e.g. explaining why racial discrimination is wrong by appeal to the facts that it is an injustice and that injustices are wrong.

As already suggested, if moral facts – even a priori facts – play roles in explaining beliefs and actions, which are concrete empirical phenomena, this would support moral realism. Suppose someone asks why Janet rejects a policy. One answer might cite the facts that she believes it is discriminatory and opposes discrimination. Her belief and opposition are psychological properties, but what makes them the properties they are depends on their content, which is moral. (She attributes a moral property to the policy.) If a moral fact, e.g. that a policy is discriminatory, can be an essential element in a fact that explains an action, then it can play an explanatory role in explaining that action. This is not to deny that her believing discrimination is wrong constitutes a kind of natural fact; the point is that it is partly in virtue of moral content that the fact is the fact it is.

Granted, we might also be able to explain her action differently, appealing to what *grounds* her believing the policy discriminatory, say its exclusions on such bases as skin color. But this would not constitute the same explanation, and it is not clear that it would be explanatorily better or, more important, that its availability invalidates the moral explanation. Compare explaining why a windshield was cracked by saying that it was hit by a pebble kicked up by a truck. The crack is also explainable by citing an impact of a certain velocity by a particle of a certain hardness and weight striking glass of a certain thickness, and so forth. This technical explanation does not undermine the macroscopic explanation and is preferable only for certain purposes.

The point, in any event, is not that in the analogous moral case, the moral fact that the policy is discriminatory is *what* explains Janet's action; it is that this fact plays an essential role in the constitution of an element, a belief she holds, which (in the context) *does* explain it.[5] The point does not even require that an explanatory moral belief be *true*. (An untrue belief's explaining an event does not necessarily depend on its being untrue.) Nor does the point require viewing moral properties as causal, or even taking such intentionalistic explanations to be causal (though many would argue that they are broadly causal).

I have been assuming for the sake of argument that the plausibility of soft moral realism depends on a moderately strong explanatory condition: on whether moral facts (or fact-like moral phenomena) can play a role in explanations of *non*-moral phenomena. If I have been correct, then one explanatory role they may play – through their place in determining the character of psychological phenomena that explain behavior – seems to meet this condition. That moral beliefs can play this explanatory role does not require reductive naturalism regarding moral properties and significantly counts in favor of at least non-reductive moral realism.

This point does not entail that playing an explanatory role of the kind illustrated in Janet's case *suffices* to show the genuineness of a purported moral fact. An anti-realist might object that since moral "beliefs" lack truth-value, they cannot even be false. How might such a view be maintained? It is understandable that just as there is a concept of a round square – which enables us to see the impossibility of there being a fact that there is one – there might be a concept of (say) wrongness but no possible fact that an act is wrong. This version of anti-realism would allow that the *concept* of

---

5 This point does not imply that no background conditions are presupposed as necessary for the success of the explanation, but the notion of a factor's being what explains something embodies a concept of some kind of salient role. How to characterize this is a complex matter that need not be pursued here.

wrongness could nonetheless figure essentially in making an action-explaining belief the belief it is and thereby play a role in explaining an action. If concepts C_1 and C_2 are not equivalent, then the belief that x is C_1 is not identical with the belief that x is C_2. Different beliefs may differ in their range of possible explanatory roles.

An anti-realist who is a noncognitivist could, to be sure, hold that sentences to the effect that an act is wrong are simply expressions of dislike in the way shouting 'Boo!' is, and that therefore there could be no such case supporting realism. This crude emotivist version of noncognitivism, however, is not plausible enough to need a response here.[6] On a sophisticated non-cognitivist view, however, it might be argued that moral concepts are not "descriptive" and, in contexts of moral judgment, instead function in framing complicated expressions of pro and con attitudes that, though not fact-stating, are not essentially emotive and may even rationally respond to reasons. This is not the place to appraise such views, though it should be pointed out that many expressive functions of, e.g., judgments of right and wrong are compatible with moral realism. What can be said here is that, minimally, the overall case for moral realism made in this book may, on balance significantly raise the bar for making noncognitivism plausible. I assume, then, that there *can* be moral facts and that (for reasons given in Chapter 7) some of those facts (such as what Janet asserts) can be empirically confirmed or disconfirmed. This confirmability supports positing the explanatory role just illustrated for moral facts and thereby supports moral realism. This support is neutral, however, between hard and (any kind of) soft moral realism, at least assuming that the explanatory power

---

6 For one thing, it cannot explain such logical operations as emphasized in setting out the Frege-Geach problem. This problem concerns (among other things) the implausibility of holding that such moral sentences as 'Lying is wrong' are noncognitive in such reasoning as 'If x lied to y then x did wrong; x lied to y; so, S did wrong'. Such points have apparently been noted by writers posing such questions after Frege and before Geach. See, e.g., Phillips's case that Ross is one such (2019: 166–167).

of a belief is neutral with respect to whether a normative property the belief ascribes is reducible to a natural property.[7]

4   A Mathematical Analogy

One way in which moral facts also play a role significantly similar to an explanatory role played by mathematical facts has been suggested in relation to the Pythagorean Theorem. Further similarities are suggested by the instructive case of the honeybees, and I assume that the Honeycomb Theorem of Euclidean geometry is important for explaining the efficiency and thus the fitness value of bees' nests as (approximately) instantiating the theorem. The theorem certainly might suggest (perhaps make quite probable) that the nests are efficient in storage, which in turn suggests an evolutionary explanation of bees' building such nests. This heuristic role, however, does not require the truth of the theorem, which is framed in terms of idealized, widthless lines. Efficiency is a multi-dimensional concept in such an evolutionary case. Efficient storage is also partly a matter of the thickness of the wax walls of the storage chambers and of preservative power, which could be better for a less spatially economical shape.

If it were an a priori truth that physical space is Euclidean, then one could at least infer from the theorem that, apart from the variables of the durability and thickness of the hexagons' walls, spatial storage capacity in hexagonal cells would be most efficient short-term. But this would leave open whether some other shape might better *preserve* what is to be stored long-term. Efficiency of storage might also vary with accessibility for use. Whether physical space is Euclidean is a difficult question to explicate (and would require specifying variables involving a good deal of physics); but the matter is empirical. Euclidean efficiency is ideal; evolutionary efficiency is physicochemical, diachronic, and causal. What we can hope to do here is ascertain whether there

---

7 For a comprehensive explanation and defense of moral realism, as contrasted with both noncognitivism and error theories, and with attention to much recent literature, see FitzPatrick (2022).

is significant analogy between the explanatory role of such a priori propositions as the Honeycomb Theorem and certain apparently a priori moral propositions.

On the heuristic side, there is significant analogy. Consider the view that a government's unjust treatment of its people entails their having a prima facie obligation to resist that government. This view seems to be a priori defensible on the basis of the moral principles, including principles of justice, supported in Chapter 7. Preserving justice plainly calls on us to resist injustice. The main point here, however, is that considering the view that it is obligatory to resist injustice a priori does not preclude discerning the systematic connections between injustice and empirical phenomena. Proponents of the view would hold that unjust treatment is partly constituted by, and is knowable by perceiving, such things as confiscation of property without due process, arbitrary body searches, unexplained domestic travel restrictions, and police brutality. Instances of the concept of resistance are also identifiable by perceptible conditions. Given these empirical connections between perceptible indications of the properties figuring in the moral proposition – between sufficient indications of governmental injustice and necessary conditions for resistance to government – are there not a number of testable hypotheses implied? Arbitrary body searches by police, which suffice for governmental injustice, might, e.g., be hypothesized to engender verbal protest, avoidance of check points, and other perceptible elements that confirm resistance. These are the kinds of things characteristic of resistance, and a subset of such indicators is necessary for behavior expressing it.

The case illustrates, then, how the moral view has significant heuristic value in leading to hypotheses which, in turn, are testable and have empirical explanatory power. This heuristic value is not, moreover, merely power to suggest explanatory hypotheses; that power could in principle come from a purely imaginary construct. The hypotheses are discovered by reflection on instances of the properties that are systematically connected with the mathematical or moral ones – for instance spatial efficiency in the geometrical case and, in the moral case, governmental injustice – and that figure in a priori generalizations. The underlying idea is that even if a normative principle of the form ⟨All Fs are Gs⟩ is a priori, where there are empirical sufficient conditions for being F, these may be expected to imply the obtaining of the necessary conditions for being G. This rational expectation may yield a goodly range of empirical hypotheses.

It does not clearly follow from the existence of such heuristic value that the moral truth in question plays any further role in explaining non-moral phenomena. But suppose, for instance, that where the grounds of governmental injustice are *believed* to be unjust there is *greater* resistance than in cases in which (perhaps owing to fanatical devotion to the government) people dislike, to a similar extent, the governmental unjust acts but do not believe them unjust. Unrecognized injustice may have causal and explanatory power; but its being generally *believed* to be injustice apparently has both. We again encounter the apparent fact that the moral content of beliefs sometimes plays a role, in a way analogous to certain mathematical contents of beliefs, in the action-explaining power of the beliefs in question. Certain moral contents of beliefs may enhance their power to affect our relations to others, much as certain mathematical contents of belief may enhance their power to affect our relations to mapping and controlling nature. In the case of resistance to government, believing a moral proposition may have a role in believing that one is being wronged and thereby play a (testable) role in explaining such resistances as blocking roads, supporting underground resistance, and hiding foodstuffs.

So far, I have raised no doubts about the possibility of mathematical knowledge or even about its apriority. But there remains much controversy about how such knowledge is possible. Particularly in the context of the sketch of the self-evident given in Chapter 7, we might appropriately consider the possibility Ross-adapted from Aristotle: that knowledge of at least elementary arithmetic is acquired, not by enumerative induction or even abduction, but by intuitive induction.[8] Ross took this mathematical

---

8 On Ross's view, "We find by experience that this couple of matches and that couple make four matches ... and by reflection on this and similar discoveries

analogy to suggest how a priori moral truths are learned. He assumed that for at least certain abstract entities, such as mathematical entities and (non-Russellian) propositions, direct non-causal apprehension is possible. To some, this will seem mysterious. But (to take a contemporary example connected with the resurgence of naïve realism) is it less mysterious that knowledge should be considered a state of mind,[9] even when much knowledge entails the existence of perceptible objects existing outside the mind? If the content of a state of mind can be outside it and even physical, why is it less mysterious that it may be abstract and non-physical? Perhaps anyone's primitive will be someone's mystery, and philosophers who countenance anything mysterious (most of us, perhaps) must continue trying to dispel the clouds.

5   The Explanatory Significance of Generic Properties

There is a less speculative and more positive point to be made here concerning realism and explanation. Most criticism of moral realism focuses on what moral facts *cannot* explain. By contrast, it is commonly assumed, at least by explanationist realists, who take having an explanatory role to be a condition for countenancing facts and properties, that natural facts by their very nature *can* explain other natural facts, in the sense of having instances that are *what* explains some natural fact. This second requirement turns out to be far from obvious. I want to show that and to bring out a role, so far not evident in our discussion but pertinent to moral realism, that certain kinds of facts, moral as well as natural, can play in explanations of empirical phenomena.

Take the natural property, shape, i.e., *being shaped*. A vast variety of objects are shaped, being round, oval, hexagonal, heart-

we come to see that it is of the nature of two and two to make four. In a precisely similar way, we see the *prima facie* rightness of an act which would be the fulfillment of a particular promise ..." See Ross (1930: 32–33).

9 As argued by Williamson in ch. 1 of (2000).

shaped, and so forth. But consider the fact that a stone has a shape. This property contrasts with (e.g.) the shapelessness of gas invisibly escaping from multiple openings in a tank. The shape fact can convey information, then, but what kind of explanatory role can it play? Compare the stone's being merely shaped (having some shape) with its being round. The latter fact would explain why it easily rolls, just as its being cubical would explain why it is stackable with stones of the same shape. It is not the generic fact of being shaped that explains these things, but particular facts that ground the former fact, in the sense that the former obtains in virtue of them. The relation between being shaped and having a particular shape is that of determinable to determinate, and it appears that the (empirical) explanatory power of shape depends on that of its determinates.[10]

Now consider wrongness, which is an important generic moral property. How significantly like a thing's being shaped is an action's being wrong? A crucial similarity is that neither property is brute; both are grounded, as are the facts constituting ascriptions of them. An action cannot be brutely wrong, any more than an object can be brutely shaped. An object is shaped in virtue of being, say, round; an action is wrong[11] in virtue of being a killing, or of being a lie, and so forth for a presumably finite list of types of grounds. The point is not that wrongness is a determinable, though it is certainly generic in a broad sense, having many kinds of "species."[12] It is like such determinables as shape and color in being such that having it requires a certain kind of structure (or anyway constitution). Much as shapes have a perimeter or a visible surface quality of a spectral kind, in the moral case wrongness

---

10 One thing that simply being shaped can explain is having a perimeter. Such an explanation would be both intra-domain and a priori – an explanatory condition certain moral facts also meet.

11 The wrongness in question is a kind compatible with excuses like self-defense; one might also speak of wrong-makingness – any morally negative term should serve for the point.

12 For a related illuminating account of goodness as a generic property see Butchvarov (1989), esp. chs. 1–4 (on his view, however, goodness is also a determinable).

requires being an act or act-related phenomenon of a certain person-related kind.

There are, of course, differences. In the moral case, an instance of wrongness can be *multiply grounded* in, for instance, lying, harming, and promise-breaking – all instantiable by a single action, whereas a shaped object cannot simultaneously have different overall shapes. Nonetheless, wrongnesss is at least sufficiently like certain determinables to sustain a similarity in relation to explanation. The fact that a thing is shaped entails that it has some (grounding) shape property, and shape properties are such that a thing's having one can explain (and presumably be *what* explains) certain facts about it. Similarly, the fact that an act is wrong entails that it has some (grounding) natural property, i.e., is wrong in virtue of being, say, a killing of a person – in virtue of having a negative moral shape, we might say. In both cases, the grounding facts can explain empirical facts.

These points of similarity between being shaped and being wrong are consistent with differences so various and important that one might easily overlook the similarities. The similarities do not require taking wrongness to be a determinable (which it cannot be, given that the different grounds, such as lying and harming, are compatible). But the similarities do provide room to argue that wrongness is not only a real property that can play roles in empirical explanations but also a natural property, as some intuitionists, being hard moral realists, presumably take it to be.[13]

---

13 Zhong cites intuitionists who are hard realists (2019: 564) but does not note an epistemological point important for his paper: that the moderate rationalism of my intuitionism is compatible with a naturalistic account of moral properties. He cites Cuneo and Wedgwood as intuitionists who are hard moral realists, but, though citing me as defending soft moral realism (in his sense), he does not note my saying, "My account [of moral perception] thus allows, though it does not require, a naturalizing of moral properties by providing a causal account of their constitution" (2013b: 55). I have also suggested that certain "moral explanations" are naturalizable, but that is where they are presented in such a way that the explaining factors are natural phenomena. I nowhere suggest that moral properties play no role in empirical explanation. See, e.g. (1993b: 95–115), reprinted in my (1997).

The analogy between moral properties and certain determinable natural properties indicates a kind of explanatory role that is, in a certain way, indirect for the determinables but direct for their determinates. A thing's possessing the determinable entails having the indirect explanatory role of entailing the existence of a determinate that can – as what some would call a "realizer" of the determinable – play a direct explanatory role: being *what explains* some empirical fact. It appears, moreover, that for both naturalistic determinables and generic moral properties, instantiation a priori entails the presence of grounding facts that can directly explain – roughly, constitute what explains – some natural fact. There are entailments (also apparently a priori) in the other direction too: being a killing entails being (prima facie) wrong – it is a way of being wrong, one might say – as being round entails having a shape, a way of having shape. Both moral facts and certain clearly natural facts have a basis in natural facts. It appears, then, that wrongness is much like shape in "making a difference to the world." This is possible without being a causal property but through playing roles in causal explanations in such a way that it would be a mistake to call moral properties epiphenomenal – real but utterly inconsequential.[14]

6 The Unifying Role of Moral Generalizations

These points suggest that certain generic properties, including both shape and wrongness, may play unifying roles relevant to

14 There is an analogy between my defense of the reality of moral properties and certain defenses of the reality of mental properties. A major difference is that the latter case (at least typically) aims at showing how mental properties figure in causal explanation, whereas I am not taking moral properties to be causal properties. For an instructive case against the explanatory exclusion principle on which the physical realizers of mental properties do all the causal work mental properties may seem to do, and in support of the causal significance of mental properties, see Yablo (1992). Using diverse examples of determinables and mental properties – properties relevantly analogous to shape – he says, "If the causally sufficient antecedent monopolizes all the influence, then the others are left with none ... rather than competing for causal honors, determinables and their determinates seem likelier to share in one another's success" (272).

explanation. The scope of instantiation of these generic properties does, after all, indicate the instantiation of at least some of the (natural) properties that partly constitute something's having the generic property. There may, e.g., be some generic explanation of the behavior of certain macroscopic objects that essentially employs the fact that they have some shape within a certain range. Shape might be important in calculating friction as a factor in movability; certain kinds of asymmetries in objects make them incapable of rolling in a straight line; and perhaps, other things equal, the more nearly round a macroscopic object is, the less the force needed to move it across a flat surface.

Similarly, other things equal, the closer to being unjust a government is, the more likely is civil resistance. This can be tested empirically by seeing whether the sufficient conditions for governmental injustice predict sufficient conditions for civil resistance. There also seem to be cases like this involving positive normative properties. Consider the normative proposition that benevolent people should be appreciated for that trait. This illustrates how a generic property such as being of good character has a specific instantiation, benevolence, that can figure in a counterpart empirical generalization: benevolent people tend to be appreciated by people aware of this trait in them. That, in turn, is a testable generalization having a measure of explanatory power.

Might there also be, associated with such testable hypotheses, some generic empirical explanation of certain types of human behavior? I have in mind explanations that essentially employ the fact that certain acts, such as resistances to a government, share one or another connection to wrongness, say being responses to seizures of property, which ground wrongness. Such responses may (though they need not) be more directly produced by moral perceptions of the seizures as unjust. The overall point is twofold: first, the property of governmental injustice can unify the many kinds of thing that ground injustice as all constituting ways for a government to be unjust; and second, it can also unify certain phenomena these grounds may produce: these phenomena may be viewed as responses to governmental injustice. This chapter suggests some directions in which empirical inquiry might pursue the question of how moral properties and their instances figure in empirical explanations or unify behavioral patterns. But quite apart from how that line of inquiry might go, the points about the explanatory roles of moral facts made in sections 1–5 of this chapter do not depend on the analogy drawn between generic moral properties and shape as a generic natural property.[15]

7   Moral Realism and Reductive Naturalism

It should be evident that I have not implied that a reductive version of moral realism cannot explain the considerations I have adduced in favor of moral realism. Presumably, it can, at least if it incorporates a priori moral truths. It might incorporate them. As Chapter 7 showed, a rationalist moral epistemology does not require the irreducibility of wrongness and all the other important moral properties. Why might it not be that wrongness, for instance, is a natural property so complex that we neither have a good overall grasp of it nor even an apt naturalistic name for it?[16]

One reductive strategy that might seem consonant with my realist moral pluralism is this. If one countenances disjunctive properties (as distinct from disjunctive concepts or something like

15 One response to the view suggested here is that both wrongness and shape may be viewed as epiphenomenal. If the point is that a thing's simply having a shape and an act's just being wrong are not causal explainers, I have not denied it. Being causal explainers is not necessary for being real or "factive" or indeed for playing explanatory roles, and it is significant that natural facts as well as moral facts (whether natural or not) illustrate this.

16 Sturgeon suggests this in (2006); and, for a recent attempt to explain and defend the causal power of moral facts along Cornell realist lines, see Luco (2019). Luco quotes the basic idea from Boyd's characterization of a causal regulation theory of reference: "A term t refers to a kind ... k just in case there exist causal mechanisms whose tendency is to bring it about, over time, that what is predicated of the term t will approximately be true of k." See 433 in Luco; 195 in Boyd (1988). Luco does not discuss the objection that epiphenomenal properties may be similarly regulated. My moral realism does not depend on this regulation view or the idea that causal regulation of property-ascriptions entails their having causal power.

states of affairs expressed by disjunctive predicates), one might use the best normative framework one can formulate to provide a reduction of moral properties to non-moral properties. Suppose we take wrongness to be the property of being either a lie or a broken promise or a killing or a failure to render aid ... for all the dimensions of wrongness. This project seems to me unpromising even if there are disjunctive properties.[17] Imagine, however, in the spirit of cooperative speculation, a different, quasi-functionalist route to naturalization.

We might begin with the idea that the institution of morality – the framework of normative standards captured in such venerable generalities as that lying is wrong, promise-breaking is unethical, and killing innocent people who block one's material success is morally outrageous – has the functional role of promoting or at least sustaining a kind of social coordination. These and other kinds of wrongness are in a sense "anti-social," and the point goes with the broad plausible idea that a function of the institution of morality is to conduce to human well-being ('human flourishing' may be a better term). This point suggests that, on the negative side, wrongness is a property of actions whose instances tend to induce fear, reduce social coordination, and engender retaliation and, on the positive side, obligatoriness is a property whose instances have contrasting tendencies. The question immediately arises whether we can naturalize all the needed descriptions of the properties we must posit to explicate moral functioning. I find this doubtful. It is in any case a significant challenge that to my knowledge has not been met.

A related point is this. It is not clear that, without appeal to such normative epistemic notions as justification and adequate evidence, we can explicate the relevant notions of, e.g., what moral

---

17 One condition for property identity is necessary equivalence, and, given the varieties and complexities of wrongness, it seems doubtful that there is naturalistic disjunction necessarily equivalent to it. A further problem is that some of the needed disjuncts, such as *failure to render aid*, are themselves not at all clearly naturalistic in character (what is relevant, of course, is failure to render aid when, within certain limits, one "can"). As to whether properties may be disjunctive, plausible doubts are raised by P. Audi (2013).

agents may be *reasonably* expected to do – a notion crucial for the theory of excuses – or what it is to know or even confirm a tendency of moral facts to yield certain consequences for well-being. Even apart from whether explicating moral concepts requires explicating epistemic concepts, from a broad metaphysical point of view there is little gain in naturalizing the domain of practical reason if we cannot naturalize that of theoretical reason, which is at least as important a realm and needs ontological accommodation. I doubt that we can naturalize it. Even if we can hope to naturalize the notion of knowledge, that of justification is quite recalcitrant in this respect.[18] If objectivity in ethics or science required naturalization of moral or epistemic properties, there would be more reason to seek to naturalize them, but there is no good reason to think that objectivity does require it. The goal may still be a worthy one with the idea of ontological economy in view. Here, however, mathematics and the a priori come back to mind. If we must be realists about abstract entities to account for mathematical and other a priori knowledge, and if these are essential for a good understanding of the natural world, I cannot see why moral realism should not also form a part of an adequate ontology.

———

We have considered a variety of explanatory roles: the role of supplying, as does mathematics, concepts or propositions whose empirical interpretations can play one or more of the four other roles described here – the heuristic role of leading, in a systematic way, to discovery of explanations; the role of being what explains something – a contextually sufficient explainer of it; the role, illustrated by believed moral propositions, of constituting a determinant of the nature of what explains certain empirical phenomena; and the role of providing a unifying explanatory account of a group of related phenomena. Moral facts are like facts of pure mathematics in their ability to explain facts in their own domain. Mathematical facts can also play a role in scientific explanations,

---

18 I have argued for this in chs. 6, 8, 10, and 11 in (1993c) and in (2010a). See, e.g., Goldman (1986) for reliabilism regarding epistemic justification.

but a similar role in empirical explanations seems possible for certain a priori moral facts in relation to empirical explanations of human behavior. Indeed, there are apparently natural facts, such as at least some ascribing determinable properties, that play roles in explaining empirical phenomena quite analogous to the roles generic moral facts may play in explaining them.

Non-reductive moral realism, then, can account for significant explanatory powers apparently possessed by moral facts and moral properties. Moreover, it appears that the explanatory role of pure mathematical truths has significant parallels in the normative realm. As to ethical naturalism, it remains a metaphysical option even for moderate intuitionists. But moral realism does not depend on naturalizing moral properties, either as a condition for moral knowledge, whether empirical or a priori, or in accounting for the explanatory significance of moral facts.

What is now before us is an action-theoretic three-dimensional approach to the theory of moral obligation – a conduct theory; a companion account of moral creditworthiness for action; a normative moral theory providing basic moral principles governing conduct; an epistemological defense of moral knowledge; and a metaphysical case for a realist construal of moral discourse. I have presupposed throughout that moral obligation entails some normative reason to do the obligatory thing and that there is a close relation between the obligatory and the valuable. If we had only what has been said so far to go on, we would have a deontological normative theory of conduct centering on commonsense moral principles formulated in Chapters 4 and 5 and defended epistemologically and metaphysically along the lines of a moderately rationalist realism. But we would not have integrated this position with a theory of value nor shown how a sound deontological theory can do adequate justice to the undeniably reasonable aims of many forms of consequentialism. Part IV is aimed at closing this gap. It addresses normative reasons – the kind most important for deontological ethics – in relation to values and, in the light of what emerges, formulates a broad conception of obligation that transcends the common dichotomy between consequentialist and deontological theories.

Part IV

Reasons, Values, and Obligations

10 Reasons, Values, and the Structure of Rational Action

In the history of philosophy, human beings have often been conceived as persons, in a sense that entails having both intellect and will. Theoretical reason, and with it theoretical philosophy, has been commonly conceived as centering on the realm of the intellect. This domain encompasses above all the fields of epistemology and metaphysics and, particularly in relation to them, of logic, philosophy of mind and language, and much else. Practical reason, and with it practical philosophy, has been commonly conceived as centering on the realm of the will. This realm encompasses ethics, including political philosophy and the theory of action. Action is motivationally based on intentional attitudes such as beliefs, desires, and intentions, and it is directionally guided by beliefs. Understanding its rationality requires accounts of action that draw on both practical and theoretical reason. Actions fail to be rational if they are guided only by irrational beliefs, a defect on the side of theoretical reason; they also fail to be rational when motivated only by irrational desires, a defect on the side of practical reason. Irrational beliefs tend to induce errors in our map of our world; irrational desires tend to send us to worthless destinations.

I have argued that some moral principles can be known and justifiedly (hence rationally) believed, and that some rational (true) beliefs clearly constitute knowledge. But we have not so far explored the rationality conditions for desires. These conditions are important because reasons for action – including normative reasons – are expressed not only by beliefs but also by desires. Reasons for action, moreover, depend for their normative status on the rationality of both beliefs and desires. Bringing about a state of affairs that it is irrational to want is prima facie irrational, and doing something to realize even a desirable end is prima facie irrational if that action is based on an irrational belief.[1]

For many philosophers, reasons for action, for instance *that one must keep a promise*, have been viewed as propositional and, often, as factive and thus truths. Beyond this propositional conception, reasons have also been considered the basic normative elements, particularly in the case of reasons for morally appraisable actions. This "reasons first" view and the contrasting view that values are normatively prior to reasons are central concerns in this chapter.

1   Normative Reasons for Action

Normative reasons are widely taken to be reasons that contribute to the rationality of what they are reasons for, and they may be practical or theoretical. The central cases of the former are reasons for action; the central cases of the latter are reasons for belief. Some philosophers would not call merely motivational reasons, such as the desire to step on an empty can in one's path, practical reasons, especially if they are based wholly on an irrational desire and thus are not good reasons. But although motivational reasons are not as such reasons *to act* – a phrase that implies having some normative force – they can at least normally be reasons *for which* one acts and, as such, reasons *why* one acts. They can sometimes explain action even when they cannot justify it.

---

1 On some views, if *S* believes, even irrationally, that *A*-ing will bring about a desirable end, *A*-ing is still subjectively rational. I can agree that *S* might be excused for such action but would argue that the primary notion of rational action is tied to the advisory point of view, in the sense that impartial advisors with *S*'s interests in view would not advise *A*-ing if their only instrumental information was that *S* is irrational in believing it would yield the end aimed at. For pertinent discussion see Brandt (1979), Scanlon (1998), my (2001b), and Cullity (2018).

Since motivational reasons can both motivate and purposively explain action, I consider them practical in the broad sense in which practical reasons contrast with theoretical reasons. On at least this score, motivational reasons are on the practical side of the contrast with theoretical reasons – reasons for believing – which, if motivational in any sense, are not motivational in the same way. We might describe someone's believing that a rival is dishonest as motivated by dislike, but although that emotion can motivate certain acts, here it is a cause of belief rather than a reason to believe. Beliefs can both produce and explain other beliefs; but, unlike desires, beliefs are not "realized" by what they produce, certainly not in the way desires are realized by what they (motivationally) produce. The point is sometimes put in terms of contrasting "directions of fit" with the world: beliefs fulfill their "aim" when their content matches the world; desires fulfill theirs when the world comes to match their content. No match of the cognitive kind, as where an instrumental belief is false, and action is ill-guided; no match of the conative kind, as with a failed attempt, and action fails to satisfy desire.

It is, however, not motivational reasons but normative practical reasons for action that are my main concern in ascertaining how reasons are related to values. The valuable elements I have in mind include, prominently though not exclusively, positive phenomena constituted by pleasures and negative phenomena constituted by pain and suffering. Broadly construed, normative practical reasons are reasons there are to do something. These are reasons in an external sense, in not being grounded in desires or otherwise "subjective." They may be either reasons there are for everyone to do something, as with reasons to avoid unjust conduct, or person-relative, as where there is a reason for me, but for no one else, to keep my promise made to you. Reasons there are to do something, whether universal or person-relative, are objective as well as external. As external, they may not be *possessed* by us (roughly, reasons we have in our deliberative ken). A consideration can be a reason for me (in the applicability as opposed to self-ascriptive sense of 'for') without my possessing it.

Given the importance of reducing greenhouse gases, there might be a reason for me as an investor to buy shares in a promising company that will extract them from the atmosphere. But until I learn about the matter I do not possess the reason and will not be motivated by it.

Distinguishing normative from motivating reasons does not imply that reasons cannot play both roles. Some reasons can (simultaneously) motivate and justify actions. Motivating reasons are reasons for which we do something, and (at least in combination with belief) they thereby provide for a motivational explanation of our doing it. They are, then, explanatory of action, possessed by agents (reasons they have), and, if the motivating reason is good enough to support the rationality of the action, also normative (at least in upshot). A motivating reason is good enough for this status when there *is* reason – or at least the agent has justification for believing there is reason – to do it. Normative reasons for action, say that one promised to help a friend, need not motivate, but are at least potentially motivating.

2   Two Paths to Understanding Reasons for Action

It has lately been common to take reasons for action to be facts. On this *factivity view of reasons*, reasons for action are expressible propositionally, and propositions expressing such reasons are true. This common view may have led many philosophers to miss an important point. Given an action, *A*, and agent, *S*, we can specify any of the kinds of reasons for action I've noted – particularly normative ones – using *either* a that-clause, such as 'that *A*-ing will yield a profit', or an infinitive clause, such as 'to save electricity'. It appears, moreover, that for any intentional action (except possibly some actions performed for their own sake) the two kinds of locutions at least typically indicate an equivalence (though not synonymy). Specifically, where *G* is a goal of action *A*, then at least typically

  (1) *S*'s *A*-ing intentionally

is at least roughly equivalent to

(2) *S*'s *A*-ing in order to bring about something, *G*,

and (2) in turn is at least roughly equivalent to

(3) *S*'s *A*-ing for a reason expressible in some instrumental
     that-clause, say *'that A-ing would realize G'*.

Call the view that (with at most a few exceptions) we can specify practical reasons for action either infinitivally or using a that-clause the *dual specification thesis*. It is plausible for both normative and merely motivating (practical) reasons.[2]

There is a certain oddity in using 'reasons' to refer both to reasons specifiable by propositional or infinitive clauses and to the psychological states – chiefly beliefs and desires – whose objects are the contents of those clauses. Nonetheless, it is entirely normal to say such things as 'Her reason for wearing a mask was to avoid spreading the virus' and 'The reason why she wore a mask was that she *wanted* to avoid spreading the virus' – alternatively, 'that she *believed* it would avoid spreading the virus'. For clarity, I propose to speak of the causally explaining reasons, say desires and beliefs, which in some sense causally explain act-tokens, as *reason states*, and of the contents of those psychological states as *reasons proper*.[3] If, in explanation of actions, reference is made to motivating reasons, it is to elements explaining act-tokens, as beliefs and desires may do. This reference is normally to reason states, especially desires. But those states may have contents that in some way rationalize act-type(s) in a way that provides for a broadly purposive explanation of the agent's

---

2 I leave open just how rough the equivalences are. They seem to hold apart from the possible exception of actions performed for their own sake; but I don't try to show this since my purposes do not require that unqualifiedly general claim. There are other rough equivalents of (3), e.g. '*S*'s *A*-ing for the sake of bringing about *G*'.

3 This distinction is explicated in detail in my (1986). It parallels the distinction between doxastic and propositional justification.

tokening them. These contents of desires or beliefs (broadly conative or cognitive attitudes) are also often called reasons, but are not psychological states – a linguistic convenience whose referential duality easily causes confusion.

To illustrate, suppose Ann's wanting to avoid spreading the virus is a motivating reason for her wearing a mask. Then, first, her wanting to do this is an explanatory reason *for* which she does it, where this is a relation between an element in her motivational system – a psychological state – and the act-token; second, *to avoid spreading the virus* is her reason proper and, in the circumstances, rationalizes, for her, the act-type, wearing a mask. This act-type is rational *for her* in virtue of avoiding the spread (or at least her rationally believing that it will); the act-token is a rational doing in virtue of (purposive) explainability by an appropriate belief and desire. Here action is parallel to belief: in virtue of good evidence, e.g., believing a proposition (a belief-type) may be rational *for S*; and in virtue of believing it on the basis of that evidence, *S* has a rational belief (token).

In broad terms, reason states can directly explain act-tokens (including indefinitely many of the act-types rationalized), and reasons proper rationalize act-types for the agent and can indirectly explain act-tokens by a presupposed reference to the propositional attitudes of which these reasons are contents. A similar example might feature a reference to a propositional reason that is the content of a belief. Asked why I bought shares in a green company, I might say *that it supports reducing carbon dioxide in the atmosphere*. This is my reason proper; but I have expressed a belief of it, and that is a state which, combined with an environmental desire I imply I have, explains my action.

The dual specification thesis concerns reasons for which an agent acts, but not (explicitly) normative reasons there are for action, which may exist whether or not anyone has them. I've introduced the thesis in terms of two ways of specifying reasons proper, but it also holds for reason states. I could have given my reason for buying the shares by saying I *wanted* to support reducing carbon dioxide or by saying I believed it would support that. A still wider version of the thesis holds for normative reasons. On this *wide dual specification thesis*, both (a) motivating practical reasons for action – reasons for which S does a particular thing – *and* (b) external normative reasons there *are* for S to act, which do not entail S's doing anything, can be specified either infinitivally or propositionally. Suppose that synthesizing a certain chemical will effectively desalinate water. Then we can say both that the fact *that* synthesizing it will yield effective desalination is a reason to synthesize it and also that *to* desalinate water is a reason to synthesize the chemical. Similarly, we can specify, in either way, motivating reasons *for* which one synthesizes the chemical.

The contrast between the propositional and infinitival ways of specifying reasons for action bears on a question rarely addressed, perhaps because the equivalence of propositional and infinitival ascriptions of practical reasons is often eclipsed by the common representation of reasons for action by using only propositional locutions (typically that-clauses). The easy propositional expressibility of practical reasons can impede recognizing something significant: on analysis, the propositional expression of practical reasons seems in at least one way less basic than the infinitival one. Before we pursue the question whether it in fact is less basic, we should explore the significance of the dual specification thesis for the question of what kinds of entities constitute reasons for action in the first place.

3   The Factivity View of Normative Reasons

To ascertain the relation between normative reasons for actions and the value of actions, we should first consider whether the factivity view of such reasons – the view that normative reasons are facts – is sound. Given the differences between the standards for practical reasons and those for theoretical reasons, it will help to note some differences between the practical attitudes, such as intention and desire, and the theoretical attitudes, e.g. beliefs and expectations. All of these attitudes can express normative reasons.

One major difference between the practical attitudes and the theoretical attitudes is that the former and, correspondingly, the contents of infinitives, are not appraisable as true or false, whereas the latter, whose contents are propositions (which are the contents of reason-expressing that-clauses) are so appraisable.[4] Intentions, for instance, are not true or false, but carried out or not carried out. One point of difference, then, is that reasons for action, propositionally expressed, can be appraised in a way that does not apply to them as expressed infinitivally, as they naturally are when given in indicating what one intends, say to get information about a flight. The that-clause, say that consulting a website will yield important information about a flight, may be true or false, whereas the infinitive clause, to get important information about a flight, is not truth-valued (as opposed to being fulfillable), and it need not express an actual (present or future) state of affairs even when the counterpart that-clause is true.

A different example will show how the difference in appraisability is connected with the factivity view of reasons. Suppose I am a host and notice that the afternoon sun is shining in the face of Sue, a guest. I now have a reason to close the blinds. My reason, which may be both normative and motivating, might be propositionally described as: that closing them will prevent the sun from making Sue squint. But it does not follow from my acting on this reason-expressing proposition that I succeed. The sun may be too bright to block by the thin blinds. Moreover, we do not act on all our reasons to act, even all our good reasons, just as we do not carry out all our intentions. These points are confirmed by considering how I might answer someone who asks, as I am closing the blinds, 'What's your reason for closing the blinds on such a beautiful day?' I can truly give as my reason: it will prevent the sun from making Sue squint. As we have seen, this is compatible with my failing to prevent the squinting (given the thinness of the blinds). I also might not have acted on the reason

---

4 Facts are not normally – in my view not properly – appraisable as true or false either. That reasons are factive is a truism if they are facts but false if they are propositions. We might speak of genuine, as opposed to ostensible, facts, but if 'true fact' does not presuppose such a contrast, it seems a pleonasm.

at all but, instead, offered Sue a different seat. In either case, there may be no fact expressed by 'it will prevent the sun from making Sue squint'.

These points do not force us, as does the factivity view, to deny the point that, in virtue of believing, even mistakenly, that doing something will achieve what we seek, we can *have* a reason to do it. The point holds whether the reason is normative, as it is if the mistaken view is justified and makes *A*-ing rational for *S*, or motivational, or both.[5] This is clear if we consider an infinitival specification of my reason: 'to prevent the sun from making Sue squint'.[6] Both propositional and infinitival specifications may answer 'What reason did *S* have to close the blinds?' Granted, if I *A* in order to bring about *G* and my *A*-ing does bring about *G*, say, actually prevents the squinting, then if (a) my reason for *A*-ing was that it would realize *G*, and (b) I *A*-ed for that reason, it seems obvious that my reason was factive, in the sense that my belief was true.[7] But, from the point that many propositional reasons for action are truths, we should not infer that I could not have *A*-ed (in order) *to bring about G* even if I were mistaken in believing *A*-ing would do so and my reason was therefore not factive. Asked my reason for *A*-ing, either before or after I *have A*-ed, I might truly say (e.g.) 'to bring about *G*'.

To be sure, if I had no idea that closing the blinds would not in fact prevent the squinting and wanted to explain myself, I might, after discovering this failure, retrospectively give as my reason: 'I *believed* it would prevent the Sun from making Sue squint'. This is not flatly false (since the belief was a motivating reason), but it

---

5 If one is inclined to think the reason is not normative because of the error, note that a justified error can explain *excusability*. That, like rendering the action rational, is a further indication of normativity (unless the term – which is variously used, is given an implausibly narrow interpretation).

6 It is significant that the infinitival form is *broader* than the common propositional form expressing a sufficient condition: *S* could *A to reduce pain* even if *S* believes only that *A*-ing will *probably* reduce it (may well reduce it, etc.).

7 Strictly speaking, I would need to have (as I might have) a reason expressible in an indicative, such as 'that it *will* prevent ...'; the truth conditions for ⟨It would prevent ...⟩ are more complicated.

is a less natural reply to 'What was your reason?' than is 'to prevent the sun from making Sue squint', which expresses a reason proper. It is important to see why it is less natural. This is in part because my (normative) reason was not the fact *that I believed this*. This fact by itself will not even entail any normative reason for the action, since the belief could be patently irrational. My believing this is an explanatory reason (explaining *why* I acted); but my normative (propositional) reason is *that closing the blinds would prevent the sun's making Sue squint*, which I mistakenly believed. If I realize that I was wrong and am asked for a reason, I can still provide a normative reason – to prevent Sue's squinting – but I may indicate that I didn't know I'd fail and add, 'I *believed* it would work'. This both explains my action and, if my belief was justified, exhibits the action as prima facie rational.

Supporting this distinction between the two kinds of reasons in question – explanatory and normative – is the point that if someone wanted to correct my error, it would be appropriate to tell me I was mistaken in thinking that closing the blinds would prevent the squinting, but inappropriate and (on my view) wrong to tell me either that I did not believe this (as where the statement is a lie) or that I had *no* reason to close the blinds.[8] By contrast, giving my reason as 'to prevent the sun from making Sue squint' stands in no need of correction even if I acted on a mistaken belief.

---

8 Here I differ with Parfit, who would say, given my mistake about the efficacy of closing the blinds, that I did not have a reason to close them but only an "apparent reason" (2011: 34–35). He did not note that, where people adduce a falsehood in giving a reason for having *A*-ed, they are seldom if ever *corrected* by saying that they acted for *no* reason, as opposed to saying they acted on erroneous information (or the like). We usually correct the error by, e.g., saying *S* was mistaken in thinking . . .). We *might* say that there was no "real" reason to believe the instrumental proposition; but – on my view – this does not entail that (e.g.) there was no "real" reason *to close the blinds*. Significantly, Parfit grants that "what it is *rational* for people to do depends on their *apparent* reasons, whether or not these reasons are real or merely apparent" (35). This view has the counterintuitive implication that the rationality of an action does not depend on the real reasons for it and the reasons *for* which one acts need not be real reasons. They are surely real even when, though rationally acceptable, they are mistaken.

My action is aimed at an end, guided by a belief, and rational, but my normative reason here is not a fact.

Cases of these and other kinds show that the factivity view of normative reasons is too narrow. Propositional reasons for action need not be facts, and reasons for action need not be propositional.[9] A factivity theorist may, to be sure, respond that facts are not propositions. Evidence for this is that we do not call facts true or false and instead conceive them as roughly obtaining states of affairs, such as the sun's making Sue squint. But this plausible view of facts is no help to the factivity view, since reasons for action are quite properly expressed by certain propositions that, being false and thus non-factive, do not even "foretell" the state of affairs the agent aims at bringing about. More pointedly, there can be perfectly good normative reasons to bring about a state of affairs (such as preventing squinting) that never is brought about. In this case there *is* no fact, say my preventing the squinting, to constitute the reason. Some might call such good reasons that embody mistakes, for action or indeed for belief, "subjective," but these reasons are not merely conjectural or otherwise unjustified.

The broader point important here is that intentional actions are characteristically explained by the *joint* work of a desire to bring about something (*G*) and a belief to the effect that *A*-ing (the action in question) bears some instrumental relation to *G*, e.g. being sufficient, being a good means, being the best way to realize, or the like. Call such beliefs *connecting beliefs* and the kinds of instrumental propositions they express *connecting propositions.*[10]

---

9 This conclusion neither undervalues the importance of facts in understanding normative reasons for action nor suggests that it is not, other things equal, preferable to act on facts rather than falsehoods.

10 The notion of a connecting belief and the theory of action-explanation sketched here are defended in my (1986). That paper accommodates *de re* connecting beliefs by broadening the belief requirement. The idea that *both* a motivational and a cognitive element are required for explaining action seems implicit in Aristotle's *Nicomachean Ethics*, esp. Book 3. Cf. Davidson's notion of actions as caused by a "primary reason," which he described as having both kinds of elements (1963: 686). I leave open whether reasons-explanations citing only a cognitive or only a motivational element – corresponding to propositional and infinitival expressions of reasons – are enthymematic, as

This conception of action-explanation is so entrenched in normal thinking that when a reason for action is given in either propositional or infinitival form, it is assumed (or at least presupposed) that the same purposive explanation may be provided for it in the other mode. If you tell me that your reason for phoning an aunt is to determine whether she has been tested for Covid-19, I take it that you believe something to the effect that phoning will determine this. If I tell you that my reason for salting the pavement is that it will melt ice, you take it that I want to melt it. In normal cases, we take it that (correct) propositional and infinitival explanations of an action each presuppose (and thereby entail) the correctness of a counterpart expressed in the other idiom. The counterpart might have a contextual equivalent of 'bringing about', such as 'realize'; and as indicated above, any of a wide range of connecting beliefs may express S's instrumental reason, including not only those representing causal connections but also indications of "constitutive" means, as where S believes swimming will *be* a pleasure.

Our examples and some important ideas they confirm – including the point that not all reasons are factive – strongly support *a cognitive-motivational conception of intentional action*: for any agent, S, act-type, A, and time, t, S A-s (instantiates the act-type, A) at t intentionally if and only if, at t, S has a goal, G (say, to melt ice), and believes an instrumental proposition, p, that connects A-ing with G, where (a) S A-s at t in order to bring about G; (b) S A-s at t on the basis of believing (hence for the reason that) p; (c) explanatory statements of *either* form (a) or form (b) provide correct reasons-explanations of why (at t) S A-s; and (d) instances of each form presuppose (and entail) the correctness of an instance of the other form. Now surely (e) in the relevant action-explaining cases, if (c) is true, then, given that explanations of form (a) do not entail the truth of p, neither do those of form (b). We may conclude, then, that reasons for action need not be factive and that neither acting for a reason nor the

opposed to simply presupposing the unstated element. I make the usual assumption that correct explanations have true explananda and explanantia.

character of reasons for which we actually do things entails the factivity of reasons for action.

4   The Normative Dependence of Practical Reasons on Values

So far, we have seen both parallels and differences between propositional and infinitival expressions of reasons and have found that normative reasons need not be factive either to account for the parallels or to do justice to the differences. Our question now is whether having a reason to do something, *A*, is normatively fundamental in a sense implying that the *value* of *A*-ing – or, in perhaps broader terms, the point of *A*-ing – *depends* on the agent's having a normative reason to *A*, say on the agent's justifiedly believing that it will reduce headache pain.[11] Such normative dependence does not entail the conceptual reducibility of the value of *S*'s *A*-ing to *S*'s having normative reason(s) to *A*. The normative dependence relation in question is important but quite different from reducibility. If there is value in doing something, there is at least some reason to do it; but it does not follow that the value of doing it is grounded in the reason(s) to do it.

It helps in answering this normative dependence question to start with the significance of the point that reason-expressing propositions are true or false, whereas reason-expressing infinitive phrases are not truth-valued.[12] Why? I suggest that in the

---

11 The idea that values are normatively dependent on reasons seems implicit in Scanlon's buck-passing view: "being valuable is not a property that provides us with reasons. Rather, to call something valuable is to say that it has other properties that provide reasons for behaving in certain ways regarding it" (1998: 96). For a concise critical appraisal of Scanlon's view, see Crisp (2005). Cf. Nagel's more explicit formulation of what seems a kind of dependence of value on reasons: "The objective badness of pain, for example, is … just the fact that there is reason for anyone … to want it to stop" (1986: 144); and Lord's related factivity view: "to possess a reason one must be in a position to know the fact that constitutes that reason" (2018: 14). A similar factivity view of reasons is held by Littlejohn (2018: 3).

12 This is not to deny that they express states of affairs that may or may not be realized; these correspond to propositions but are not identical to them.

practical domain, action is central and its rationality has a double dependence. First, it depends, as is widely agreed, on propositional reasons that indicate the relation of the action to the agent's end (say, sufficiency to desalinate water), and these propositions may be false or unjustifiedly accepted by the agent. Second, and more important for our purposes, the rationality of action depends, as is not widely agreed, on infinitivally expressible reasons that guide the choice of means (say, means to relieve pain, a good thing to do). An important contrast that confirms this second dependence is this. That *A*-ing will bring about *G*, when *G* – say, reduction of pain – is desirable (valuable either in itself or instrumentally), counts as a normative reason there is (for anyone) to *A*, in virtue of the desirability of *G*, but the desirability of *G* does not similarly depend on whether *A*-ing or anything else we have power to do will bring it about.[13] Being enjoyable – in the experiential sense illustrated by delight in hearing music – instantiates one kind of desirability; so does fulfilling a moral obligation, or happily singing a beautiful aria, or honoring a courageous good deed. Desirability is a highly pluralistic notion.[14]

It is important here to include instrumental desirability as one kind of value and to include external as well as possessed reasons. Recall the desalination case. There is reason to desalinate water, but that reason is (among other things) *to increase the potable water supply*. Moreover, we now *have* this instrumental reason; but even before we knew of desalinization, there was a reason to

---

13 This view does not preclude an equivalence between there being normative reason to *A* and the desirability of *A*-ing, but I am presupposing that the *in-virtue-of* relation is asymmetrical. The view is also neutral with respect to hedonism, even conceived broadly. For defenses of the basic role of pain and pleasure in the practical realm see Crisp (2006) and Parfit (2011), esp. chs. 1–2.

14 Fittingness is similarly pluralistic, as is shown by many cases described by Cullity (2018). Fittingness may be entailed by desirability but need not entail a reason for action – even if *un*-fittingness entails a reason for abstention. As this suggests, fittingness supports the normative *eligibility* of an action in a set of circumstances and in that way bears on permissibility, as I have suggested in, e.g., Chapter 6.

desalinize, and we would have seen (and possessed) it if we'd known more. There can *be* a reason to realize an end (or any actualizable state of affairs) even if there is no action accessible to us that will do so. This again illustrates the priority of values realizable in action over instrumental facts that constitute propositional reasons.

On this dependency view regarding such propositional reasons for action – those indicating a kind of instrumental relation to the goal of action – for any act-type, *A*, the fact that *A*-ing will bring about *G* owes its normative authority (if it has such authority) to a normative property of *G* (*G* may be an act-type conceived as a behavioral state of affairs). By contrast with the case of propositional reasons (which we might also call instrumental reasons), where the reason for action is to bring about *G*, for instance where the reason is to reduce pain, this authority seems intrinsic to the desirability of reduction of pain. Why? One answer is that if we should come to believe that there is nothing good (worthwhile, valuable, useful . . .) about reduction of pain, we would take that to defeat our would-be (normative) reason. Beyond this, and on the positive side, reduction of pain seems intrinsically good and also normatively basic. Dimi-nution of pain – which, in the context, is entailed by the behavioral state of affairs, *reducing pain* – is desirable in itself in a sense implying that there is (some) reason for any action that contributes to that diminution.

As our examples indicate, reduction of pain (and of course eliminating it), though desirable *only if* there is reason to achieve it, is not desirable *in virtue of* their being reason to achieve it. The converse seems more plausible: it is in virtue of the desirability of reduction of pain that there is reason to reduce it. (How desirability provides a kind of explanation of there being a reason, and such explainability will be illustrated shortly and in Chapter 11.) Reduc-tion of pain, like yielding (or enhancing) pleasure, is – and is widely agreed to be – a constitutive aim of practical reason. Granted, the desirability of states of affairs is not brute, but grounded in some set of natural properties, such as being enjoyable or reducing pain. These are phenomenal elements that have great prominence in human consciousness, immense power in our motivation, and a major role in our flourishing. But that meta-physical grounding is consonant with the normative dependence view just proposed.

In the light of this objectivist partial account of the normative basis of practical reasons, we can say that even for rational actions, agents sometimes have only apparently objective ("external") reasons to do the things in question. But (as illustrated in the sunlight case) an apparently objective but actually mistaken reason need not be a merely apparent reason. Suppose I rationally yet falsely believe, on excellent though ultimately misleading evidence, that something is desirable, for instance that viewing certain sculptures would be enjoyable (where I consider this an instance of the desirable). I can still act in order to realize this end. This is a case of acting for a good reason, and an action's being based on a good reason counts toward its rationality. I can give my reason for going to the relevant museum by saying 'to enjoy the new sculptures'; and I can rationally act for this reason. But my action may still fail to achieve the good I sought, just as a rational belief can fail to be true. When all goes well, however, we can act in the light of justified true beliefs, for reasons that are objectively good – evidentially if they are propositional reasons and valuationally if they are infinitival reasons – and achieve practical success. *Overall* good reason for action is a complicated combination of both cognitive and motivational reasons for it.

It might be thought that only a relation weaker than normative dependency holds between the value (roughly, desirability) of realizing a goal and the normative authority of a propositional reason to realize it. One might object that what has been said shows at most that propositional reasons for action are *defeasible* by considerations of value, not that the former positively *depend* on the latter. The distinction between negative and positive normative dependence is important. Positive normative dependence is at least a partial derivation of reason-giving power from some basis of that power, such as the desirability of reduction of pain; negative normative dependence is a vulnerability to disempowerment, as by overriding counter-evidence. But does showing that there is no value in bringing about G (the goal of action) only defeat the normative authority of the agent's reason – say, that *A*-ing will realize *G* – or does it also show that there is no normative reason for the agent to *A* at all?

On my view, showing that there is no value in bringing about something does show that no agent can have normative reason to bring it about, *provided* desires cannot themselves yield such normative reasons. Humeans and even less thoroughgoing instrumentalists maintain that (intrinsic, non-instrumental) desires can by themselves yield reasons to act. I doubt this thesis.[15] But suppose it is true. If there is no value in bringing about *G*, this still eliminates any reasons *other* than those based on desire. On this Humean view, being (non-instrumentally) desired is reason-giving but not value-conferring. It is as though one's passional nature alone, constituted by what one most deeply, strongly, and non-instrumentally desires, could give one reason to realize some end, with no implication that the end has value. Thus, the normative authority of a propositional reason, say that *A*-ing will realize *G*, depends on the *desiredness* of realizing *G* – being actually desired or, for hypothetical reasons, potentially desired. This conative property functions like value in grounding propositional reasons but is psychological and non-normative. The significance of the dual specification thesis concerns reasons in general and, though neutral regarding this Humean view, helps to explain why Humeans are not committed to a reasons fundamentalist view of practical normativity.

5   Normative Reasons and Their Grounds

From what has emerged so far, I hope it is clear that contrary to what one might expect from the view that practical reasons are essentially propositional and factive, they may be expressed by non-truth-valued infinitive clauses. This point facilitates arguing that the normative authority of reasons for actions depends on the value of the states of affairs those actions may be taken to

---

15 I have critically assessed this thesis in (2002).

realize.[16] There is another way to view both reasons and values which supports the idea that, in the practical sphere, values are more basic than reasons. Let me explain.

If, like a number of prominent moral philosophers, one regards the notion of a reason as normatively basic, it is natural to see no need to explore whether reasons themselves may be grounded: roughly based on something else from which they derive their normative authority. I doubt that this has often been systematically done. Suppose, however, that reasons themselves are grounded. This would not preclude their also grounding something else. Where p and q are propositions, one's belief that p might be based *on the ground that q*, where q entails p. Here one also believes *p for the reason that q*. Indeed, 'believing on the ground that' seems roughly equivalent to 'believing for the reason that', though the latter may more strongly suggest that the belief is inferential. Moreover, where we believe that p on the ground that q, we may still have further grounds of the same kind. We might believe that q on the ground that r. Here r is also propositional and may or may not be one's "ultimate" ground for believing p. Grounds of a propositional kind, then, can be based on one or more further grounds, much as premises can be based on one or more further premises.

Where (normative) grounds of beliefs and other truth-valued attitudes are constituted by reasons, they are normally best expressed by that-clauses. For instance, believing, judging, and conjecturing that p can be alike in implying that the attitudes in question are based on the reason that q (where q supports p). Grounds of actions (at least actions for reasons) are also propositionally expressible. You might A on the ground that you promised to A. This that-clause expresses a proposition, but the case

---

16 This allows both for normative reasons given by false but justified beliefs, as already described, and for justified but mistaken attributions of value. In one tradition, this corresponds to ways to distinguish between subjective and objective rightness, but I find 'subjective' misleading here because I do not consider the justification in question "subjective." Its grounds are *internal*, as described in my (2020a), but that accommodates justification as a state that transcends mere opinion and deserves interpersonal respect.

would also be one in which an action, here promising, itself grounds the obligation to A. One has the obligation to A in virtue of that promissory action. In this kind of a case, an action constitutes a non-propositional (and metaphysical) ground of an obligation. In virtue of promising to A, one has a reason to A. That the fact that one promised is also a reason is normatively significant; but, understood as the fact that promise-makings are reason-giving, it does not show that actual promising is not also normatively significant. It is a non-propositional ground in virtue of which one has a (promissory) reason to A.[17] What the fact shows is that the existence of a (normative) ground for action, such as actual promising, entails the existence of a propositional reason for action: a reason having content that entails the existence of that normative ground.

A difference between reasons and grounds is also evident in the theoretical case. Some grounds for believing are not properly considered reasons for believing (some may call them reasons, but this is not felicitous where a that-clause is not what expresses them). Think of perceptual belief. Suppose I hear voices coming from a dark house I pass on an evening walk. I may immediately believe that someone is inside. My ground for the belief – both the normative and the psychological basis of the belief – is my hearing voices, which is an experience and not a proposition. As just indicated, however, this ground is also the basis of a normative reason for belief. My hearing voices is, to be sure, a reason *why* I believe someone is inside; but that is an explanatory reason, not a normative one. The perception itself – hearing voices – would not normally be cited as a reason *for* believing someone is inside. My reason is *that I hear them*; it cites my ground, and the proposition that I have that ground is a reason for others to believe someone is inside: it is sharable in a way my visual ground for it is not. My ground is experiential and indeed

---

17 In terminology stressed by Chang (2013), one's promising to A creates a reason to A, whereas the fact that promise-making is reason-producing is not created. This normative fact is *given*, much as a scorching fire's approaching one is a given reason to retreat.

non-conceptual.[18] Reasons for believing (and to believe) are normally expressed by that-clauses, and these clauses are conceptual. But, as the example indicates, such reasons have grounds in experience and depend on experience for their normative force.

To see the relevant relation between the grounds and reasons in question, suppose I am walking with a companion who is hard of hearing, thinks the house has been vacated, and asks my reason for believing someone is inside. I might give my reason by replying: '(that) I hear voices coming from it'. This response expresses a propositional reason there is for my belief, and the case shows the naturalness of taking propositional elements, as commonly expressed by a that-clause, as reasons for belief. But my original, occupant-ascribing belief itself is normatively grounded in my experience, my hearing voices, not in some further belief, e.g. the self-descriptive belief that I hear voices. It is natural to use that-clauses to express a reason for believing something. This fact partially explains the correspondingly natural tendency to think of reasons as intrinsically propositional.

Reasons for action are also very often propositionally expressed, and that, too, contributes to the strength of this tendency regarding those reasons. Related to this is the point that the high relative frequency of plainly true propositions as what ordinary (honest) people cite as their reasons for believing partially explains why reasons are often considered facts. Perhaps Reid had such cases in mind in saying, "Truth is always uppermost and is the natural issue of the mind."[19] We very commonly know what instrumental proposition(s) underlie our action and, in favorable circumstances, those propositions are both true and known by us.

The view outlined here highlights a distinction only occasionally observed and at least not widely noted. Non-propositional grounds give us reasons to believe (or to act) but do not themselves

18 This is not uncontroversial but is widely defended and recently argued in detail in ch. 2 of my (2020a).
19 See Reid (1863/1983: 94–95). The passage suggests both an effortful element in lying and the spontaneity of truth-speaking in ordinary communication.

constitute such normative reasons – or, in any case, are not best construed as constituting them.[20] My auditory belief, which expresses an answer to my companion's request for a reason, is not my ground for believing someone is in the house. Grounds provide a basis for beliefs, and accordingly, for reasons those beliefs may express. But the ability of grounds to justify reason-expressing beliefs we may form does not depend on our actually forming those beliefs. A ground such as my hearing voices can provide justification for beliefs even if I do not form any. It is possible to walk by a house from which one hears voices but, being absorbed in conversation, not form the belief that there are people in it.[21]

6   Experiences as Sources of Normative Grounds

The points made so far in this chapter should indicate why it is natural to take non-propositional grounds such as sense-experiences to have a kind of priority over reasons and the propositional grounds that reasons may constitute. This point seems to hold for practical reason as it does for theoretical reason, and I take the applicability of the priority view to both theoretical and practical reason to be a consideration supporting the point. Surely the (normative) reason-giving force of my reason for taking aspirin – that it will cure a headache – is grounded in (roughly, possessed in virtue of) the aversive qualities of the headache. One might speak also of their normative force being grounded in the painfulness of the headache,

---

20 In some cases, this distinction is minimized. Parfit says, e.g., "Reasons are given by facts, such as the fact that someone's fingerprints are on some gun ... some people say that these facts *are* reasons ... these are merely different ways of saying the same thing" (2011: 32–33).

21 One is *disposed* to form such a belief if asked whether there are people there; but many dispositions to believe are unrealized. If I do form the belief, my auditory perception of voices is the reason why I believe, and thus explains my then believing, that there is someone inside. But not every reason why someone holds a belief is a normative ground of it. Brain manipulation can cause belief-formation without being a normative ground of it. My (2018a) explains these points in detail.

but this is less specific, and in any case that painfulness is grounded in those qualities. If, as I assume here, the relevant grounding relation is transitive, these qualities also ground the reason-giving force of the fact that the aspirin will relieve the headache.

Moreover, if, as seems clear, the grounding relation is also explanatory, then the aversive qualities in the abstract explain the normative force of the reason in the abstract, as a factor favoring a kind of act-type. *That* a kind of experience is painful explains why there is reason for act-types that prevent (or eliminate) experiences of this kind. The psychological fact that an experience is painful is not itself normative in content but only in upshot (a difference explained in Chapter 7). But that doing something is obligatory is a normative fact and can be called a propositional ground: one could, e.g., believe that one should risk embarrassing a friend on the ground that the potentially embarrassing deed is obligatory. This illustrates a sense in which a ground can be a kind of reason. Such propositional normative grounds, however, are themselves metaphysically grounded. I assume here that normative properties and, correspondingly, normative reasons, are ultimately grounded in natural properties, but I leave open how diverse and how far "down" some grounds may go.

In the concrete realm, there is a psychological parallel: the unpleasant state itself – say a headache – causally explains the desire to eliminate it, and this causal relation parallels the grounding relation that the unpleasantness of the state bears to the rationality of the desire. The unpleasantness of the state, its distinctive unpleasant qualities, may be called its badness, but it may be more accurate to call the unpleasantness the ground of that badness – of its hedonic disvalue, we might say. The desire to eliminate the headache is a reason state with the intentional content: *to eliminate* the headache. A corresponding cognitive reason state, which has an overlapping causal basis, is believing that the medicine *will eliminate* the headache. These states, as psychological elements in the agent, can serve as action-explaining reasons. Whether their contents, propositional or infinitive, express external normative reasons for action – reasons there *are* to *A* – is a matter of the desirability of the agent's end. Whether that end is desirable depends, in turn, on the character of the end as, say, painful or enjoyable.

It may seem that to attribute to aversive qualities of experience the power to serve as metaphysical grounds of the intrinsic bad-ness of a headache and thereby the normative power of certain reasons for action to eliminate the headache is to exaggerate the normative importance of experience. But compare the theoretical case: if the representational qualities of the auditory experience of voices have the power to ground epistemic justification for believing that there are voices, why should aversive and other experiential qualities not have the power to ground practical justification for action, such as taking an aspirin? There are of course differences between the cases, but the grounding of rea-sons for belief seems strongly analogous to that of reasons for action.[22]

7   Are Ascriptions of Intrinsic Goodness Incomplete?

We have seen reason to consider goodness to be grounded in other properties. Indeed, intrinsic goodness is generic in much the way wrongness is. Might 'good' be a place-holder for some less 'thin' normative term – or for a natural property in virtue of which something is good and there is reason to realize it? With these points in mind, it should be clarifying to locate the view of reasons taken here in relation to the "buck-passing" view of goodness. This is a kind of *place-holder view of goodness*: to call something good is equivalent to saying, with a contextually indicated force, and in clearer, more basic terms, that it has one or more properties constituting one or more reasons favoring it, say to realize, pre-serve, or honor it.[23] Several points should be made here.

---

22 For a full-scale theory of the importance of experiential phenomenal properties in the theoretical case, with parallels to the practical case, see Smithies (2019).

23 As Parfit briefly expresses the buck-passing view, "for the most important uses of 'good'... goodness is the property of having *other* properties that

Let's suppose for the sake of argument a widely held view, partially sketched in section 4 of this chapter, that is maintained by both leading consequentialists and leading non-consequentialists: that at least some of the basic bearers of intrinsic goodness are experiences, and that they may have many differing good-making properties, such as being enjoyable, being engaging, and being a diminution of pain. I regard these as kinds of rewardingness. On the view in question, some experiences are good in virtue of being enjoyed (as having hedonically positive qualities), and are not good in a merely derivative way. Enjoying a walk on a beautiful mountain path may be a good experience quite apart from its contribution to, say, health, which would also give it instrumental value. This position is compatible with the view that the presence of badness – being "punishing" in salient cases – which is similarly grounded, has the kind of normative authority I attribute to intrinsic goodness.

Given this experiential grounding conception of value, whether positive or negative, it is to be expected that (as the place-holder view also requires) calling something intrinsically good *commits* one to taking it to have at least one appropriate grounding, reason-giving property. Being enjoyable (broadly, pleasurable) is a prominent example, but the view allows for such non-hedonic properties as being intellectually engaging. Fulfilling the commitment implicit in attributions of intrinsic goodness, even by citing all the relevant grounding properties one can think of, need not exhaust the *content* of the attribution of goodness to an experience. There may be no disjunction that can fulfill this conceptual role. Moreover, one could attribute to an experience a sufficient ground of (some) goodness, such as being enjoyable, admirable, or intellectually stimulating, without attributing overall intrinsic goodness to it. Overall intrinsic goodness need be neither entailed by even a

---

might give us certain reasons" (2011: 39). He also says, "Pain is bad, some of us truly believe, *in the sense of* being something that we have reasons to avoid" (2011: 371 [italics added]). More recently, Scanlon has further argued for the view (cited earlier in his 1998 formulation) "that the basic element of the normative domain is a relation, *being a reason for*, can be seen as a claim about the metaphysics of the normative" (2014: 25–26).

high degree of any one kind of such goodness nor analyzable in terms of a disjunction of kinds of intrinsic goods.

The buck-passing (place-holder) view should not, then, be taken to imply (as it seems to) the possibility of a disjunctive account of intrinsic value. Could there be a disjunction of grounding properties such that to attribute intrinsic desirability to an experience is simply to take that disjunction to be true of it? I doubt this. Granted, attributing intrinsic goodness to something presupposes that it is of a certain kind and commits one to the existence of a reason-giving property appropriate to that kind. This point would hold even if, as our discussion makes plausible, values are normatively more basic than reasons. Passing the buck, we might say, does not entail trashing it. It also does not require rejecting its usefulness or value. To see this, suppose that values are normatively more basic than reasons, and imagine asking a friend one knows to be reliable what would make for a good evening in the city one is visiting. If the answer is 'a walk downtown', would one not acquire a reason to walk there? One need not know what grounding property determines the attributed goodness – what spending the buck would buy – though, as a condition for understanding the advice, one would need a conception of the *sorts* of properties that are good-making for walks. One could understand and rationally accept the attribution by such testimony from a highly credible person without knowing what property or set of properties is in question.

If buck-passing is seen as I have suggested, as a kind of explicitation of ascriptions of value through which they are appraisable – roughly, in terms of the reasons that specify the kind of good in question – we can apply the same sort of demand to reasons for action. If reasons-first theorists are right in passing the buck from values to reasons, my view might similarly call for passing it at least one more time: from reasons to grounds. The goodness of drinking cold water on a hot day has, as its "cash value," relieving acute thirst. But it is the unpleasant qualities of that thirst which mainly ground the normative force of the reason. To discern this conferral relation, we need only reflect adequately on the actual experience. No one wonders whether thirst provides a reason to drink. The buck stops here, with this kind of experiential reason.[24]

If reasons can be grounded, and if, in particular instances, practical reasons derive their normative authority from the value of the relevant goal – strictly, from what grounds that value – does this support, in metaethics, the reducibility of reasons to considerations of value or, in normative ethics, consequentialism? Although (as indicated earlier), I do not take grounding to be a reducibility relation,[25] in a way my view does support a kind of consequentialism in ethics. If reasons for action, conceived prospectively, say in the context of deliberation or intention-formation, derive their normative authority from what the action may be seen as bringing about, it is highly plausible to consider the value of its consequences as determining how good the reasons are. What count as consequences, however, and how to weight their value are left open here and will be considered in Chapters 11 and 12. A consequence of action may be finding a cure for the coronavirus, thereby reducing suffering and mortality, something utilitarians among others would applaud; but a consequence of action (or activity) might also be treating persons as ends in themselves by giving them equal access to education, a consequence of action that establishes a public policy. This consequence Kantians among others would applaud. Moreover, even the consequentialist view that if nothing has (intrinsic) value, then there are no reasons for action does not imply any particular version of consequentialism.

---

24 In a passage that contrasts with the Humean desire-satisfaction view of practical reason, Hume says, "Ask a man *why he uses exercise*; he will answer *because he desires to keep his health*. If you then enquire, *why he desires health*, he will readily reply, *because sickness is painful*. If you ... desire a reason *why he hates pain*, it is impossible he can ever give any. This is an ultimate end and is never referred to any other object" (1777/1975: 293).

25 The literature on grounding is now extensive, but it should be noted that as early as Ross (1930), grounding played a major role in explaining obligation, for Ross a "resultant attribute." He considered the resultancy relation both explanatory and asymmetrical. He used 'consequential' similarly. See, e.g. (1930: 22 and 28–29).

In the widest terms, we have been considering the structure of practical reason. Since Aristotle, it has seemed to many philosophers that the realm of standards for guiding the will is that of the good and that the realm of standards for guiding the intellect is that of the true. The will, so conceived, is the aspect of our agential nature that functions to yield intentions directed toward realizing the good. The intellect, so conceived, is the aspect of our reflective nature that functions to yield beliefs that map the true – including pathways to the good. Our exercises of will bring about states of affairs. It is essential to see that even if, in bringing about anything at all, we enter the causal order, not everything we bring about is something we cause. With some of our actions, our very performance of them achieves a good, for instance doing justice to victims of crime. Similarly, issuing compensatory funds to repair a home we've damaged can *be* the good we realize. Such realizations of value can be intrinsic to what we do – a point crucial for deontology. Realizing the good, understood pluralistically and, whether causally or otherwise, is the governing "aim" – certainly a central aim – of practical reason. If our actions are to achieve this aim, they should be guided by beliefs, ideally by true beliefs that are both justified and constitute knowledge. But our beliefs apparently do not rise to expressing normative reasons for our actions apart from the value of what those actions are aimed at bringing about.

Nothing said here implies that reasons are reducible to values or that values are reducible to reasons, but we have seen a good case for taking the normative authority of reasons for action to be axiologically grounded. In broad terms, my position has been that the normative authority of reasons for action – roughly, their power to support its rationality – depends on value: on the overall value of consequences, which may be of many different kinds and may include any constituent moral results actions may have. Is the position of this chapter, then, a value first view? It is not clear just what 'first' in this usage means. It may seem to imply reductivism, though (as argued in sections 4 and 5) one could take reasons as the most basic elements in the normative order and still resist maintaining that values are reducible to, for instance, considerations of what we have best reason to do. But this would be a natural economy in ethical theory, and even a non-reductive reasons fundamentalism can easily make that reductive view seem plausible. If, by contrast, mine is a primacy view, it is a grounds-first theory. In outline, the idea is that the qualities of experiences of certain kinds, such as painful and pleasurable experiences, ground desirability, which in turn grounds normative reasons for action. Chapters 11 and 12 will say more about the complexities that go with these ideas and how they bear on moral decisions. But at this point we can at least see what kinds of variables are relevant; we know how to compare them; and we have sound principles of prima facie obligation to guide our practical judgments.

If it is true that the normative force of reasons for action depends on value, and if it is also true that what we morally ought to do is what is supported by the best reasons, it does not follow, and I have not implied (nor do I hold) that the rightness of an action is definable in terms of the value of its consequences. How and to what extent the rightness of an action depends on the value of its consequences is something ethics must determine. In many discussions of consequentialist ethics, especially utilitarianism, it is often unclear what constitutes a consequence of an action, and in much ethical literature it is often unclear what kinds of value are in question and whether, as utilitarians have thought, we can make good enough sense of maximization of value to allow that goal to count even as the criterion of right action. These and related questions must be in some way resolved if we are to complete the statement of a comprehensive ethical theory as an aim of this book.

11   The Diversity of Value

In one way, normative ethics can proceed quite well without being guided by an account of the relation between the good and the right. It might be, for instance, that acts are right if and only if they appropriately realize the good, and perhaps which side of this equivalence one concentrates on in framing criteria for right action need not matter in determining what to do. One may be guided either by considerations of rightness and obligation or by considerations of value – of goodness (desirability) and badness (undesirability) – and make morally right choices either way. Perhaps we can work on either side of the equivalence with the same day-to-day results for conduct or, sometimes, work on both sides or learn to work mainly on one side or the other depending on the situation. It is possible, however, that normative ethics is best understood when either the deontic concepts of right and wrong or the value concepts of the good and the bad are seen as more basic than their normative counterparts, especially reasons for action. This chapter explores this fundamentality question with a view toward a unified position on which the normative dependence of reasons on values explained in Chapter 10 is seen as a basis for viewing morality as calling on us at least to approach optimally realizing the good. A major aim of this chapter and the next is to transcend the dichotomy between deontological and consequentialist perspectives, not by taking reasons, or even values, as unqualifiedly fundamental in the normative order, but by accounting for reasons, obligation, and value in an integrated ethical framework in which conduct is a morally central element.

1 Axiological Pluralism, Inherent Value, and Reasons for Action

It should be clarifying to locate the account of practical reasons proposed here by revisiting the place-holder view of goodness: the position that to call something good is equivalent to saying, in more basic terms, that it has one or more properties constituting an appropriate set of reasons favoring it, for instance to realize, preserve, or honor it. This position is especially important as applied to intrinsic value, which is usually what is referred to in speaking of such things as enjoyable experiences as good in themselves. In ways indicated in Chapter 10, the position accommodates what is plausible in the *attributive view of goodness*, on which calling something good is not even clear in meaning unless the kind of thing in question is indicated.[1]

It is significant that we speak of very different kinds of things other than experiences as good in themselves – paintings and sculptures, musical and dramatic performances, just distributions, virtues of character, policies even abstractly considered, and much else. It is not generally noticed that the great diversity of the things good (or bad) in themselves is inadequately represented by the single term 'intrinsically good'. The wide use of the term tends to obscure significant differences among the things that are good in themselves. Even a broad hedonism is inadequate to the diversity and complexity of value. If, for instance, pleasure is intrinsically good, how can sadistic pleasure, even in itself, be overall intrinsically bad?

From the perspective of justice to the diversity of value, the attributive view is a welcome corrective for narrowness. But insofar as the view is taken to refute the position, common

---

1 The attributive view that 'good' is properly attributive rather than predicative, is argued by Peter Geach, apparently following Aristotle, and by Thomson, among others. See her (1997) and chs. 1–2 of her (2008); and, for critical discussion of the attributive view about goodness, Rowland (2016). I see no inconsistency between a properly qualified attributive view and mine, since *experiences* of the relevant sorts can be of value-anchoring kinds that meet the appropriate demand.

among moralists as different as Mill and Ross, that certain things are non-relationally good, it is misleading. Granted, whatever is intrinsically good is of some kind, and granted that the kind is important for understanding the goodness of the thing, it does not follow that its goodness is relational.[2]

If the basic kinds of things good in themselves are experiential, we have a pathway to understanding myriad other kinds of things good "in themselves." The notion of intrinsic value as non-relational needs analysis, and what follows explains part of what is needed. I propose to clarify intrinsic value and related notions in part by using a different term for things that are good in them-selves – intrinsically good, in the common, generic sense – but, unlike pains and pleasures, are not experiences. These other things are appropriately called *inherently valuable*. (There is also inherent disvalue, but it will suffice to concentrate mainly on positive cases.) Inherent goodness is non-relational. Something's having it does not entail a relation to any other thing, and it is not possessed in virtue of relational properties such as reducing greenhouse gases. We need a terminology that distinguishes inherent goodness from intrinsic goodness as a property of experiences and preserves the contrast of both with instrumental value. The terminology should also highlight the non-relational "internal" (thus inherent) char-acter of the diverse kinds of things good in themselves. Artworks provide examples. Their inherent aesthetic value is grounded in their non-relational properties, as with the colors and shapes in paintings. Things of inherent value may also have instrumental value, but they can have aesthetic value even apart from any causal or other relations to anything else.

This kind of non-relational value that inherently valuable things have does not, however, entail that they are (as such)

---

2 Good experiences entail experiencers having them. I am not conceiving this kind of entailment as a relation, certainly not of the kind that connects metaphysically independent entities, and am thinking of typical two-place relations such as *taller than*; but an account of relationality is not possible here.

valuable in the basic way that what is intrinsically valuable proper is. What has inherent value, such as a beautiful sonnet, a breath-taking mountain vista, or an admirably crafted logical proof, has such value *directly* in virtue of (certain of) its intrinsic properties. This is a *grounding condition*. But what *constitutes* inherent value in something is a power: its power to yield intrinsic value in an experience that is appropriately responsive to the right kind of focus on its intrinsic properties. The *manifestation* of this power in such experience of the inherently valuable thing entails a relation to some person (or appropriately responsive living thing); mere possession of the power does not. I am assuming that inherent value is grounded objectively, for instance in properties intrinsic to the artwork that has it, and that the aesthetically rewarding experience of the work is responsive to at least a subset of its intrinsic properties.

To illustrate, consider sensitive readings of a fine sonnet. These tend to be aesthetically rewarding, as the experience of writing it may also be.[3] The rewarding elements in such readings and writings are experiential. More specifically, they are occurrent elements in the life of some person or other being capable of the kind of rewarding experience in question. Where an experience is appropriately focused on something of inherent value and the experiencer discriminatively engages its intrinsic properties, this experience may be rewarding. Aesthetic pleasure is one clear

---

3 The term had a similar though insufficiently explained use in Lewis (1946: 391) and his (1955): "An art object ... has inherent value: it conduces to a satisfaction to be found in the presence of it. All aesthetic values are such inherent values" (1955: 69 and 58–68). As shown in my (2003: 30–56) (but is not noted by Lewis), something intrinsically valuable may *also* have inherent value, e.g. a child's (intrinsically good) delight in hearing virtuoso finger-work on the piano. This delight might or might not be aesthetically good. If it is aesthetically good, it might illustrate aesthetic value apparently not, in Lewis's sense, inherent (since he took that to be non-experiential). I would experience the child's delight with pleasure, an intrinsically valuable response, and this would manifest its inherent goodness. By contrast, a negative experience of observing, with horror, atrocities perpetrated by a dictator has intrinsic dis-value; and it also has inherent disvalue in that reflecting on it in the right way will be distressing and in that way intrinsically bad.

example, and such experience is intrinsically good on the basis of certain of its phenomenal qualities. Much could be said about these rewarding qualities, but they are familiar enough not to need detailed description here. When experience is, in a certain non-instrumental way, rewarding, it is intrinsically good.[4]

Poems are not themselves experiences; but they are by their nature experienceable, and their character, which is intrinsic to them, gives them the power to yield experiences – commonly intrinsically good experiences of kinds many people have had. Not just any focus on the relevant properties, however, is competently discriminative relative to the kind of value in question, and it is also possible for some competent observers to fail, on one or more occasions, to find even the right kind of focus rewarding. But if poems could not be experienced rewardingly (as least by creating them), then (apart from their instrumental value) there would be no point in writing them. By contrast, what is intrinsically good in the experiential sense – "intrinsically good proper," if you like – is, by its very nature, an experience with certain qualities and is the kind of thing that there *is* a point in bringing about. As explained in Chapter 10, these basically good elements in life are such that there is (defeasible) non-instrumental reason to realize them.[5]

Inherent value is like intrinsic value in being non-relational in a way that rules out its being instrumental. The inherent value of a good sonnet lies not in its *causing* or even having the power to cause an intrinsically valuable experience of it – that would be an instrumental value. Its inherent value lies in its power to be a *constituent* in such an experience. This constitutive element in an experience of reading a sonnet is not a relational property of the

---

4 Rewardingness is many-faceted. A sketch of it is provided in my (2001b: 96–97).

5 These points presuppose a difference between valuable *tokens*, e.g. actual pleasures, and valuable *types*, say the exact type of experience I am having that you might also have hearing the same music. Our examples will be mainly (token) experiences that actually instantiate some type of value (or disvalue), but value theory must take account of both the abstract values that can be realized and concrete instances of them.

experience. A sonnet that someone is enjoyably experiencing in the discriminative way appropriate to aesthetic pleasure is the object of that enjoyment, not its cause. Its inherent value is aptly so called both because that value is grounded in intrinsic properties of the object and because the intrinsically valuable experience the object makes possible embodies responsiveness to its intrinsic properties. The same experience *may* embody an awareness of instrumental value. This is common with architecture. We can simultaneously enjoy the beauty of a building and realize its efficiency. But aesthetic rewardingness is not grounded purely instrumentally. Moreover, a natural object not experienced by anyone can be inherently valuable in being *capable* of being rewardingly experienced on the basis of an appropriate focus on its intrinsic properties.

Inherent value, then, may be viewed as a kind of potential for its possessor to be a constituent in a rewarding experience. This introduces a complication in the theory of value. Persons can have higher-order experiences; and some experiences, as objects of higher-order experience, may themselves be both inherently and intrinsically valuable. Certain moral and aesthetic experiences can be of this kind. Consider first a moral case in which a *non*-experiential instance of moral value is inherently good. Take, e.g., a just distribution of emergency medical supplies, which is inherently good as meeting the needs and circumstances of the recipients. One package sits appropriately labeled for each person. Related instances of moral value are intrinsically good, in the basic, experiential sense: such moral value might be a gratifying element in an experience of *making* such a distribution. If everything of inherent value were a substance, we could speak of inherent value as substantive value. But given that some things of inherent value are experiences, it is preferable to call inherent value *objectual*, allowing for it in any suitable object of experience. By contrast, intrinsic value proper is experiential, belonging to experiences in virtue of their intrinsic properties.

To illustrate inherent value further, think of morally sensitive observers *witnessing* someone's making a just distribution. This is a potentially approbative, possibly also empathic, experience that may be morally positive and good in itself. The experience is likely still more valuable if one is made happy in perceiving the agent overcoming temptation in making the distribution, say refusing bribes. A moral response to creditworthiness would then be combined with the positive response to self-control. In both cases, the positive moral experience has non-instrumental value. The just distribution itself is a perceptible activity that is morally right and inherently morally good; the positive *experience* of it as right is intrinsically morally good. We have, then, a distinction among kinds of inherently valuable entities: making just distributions is inherently good, and experiences of them may be both intrinsically good and also inherently good. Higher-order rewarding experiences *of experiencing doing justice,* appropriately and responsively focused on its intrinsic properties, including those grounding its moral value, are intrinsically good.

We could instead use terms that allow attributing intrinsic value of the basic kind to fine poems themselves, contrary to many consequentialists, for instance hedonists who require that what is intrinsically good be a kind of consciousness or at least an element in it. But this is less clear terminology and can easily mislead, for instance by inviting the view that only experiences can be a source of non-instrumental reasons for action. On my view, by contrast, things of inherent value – beautiful paintings, fine poems, and indeed justice in action – are sources of non-instrumental reasons for action, especially of enjoyment, preservation, and promotion. This is a major reason for the importance of inherent value as a distinctive and diverse kind: it accommodates the practical importance of the multiplicity of good things that give us non-instrumental reasons for both pro-attitudes toward them and positive acts regarding them. The beautiful painting has value beyond being instrumentally good, say as a means to producing educational visits to museums. It is a potential constituent in valuable aesthetic experience and, as such, can be non-instrumentally valued and thereby yield positive actions such as praise and preservation.

The proposed axiology, then, brings out differences among kinds of values, the diversity of the possessors of non-relational value, and the relation between those that are non-relationally valuable and reasons for action. Rewarding experiences of moral phenomena, and of aesthetic entities, on the basis of their intrinsic properties, ground non-instrumental reasons for action, say a reason to read Shakespeare's sonnets. Being a source of non-instrumental reasons for action is common to both the intrinsically and the inherently valuable. In this respect, both contrast with what has only instrumental value, though that can be possessed by things of either kind: things commonly called good "in themselves," the generic sense of 'intrinsically good'. Reciting a poem can be intrinsically good as an experience of yours, inherently good as an object of my aesthetic pleasure in hearing it, and instrumentally good in lulling a child to sleep.

These and related points support recognizing inherent value as a distinct kind and replacing the traditional two-dimensional conception of value – as either intrinsic or instrumental – with an axiology that is at least three dimensional. One dimension encompasses experiences that are intrinsically valuable in the most basic way and are occurrent elements in a life. The second dimension is that of the inherently valuable, which has power to figure in a certain way in lives but does not require any relation to any actual life. The third is instrumental value, which is instantiated by means to ends, means that are contingent routes to these and not, like artworks as best conceived, constituents in the ends they serve. On this view, experiences are the bearers of intrinsic value; inherent value is the power to yield intrinsic value in appropriate experiences; and the basic value properties are certain qualities of experience, notably but not exclusively pleasurable and painful qualities.

2   The Scope of Inherent Value and Its Importance in Ethics

The three-dimensional conception of value just introduced concerns both value properties and what specific sorts of thing have value. A given thing, such as an experience, can have all three kinds. My hearing an aria can be intrinsically good in virtue of aesthetic pleasure in the auditory experience; inherently good as an enriching focal constituent in my host's rewarding experience of my evident enjoyment; and instrumentally good in relieving tension. Using 'intrinsically valuable' only in the generic sense tends to obscure differences of this kind and among types of reason for action. Again, something's having intrinsic value does not preclude its also having inherent and instrumental value. A distressing experience of envisaging firing an employee may lead to a good decision to delegate the termination decision to someone else. As distressing, the experience has negative intrinsic value. But that neither prevents its having inherent value as morally enlightening or instrumental value as leading to solving an important problem. Such higher-order experiences are significant. They are also quite common if we include, as I do, cases where, in making decisions, we reflect on our own anticipation of outcomes or on intuitions and feelings regarding our options. Anticipatory reflections and the intuitions they elicit may be insightful, and they are in many cases evidence of the kind and extent of the value of realizing one or another kind of conduct.

Observing the distinction between intrinsic and inherent value has still other advantages for exploring the relation between values and reasons and, more broadly, between value and obligation. In highlighting differences among the kinds of things valuable in themselves, the distinction clarifies the range of phenomena important for structuring a good life. In focusing on kinds of actions that realize intrinsic value, such as those that, like artistic creation, bring aesthetic value into our lives, the distinction connects reasons for action with the values achievable in human life as a whole.[6]

---

6 In at least one place Ross could be implicitly recognizing inherent value: "good is a characteristic belonging *primarily* only to states of mind ... in virtue of three characteristics included in them, the moral virtue included ..., the intelligence ..., and the pleasure included in them" (1930: 122, italics added). But he later says, "to pay a certain debt ... is itself no addition to the sum of values in the universe. If he does it from a good motive *that* adds to the sum ..." (132). He also includes virtuous dispositions as "intrinsically good" (134). It is noteworthy that he does not consider *experiences* of acting virtuously, or indeed

A different example of how the intrinsically valuable can have inherent value may help here. For me, an experience of guests' enjoying a meal together – an intrinsically valuable episode in their lives – is intrinsically good. My experience of that evident pleasure is both enjoyable and, in one of its aspects, socially rewarding. Moreover, the intrinsic value of such experiences can provide the anticipation of experiences like them with normative power. If clearly anticipating a state of affairs one can bring about is intrinsically good, as with the happy anticipation of having friends at dinner, it gives one (some) reason to bring it about; if intrinsically bad, reason not to do so. Perhaps an explanation of this normative power of (a certain kind of) anticipation is that it is often one's best future-oriented way of appraising the prospect in question. Happy anticipation is good in itself, but it may also support our realizing an anticipated state of affairs. That realization in turn may be a good experience, as writing a story or a poem may be. These concrete creations may be both inherently good and, if they lead to intrinsically enjoyable readings, instrumentally good.

As these examples illustrate, countenancing inherent goodness helps to unify two quite different aspects of the morality of conduct. It does this in part by facilitating an understanding of how what we can bring about – including moral conduct – is connected with what we cannot bring about, such as persons themselves. One aspect of morality is the ethics of *producing* what is good – which includes reducing or preventing what is bad. Another aspect is the ethics of *respecting* the good. The former concerns guiding our choices that, by realizing or producing good experiences and good things, give us a worthwhile future; the latter concerns both that and our conduct regarding what is

---

of gratifyingly contemplating such action, as adding to the "sum." It is perhaps clearer that *disapprovingly* contemplating vicious dispositions is an intrinsically negative experience, but he apparently does not consider such experiences nor explain how everything intrinsically good, including the "apportionment" of happiness to virtue, is related to states of mind.

valuable and already actual – above all, persons. The inherently good is an incalculably rich realm of things worth experiencing. Intrinsically good experiences would be drastically limited without it, and they are enriched by enjoying, preserving, and honoring it.

It is important not to underestimate the range of things that are valuable in themselves. The theory of value must do justice to the idea that rewarding experiences are valuable in themselves, to the Kantian idea that persons have value as ends in themselves, and to the diversity of non-living things good in themselves – for instance artworks, things of natural beauty, and sentient beings. One advantage of taking experiences as the bearers of intrinsic value (intrinsic value proper) is that they stand to be brought about in action – by doing things that constitute or lead to rewarding experience. This makes it easy to understand how they can be objects of desire and intention (as explained in Chapters 1 and 10) and have a major role in rational action. We do not, of course, bring persons about, but we do bring about (and have intentions to bring about) interactions with them and actions that manifest respecting them.

3   The Value of Persons

What has inherent value – above all persons – figures centrally in structuring our conduct, particularly in relationships with other people. The value of persons is too large a topic for extensive discussion here, but several points will indicate some important aspects of it.

The simplest point here is that persons – or anyway living beings capable of a certain kind of consciousness – are metaphysically essential for the realization of intrinsic value in human life: its realization depends on experiences, and the experiences had by persons are apparently the axiologically most important kind. This ontological status of persons is crucial for experience of inherent value and could be called *substratal* value, though the term is misleading since that is a condition for value and not a kind of it. Without persons, what appear to be the highest kinds of intrinsic value and inherent value (even if not all the kinds) could not be manifested in experience.

The inherent value of persons includes dignity. Whatever else dignity is, it gives us the kinds of reasons for action that call for conduct that expresses respect for persons and caring about their good.[7] Dignity is not easily characterized, but among the elements that apparently ground it are moral agency; the capacity for constructive and vibrant personal interactions; the potential for self-realization; sentience; and aesthetic sensibility. These are appreciated in our contemplation of their intrinsic character and our imagining their manifestations in us, but – as is crucial for ethics – interference with them, as in coercion, tends to be intrinsically disvaluable, at least in those coerced. Persons also commonly reflect on, or are at least conscious of, their own qualities and experiences. Such experiences of selfhood may have intrinsic value or disvalue and in either case ground reasons for action. Sound morality in agents – moral virtue in some terminologies – is above all the right kind of steadfast and sufficiently pervasive responsiveness to the inherent value of persons.

If persons have inherent value, why is it at best odd to say simply that persons as such are good in themselves? This is partly because 'good person' is generally used with high moral standards in mind. Even if, as Kant and others have thought, moral value is the axiologically "highest" kind, a wholly moral perspective on persons is too narrow to account for their overall inherent value. Moreover, the evaluation of persons, especially in its inescapable moral dimension, admits of disapprobative descriptions like 'malicious', as well as positive ones like 'benevolent'. But even a malicious person has intrinsic properties whose appropriate contemplation – which has non-moral as well as moral

---

7 Kant's conception of dignity is clarified by O'Neill in, e.g. (1989), and by Ameriks, e.g. in (2020). Here fittingness provides an alternative (though compatible) conception. As Garrett Cullity has suggested (2018: 60–62), we could say that a person's dignity consists in being a fitting object of certain respect-responses. I can imagine a development of this view extensionally equivalent to mine regarding what beings have dignity. This would leave open which conception, if either, should be considered basic.

dimensions – has intrinsic value. Granted, the experience of reflection on a malicious person might be distressingly disapprobative. This would be expected if, overall, the person is inherently morally bad. But even inherently morally bad persons may still be sources of non-instrumental reasons for action. They can suffer in ways that arouse pity and merit palliation. Even malice rising to punishability need not block potential for reformation or achieving some good. Contemplating that potential may be, overall, rewarding in itself. Related to this is the value of reflection on the moral standing of even malicious persons. This standing includes rights against cruel punishment and (in my view) the possibility of remorse and reparation. Such reflection may have moral value in embodying a sense of understanding of the vulnerabilities, aspirations, and possibilities that go with the life contemplated.

If, however, all of us have inherent value, for instance in the capacity for rational agency and moral goodness or at least reformation, then an appropriately informed contemplation of our intrinsic properties, despite our possession of some inherently bad characteristics, may not be unqualifiedly negative but mixed. Perhaps, for some cases, it can be positive on balance, if only because competent observers have a sense of potential improvement or rewardingly contemplate the vicissitudes of a life gone wrong.[8] Quite apart from this, if, in virtue of their intrinsic characteristics, persons are sources of non-instrumental reasons for action – including of course moral reasons – the axiology I am proposing provides for taking them to have inherent value.

The metaphysical side of the inherent value of persons has already been noted in relation to intrinsic value: they are essential

---

8 Much is left open here regarding how persons are best conceived, e.g. materialistically, mentalistically, or in some more complicated way. In any case, they can be experienced and the proposed conception of intrinsic value can do justice to the point that the richer our experience of persons, the more fully we can value them. For a very different approach to the value of persons see Theunissen (2020), and for numerous conceptions of the value of humanity bearing on the matter see Buss and Theunissen, eds. (2023).

for the vast variety of experiences that are the bearers of intrinsic value, including life's greatest joys. Elementary pleasures and pains are also possible for animals – though even these experiences depend on an agential quasi-personal status that makes possible experiences of kinds shared with persons. Persons, however, can have intellectual and aesthetic experiences that count heavily among elements that make human life good. In a way, it is misleading to call this metaphysical status of persons inherently valuable, but it is indispensable for a huge range of values; and, given normal human lives, in which persons instantiate intrinsic value properties (positive or negative), such a status – call it personhood – is incalculably valuable in upshot. Persons clearly have inherent value in at least one important way: their existence entails that there are non-instrumental reasons to treat them in certain broadly respectful ways. If intrinsic value, in its experiential embodiments as I have characterized them, is axiologically basic, there is a plausible account of the moral and valuational importance of persons (and other conscious beings) whether or not they are explicitly called inherently valuable.

4   Moral Value as a Distinct Kind

Despite the diversity of things valuable in themselves, inherently or intrinsically, it may be objected that the proposed three-dimensional value theory still lacks the breadth needed to account for all our moral reasons.[9] I have illustrated the diversity of value, and I consider each dimension one in which we have morally significant reasons for action. But may we not say that well-being (e.g.) is explicable in terms of its rewardingness in the life of sentient beings, understood in relation not just to pleasure and pain but also to the multifarious inherently valuable elements in it?

9 It has been noted, for instance, that "The desirable, the estimable, welfare, and dignity are different kinds or dimensions of value." See Darwall, "Normativity in Contemporary (and the History of) Ethics" (in preparation), which cites Anderson (1993) on the point.

The bearers of moral value that have received the greatest emphasis in some of the moral philosophers we have considered are complex behavioral patterns in which an agent acts from moral or at least virtuous motivation, say a sense of justice. Arguably, there is moral value in such concrete actions even if the agent is (excusably) mistaken in thinking the action is right. This is not to imply that rightness is a kind of goodness. The point is that there is a kind of value – inherent moral value – that right actions have. Even actions justifiedly but mistakenly believed to be right can have it, partly because of their connection with good intention(s). Some philosophers call these unfortunate actions "subjectively right," at least if the agent has good enough reason to consider the act right. If such morally directed action does not manifest moral virtue – another instance of inherent moral value – at least it manifests a condition of the will that is appropriate to moral virtue. Such conditions may indeed be natural stages in moral development toward virtue.

I grant that the dignity of persons is more difficult to account for than their inherent moral value taken in general terms. This is partly because the notion of dignity is itself elusive. But surely dignity in persons is in part a moral status and entails having moral rights. Moreover, it is possessed on the basis of inherently valuable properties, such as autonomous rational agency, which is stressed by Kant as, if not the basis of dignity, crucial for possessing it.[10] On

10 Kant maintains, e.g., that "the law-giving [under the categorical imperative] itself, which determines all moral worth, must for that very reason have a dignity ... *Autonomy* is therefore the ground of the dignity of ... every rational nature" (1785/1997: 436). Here autonomy emerges as the best candidate for the Kantian ground of dignity, with lawgiving taken as exercising autonomy. I leave open the relations among inherent value, dignity, and autonomy (and whether a certain kind of *potential* for autonomy and other bases of dignity may suffice for dignity). But *experiencing* the possessors of these characteristics in terms of their intrinsic properties such as admirable exercises of autonomy, normally has intrinsic value, doubtless including moral value. I also leave open whether the normative framework of Part II is incomplete without an account of rights. Perhaps so, but rights can be at least extensionally accounted for in terms of moral principles. Cf. Thomson: "[r]ights reduce, in a certain way, to what – other things being equal – we

my view, these points imply that there is intrinsic value – sometimes including intrinsic moral value – in certain kinds of experiences of honoring persons, treasuring them, interacting with them intellectually, and, looking outward from activities, simply experiencing perceptions and emotions regarding them. We may feel pride in being positioned to honor a successful student; happy in affectionately embracing a child; zestfully alive in arguing with a friend; and elated in seeing pleasure in a loved one's receiving a gift from us. We have moral reasons to act consonantly with values of all these kinds.

In assessing the usefulness of employing the categories of intrinsic and inherent value as I do, we should consider practical reasons whose strength partly depends on the intrinsic value of anticipatory experiences of considering one's options. Ethical literature has long been concerned with such questions as whether a life of experiences that are intrinsically good suffices for living the good life understood as a kind we may rationally seek – and take to be a case of living morally. Many philosophers have considered deception scenarios in which an apparently happy person is systematically deceived about such things as the devotion of others, including family members. Who would flip a coin between a life of "subjective" pleasures in interpersonal relations pervaded by such deceit and one that is hedonically (and otherwise) alike but having true beliefs replacing the false beliefs essential to the first scenario?

The central point here is that the content of our reasons in such cases includes at least some of what is essential to each scenario and is accessible to reflection on it in a way that affects the rational appraisal of the options on which one's reasons bear. The anticipation of the deceptive scenario is aversive, even morally distressing, and surely these negative experiences are rational responses to clearly envisaging its realization. Is there any doubt that aversion based on such anticipatory experience provides a reason to avoid realizing the scenario that evokes it? Indeed, it is

ought or ought not to do, and may or may not do" (1990: 33). My (2005) provides reasons for a certain priority of principles to rights.

surely a principle of practical reason that clear-headed rational moral aversion to a prospect provides good reason to avoid realizing it. Even moral doubt of its permissibility or moral disapproval of it is some reason against it.

We have, then, reason – I believe strong reason – to prefer realizing the scenario with the "true" pleasures over realizing its counterpart with false pleasures, and so for other intrinsically good experiences. This holds even if the veridical and hallucinatory pleasures in question are equally valuable "intrinsically." Intrinsically valuable experiences may themselves have inherent value or inherent disvalue. That can account for anticipatory reasons not to realize experiences embodying falsehood and error – these experiences are inherently objectionable. The inherent disvalue of the projected scenarios, like that of actual instances of them, entails the intrinsic disvalue of appropriately focused anticipatory experiences and thereby reasons for the preferences we find intuitive.[11] In these cases, there are non-instrumental reasons to avoid bringing about what is inherently bad, morally or otherwise.

Suppose, then, that we first focus on non-instrumental value, leaving open how we might accommodate the diversity within this category. A major view defensible for any adequate account of non-instrumental value is that, as at least deontologists should hold, one irreducible kind is moral value. If so, there are deontological reasons for action – at least if we may include doing something prima facie obligatory or prima facie wrong as an intrinsic consequence of certain actions. Intrinsic consequences as understood here are entailed, rather than simply caused, by

---

11 This treatment of the delusional scenario problem, as we might call it, for experientialism about intrinsic value is developed differently in ch. 11 of my (1997), which addresses the experience machine problem raised by Robert Nozick. For a related treatment, which proceeds by distinguishing pure from enriched welfare (where the latter excludes deceptive scenarios), and compares that approach with the strategy of Kagan (1994), see Feldman (2019). Feldman's approach is mainly compatible with mine but less conceptually comprehensive in, e.g., his narrower notion of welfare by comparison with the scope of my three-dimensional account of value.

the actions that yield them. Unjust deeds and broken promises, for instance, are, in themselves, morally bad. For many deontologists, the prima facie wrongness of such acts is a priori entailed (as I argue it is) by the grounds of fidelity or justice. Consequences of what we do are not limited to phenomena we cause.

Taking 'consequence' this broadly, as including not only effects in the causal order but also what have been called results of action, is compatible with its being a priori true that the moral disvalue of lying, like that of doing an injustice, gives one a reason not to lie. The moral wrongness of lying – wrong-makingness – which does not entail being wrong on balance, is a morally bad consequence (and here a result) of the action. If that moral status of consequences partly grounds the moral authority of reasons of veracity, we could speak of a pluralistic consequentialism. There is a plurality of moral values corresponding (at least) to the moral principles discussed in Part II. For instance, the moral disvalue of promise-breaking, killing, and failing to make reparation for injury are results of certain actions. Dying is a result of (e.g.) directly causing a death, as misapplied punishment is of imprisoning someone for a crime the person did not commit. These are all morally significant results. We can leave open priority relations among the various kinds of reasons as well as how to weigh combinations of reasons where we face competing obligations and must determine what we have most reason to do. This kind of consequentialism, attributing moral value as it does to certain entailed – and in that minimal sense essential – properties of acts, has a perhaps surprising character: it is compatible with a certain kind of plausible deontological ethics. Seeing this requires further exploration of moral value, and I turn to that now.

5 Moral Value and Moral Obligation

Our examples suggest that hedonism is too narrow to capture the full range of non-instrumental values, even if, as with Mill, experiences are treated as the bearers of such value, and pleasures – presumably also pains – are taken to admit of differences in quality. A liberal hedonism, however, should not be underestimated.

Given how diverse pleasures and pains can be, one might argue that negative moral experiences, such as the sense of being cheated, are a kind of suffering, and their positive counterparts, such as the satisfaction, sometimes a joyous relief from anxiety, of freeing someone from a debilitating fear, are one kind of pleasure. There is some plausibility in such a case, but there are also experiences of moral approval of, say, a plan of action, where this is a guarded satisfaction rather than a hedonically positive gratification.

For reasons of this kind, taking the bearers of intrinsic value to be experiences does not commit one to hedonism. I grant, however, that perhaps an experience could not be good overall if it is, on the whole, highly painful.[12] Pain can be a kind of defeater of (overall) intrinsic value – which is a significant though negative normative role – even though the mere absence of defeaters is not a ground of such value. Being eliminable by pain is only a negative dependence on it. An experience that is good overall is not such even in part *in virtue of* not being painful, even if it may fail to be good overall unless it is *not* painful. In any case, even if overall rewardingness in an experience negatively depends at least on its not being excruciatingly painful, there could be rewarding experiences that are intrinsically good without being pleasurable overall, as perhaps with some intellectual experiences. This applies especially to some that are laborious and challenging.

Rewardingness is a broad category and includes non-hedonic positive experiences. Among these are experiences of positive experiential change. The simplest example (introduced earlier) is that of felt diminution of excruciating pain: such experience can be a welcome relief without being a kind of pleasure. *Broad hedonism* – roughly the view that intrinsic value is determined by pleasure and pain – might claim that the experience is still hedonic. Suppose it

---

12 Moore went further: "[N]o whole can ever have any intrinsic value *unless* it contains some pleasure." See (1912/1965: 103). He apparently did not take adequate notice (at least here) of the implausibility (or anyway unclarity) of positing non-experiential wholes that "contain pleasure."

is. It still shows that the pleasurable and the painful are not the only experiential intrinsic values. Think of a growing gratification as one experiences improving technique in a difficult exercise painful throughout. This sense of progress can be a good feeling without being pleasurable.

Given the importance of moral experiences that (as such) are intrinsically good or bad, other cases should be considered. Surely the experience of being done an injustice can be intrinsically bad. Think of the experience of receiving a guilty verdict for a crime one knows one did not commit. It might evoke moral outrage; it might also embody an excruciating sense of moral defamation, especially if the trial is procedurally correct and its verdict will clearly be respected. Between these two strong reactions, especially if the wrong is not major, there may be an experience of moral embarrassment, which could be acutely unpleasant but – though in a sense suffered – need not be a kind of pain. Not everything aversive is painful. Similarly, one might suffer a kind of moral disappointment on discovering that, say, an enterprising young nephew selling magazines to passers-by regularly cheated them. The most important point here is that the experiences in question have moral value or moral disvalue. Whether a broad enough hedonism can accommodate them is secondary.

There are contrasting cases we should also note, where the moral experience is positive. Consider the morally good experience of making a just distribution, especially when felt as the completion of difficult careful deliberation, as in grading essays.[13] One might have a similar positive experience in contemplating a fulfillment of a duty of gratitude: one knows what would be just

---

13 For Ross, "... it is in virtue of the motives that they proceed from that actions are morally good" (1930: 156). Ross's quite reasonable distinction between the *rightness of what one does*, conceived as a property of instancing an appropriate act-type, and moral *creditworthiness in what one does from a moral motive* does not commit him to denying that act-tokens of, e.g., doing justice may *also* be (inherently) morally good. It apparently did not occur to him to countenance inherent value as I conceive it; see, e.g. (1930: 70 and 86), but cf. 127. My (1988) offers further points on moral experience and its intrinsic value.

the thing to express thanks and provide appreciation. On the negative side, the experience of guilt is significant. Even apart from being hedonically bad, distress in contemplating a wrong one did, or that a loved one did, can be a morally bad experience, fraught with self-loathing.

Granted, it can be good *that* a wrongdoer feels guilty about having done wrong – a morally good state of affairs – and feeling guilty can have a morally good-making property in virtue of its fittingly remorseful element, even while it has a hedonically bad-making property in virtue of being distressing. The former element can, given the remorseful element, make the experience of feeling guilty a case of fittingness of the overall reflective experience to its content.[14] The experience may indeed be inherently good overall even if it is not overall intrinsically good. If it is inherently good, that may be part of the reason why it can mitigate the punishment that might be due. Such goodness can also contribute to the fittingness of forgiveness, whether or not the sense of such fittingness is, as it may be, moral. A kind of unfittingness may also play a role in overall value: I would find intrinsically bad the experience of a friend's lying to me even if I expected it. There might be a kind of moral distress due to a sense of attempted manipulation. Disappointment over someone's breaking a promise may also be an experience with negative moral value.

If these examples show what they seem to, then lying and injustice are inherently morally bad in my sense: an appropriate – in this case morally comprehending – experience of them as having the moral status they do is intrinsically (morally) bad; and experiencing one's doing of justice can be intrinsically (morally) good. Indeed, surely one way we ascertain reason to consider certain acts wrong is by the moral negativity of vividly

---

14 For informative discussion of fittingness as a normative notion and of much else relevant to this chapter, see Cullity (2018), esp. chs. 2 and 8. A historically important discussion of fittingness usefully compared with Cullity's is Broad's (1930). For a still earlier conception of fittingness, see Price (1787/1974), esp. ch. VI, and for examination of Franz Brentano's fittingness theory, see Chisholm (1986).

contemplating them. This may range from an intuitive sense of wrongness to acute disapproval to indignation. Suppose, as hedonists may claim, such negative experiences are a kind of pain. So long as the negative experience is moral, it can play the normative grounding role sketched here regarding reasons for action. Prospective distress in contemplating an act can ground the intrinsic moral badness of that foresightful experience, and that anticipatory distress in turn can ground a reason not to do the deed.

6   Organicity in Value and in Reasons for Action

For a good understanding of value and its relation to reasons, we should consider an idea widely thought plausible for intrinsic value but, on my view, applicable for similar reasons to inherent value. I refer to the idea that intrinsic value is organic. This entails that the intrinsic value of a complex whole need not be the sum of the intrinsic values of its parts or aspects.[15] Positively, the intrinsic value of a complex whole is not only non-additive but also depends on certain relations among its parts or aspects. If we integrate this idea with the view (argued in Chapter 10) that considerations of intrinsic value are grounds of reasons for action, we would expect that the cumulative weight of reasons for action is also organic rather than additive, and in similar ways. That is surely so. Consider a promissory reason to do something that one later sees will be painful. I promise to take a child to the zoo on the coming Saturday, but I then suffer a knee injury that would make the visit painful. Quantification is impossible here except in rough terms. But we can imagine plausibly concluding that even if the child's disappointment at rescheduling would pass after a flood of tears over the delay, the reason to keep the promise is

---

15 I here add to Moore's (negative) formulation in (1903) a reference to aspects as distinct from *parts* (as most commonly understood) of a valuable entity, and my broad positive formulation explicitly takes account of inherent value, as Moore apparently did not. For an informative discussion of organicity, see Lemos (1994), esp. ch. 3, and Appendix A on Chisholm's definition of organic unity.

stronger than the excusatory force of avoiding pain. This could hold even if I have a second reason to reschedule: to help a student with a paper due too soon to assist with if I lose hours at the zoo.

Here reasons of fidelity and beneficence oppose a reason of self-protection, and the case shows three things. First, we are in no position to assign values in a way that permits additive comparisons among them. Second, even if one thinks the intuitive weight of the promissory reason taken alone is not great, one might reasonably decide to grin and bear the zoo trip. Third, even for hedonists, as for non-hedonist consequentialists like Moore, one need not take pleasure or pain, or the hedonic reasons based on them, to be either measurable quantitatively or additively combinable. Where reasons bear on practical decision, comparing their "weights" is holistic: it must take account both of all the relevant reasons and of the relevant relations among them. Given this requirement, such decisions as whether to keep a burdensome promise should take account of numerous contextual variables that might strengthen or perhaps weaken the reason to keep it.

A quite different ethically significant illustration of the organicity of intrinsic value, and implicitly of normative reasons, is afforded by sadism. Consider a sadist's pleasure in paining a victim (where the pain is not requested or desired by the victim). Suppose the pleasure far exceeds the pain the latter suffers from the sadist's enjoyable activity, say acutely embarrassing the victim. In at least most such cases, the overall intrinsic value of the state of affairs, the sadist's enjoying giving pain to the victim, seems negative. It is, say, cruel, disrespectful, patronizing, and the like. One reason to say this is that the pleasure ill-befits its object. An unqualified Benthamite utilitarianism would treat pleasure and pain additively (so far as possible), thereby being committed to calling the experience intrinsically good overall.

The organicity of intrinsic value is reflected here – or in any case paralleled – by that of reasons for action. Insofar as such sadistic experience is pleasurable, there is some reason for sadists to realize it. This is why it can "make their day." But insofar as the overall experience of enjoying giving the victim pain is intrinsically or inherently bad (morally or otherwise), there is reason (for sadists or anyone else) to avoid it. Imagine a friend who gets sadistic pleasure from teasing a hardy though sensitive colleague to the point of some distress. One might say 'You have no reason to tease like that'. One answer might be 'I do: it's great fun for me and he gets over it quickly'. Especially if this is the highlight of the sadist's day, it seems wrong to say 'That's no reason', but one might say that it isn't a good enough reason to justify distressing someone. Some sadists might disagree, but at least from a nonhedonistic point of view, and surely from the moral point of view, the latter, harm-avoidance reason would typically outweigh the enjoyment element that supports teasing. If, however, normative reasons depend on values in the way I have described, it is expectable that their overall force should depend on overall value and that the magnitude of this force is no more additive than the pluralistic grounds that are its basis.[16]

The non-additivity in question goes with incommensurability but does not entail incomparability. We may reasonably judge that one state of affairs is intrinsically better than another even if we cannot express the superiority numerically. With inherent value, the measurement problem faced in making certain comparative judgments is perhaps even more difficult. The inherent value or disvalue of something, say the state of affairs, a sadist's giving pain to a victim, increases with its power to yield intrinsically good (or bad) experiences of the right kinds. Here readiness to yield them is one complex factor, but so is the "amount" of intrinsic value they will or probably will produce given an appropriate focus on the intrinsic properties of whatever is in question. Any plausible theory of value will face comparable, or at least comparably difficult, problems in justifying comparative value

16 I refer here to the value of "wholes," including complex states of affairs. If there is additivity for non-instrumental value, it might be where perfect duplicates have experiences of exactly the same kind and duration. A world with both experiences might, in that respect, be considered twice as good as a world with just one. Such *duplicational additivity* is of course an idealization.

judgments, but perhaps enough has now been said to suggest what kinds of questions must be pursued if we are to develop a more detailed theory of the justification of value judgments.

7   Contributory Value

It is not unreasonable to object that the sadist's (overall) pleasure is not possible in the abstract, since it is taken *in* the victim's suffering, and so is a kind of pleasure whose goodness is vitiated. How, then, can sadistic pleasure be intrinsically good (assuming it is) and reason-giving at all? The objection poses a problem for the view that pleasure is intrinsically good in a sense implying that (as we may assume here) it is necessarily so. This view, however, is consistent with denying that pleasure is necessarily a *contributory good*, one that contributes positively to the overall good of a complex of which it is a part or aspect. Pleasure need not do this. This point is consistent with maintaining that pleasure is intrinsically good-making, where this is roughly to say that it necessarily counts toward that overall good *defeasibly*, just as a prima facie reason to act defeasibly favors an action, so may be overridden by a stronger competing reason (or a set of reasons that are collectively stronger). In this case, pleasure may be considered a prima facie contributory good; but it counts defeasibly, in the sense that its positive contribution to the value of the complex whole in question need not exceed any negative contribution it makes.[17]

As some cases like this illustrate, an experience having more than one aspect – as experiences usually do – can contribute positively (say, to an episode in one's life) in virtue of one aspect and negatively in virtue of another. Contributory value (as

---

17 Cf. Feldman (2000) and (2019), for indications of how the goodness of pleasure may be defeated when it is, as with sadists, of "the wrong kind" and thereby without intrinsic value. I could with some revisions accommodate this approach, but determining defeasibility is difficult and may require judgments of contributory value whether the defeat is of some basic value, such as that of pleasure, or (as I prefer to maintain) of its "normal" contribution to the value of an experiential state of affairs of which it is an aspect.

conceived here), moreover, is not best viewed as instrumental – or, strictly speaking, as a *kind* of value given how it is role-defined by contribution *to* value. The contributory badness of sadistic pleasure to the overall intrinsic value of the sadist's experience is not a means to that negative value nor related to it only contingently. Insofar as the negative contribution is explainable, it may be at least partly in terms of unfittingness. The unfittingness of sadistic pleasure to its object contributes negatively to the overall intrinsic value of the experience, and that unfittingness is also non-instrumental and non-contingent.

When an unfitting pleasure makes a predominantly negative contribution to the overall value of a sadistic experience, that experience may be, as an element in the life of the sadist, intrinsically bad overall: discolored by feelings of guilt that can overshadow the pleasure. It may also be inherently bad, even perceptibly so for the sadist, who may or may not properly reflect on the sadistic activity. But we may still ask: *Must* the appropriately focused, comprehending experience, by a relevantly competent third party viewing the sadistic pleasure, be morally distressing overall? That it would be is plausible but not obvious. We might, however, say that, first, if the sadistic experience is, overall, intrinsically morally bad, then it has some morally bad-making property and, second, it is likely to be inherently morally bad overall: an appropriate experience of it focused on its intrinsic properties will have at least one bad-making element such as a felt disapprobation, and this experience will likely be overall intrinsically morally bad. Admittedly, an experience that is (overall) morally bad could be (overall) aesthetically good. We can perhaps imagine a witty enough exchange between sadist and victim, and in some cases, with both exhibiting aesthetic excellence, this excellence might outweigh the moral negativity. Still, this organic combination of good and bad is compatible with the experience's being intrinsically bad in an overall way. But given the organicity of both intrinsic and inherent value, some questions of overall intrinsic goodness in such mixed cases have no easy resolution.

Pleasure can be both intrinsically and necessarily good-making (providing an element of goodness) consistently with its being a defeasible contributory good. Perhaps the best answer to the objection that sadistic pleasure can be in *no* way intrinsically good is that the complex hedonic state in question may contain an intrinsically positive experience of an isolable kind – something like a feeling the person delights in having. This phenomenal kind of experiential element might be common to certain other experiences, including non-sadistic ones, yet has negative contributory value in the sadistic case.[18] This element, like certain pains or certain unfamiliar sensuous pleasures, is, first, not intentional, since, as a "raw" feeling state, it has no intentional object; second, partly for that reason, it is possible apart from the object of the wider sadistic pleasure of which it is an element. That hedonic experience could account for why (in some cases) there is a normative, though defeated, reason for the sadist to give pain to the victim and why the sadist's wanting to do this need not be irrational. This does not imply that doing it is rationally required or even rationally preferable to abstaining.

It is not necessary, however, that such a raw hedonic positive feeling – perhaps some pathological thrill – is a constituent in the sadist's pleasure in the victim's suffering. The pleasure may be less visceral and need not have any hedonic aspect that can exist in isolation. The sadist's pleasure could embody a phenomenal integration of pleasure and a dominating satisfaction in paining the victim. This kind of pleasure tends to raise the overall moral disvalue of the experience. Similarly, when the sadist simply enjoys paining the victim for its own sake, the pleasure taken in the experience again fails to contribute positively to the intrinsic value of the overall state of affairs: the enjoyment of giving pain to another.

Implicit in some of what has been said is that for some of us, even vividly imagining the higher-order experience of this unfitting sadistic pleasure would be intrinsically bad. I find aversive the very prospect of watching the sadist's enjoyment in paining

---

18 Cf. Hurka's assumption that pleasure (of at least one kind) is "a sensation distinguished by an introspectable quality of pleasantness" (2001: 12), a view he attributes to Bentham.

the victim, and I think I am properly responding to my vivid picture. This is partly why I view that sadistic enjoyment as, overall, inherently bad. Even if the sadist is witty, it would be as if I saw, in a single viewing, a fine sculpture and, unignorable, just next to it, a man repeatedly slapping a child. My overall experience would be bad, despite having an element – the viewing of the sculpture – that is good. In this way, we can account for the rationality of retrospective remorse on the sadist's part, as well as for the possibility that the sadist's prospective reason for giving pain to the victim is defeated but not unintelligible. An analogy might be that of a sadistic artist's enjoying doing a very fine drawing – something there is good reason to do – but on the victim's back and with boiling hot inking needles. There is overriding reason for such sadists to abstain from producing such an interpersonal experience and to seek the apparent aesthetic rewards in better pursuits.[19]

There is a great plurality of things good in themselves. Some of these are intrinsically good: occurrent elements in experiences that are good in themselves. Others are inherently good: objects of greatly diverse kinds with powers to be constituents in intrinsically good experiences. I have illustrated how both kinds of good things – often indifferently described as good in themselves or good "as ends" – may characterize complex entities whose overall value is an organic integration of the values of their parts or aspects. Taking intrinsic and inherent value to be organic is neutral between deontology and certain kinds of consequentialism. So is countenancing inherent value. Moore and surely Ross might have countenanced inherent value. But contrary to deontology as I propose we view it, Moore took rightness, and implicitly moral reasons for action, to derive from considerations of non-moral value, and he took obligation to depend on

19 For discussion of the case that fittingness considerations suffice for this overall conclusion, see Cullity (2018), e.g. 35–41; and for a plausible defense of the organicity of reasons, with significant bearings on sadism, see Oliveira (2016: 173).

maximizing value. If he seriously considered whether there is moral intrinsic value, he made no commitment to viewing moral value as irreducible. He had room to argue that, for instance, there is an unfittingness of pleasure to causing pain and that this at least partly accounts for the overall badness of sadistic activity. On my view, by contrast, moral value is an irreducible kind. This position is characteristic of deontologists, including Kant and Ross, but, as may now be apparent, compatible with certain kinds of consequentialism. Might the position also point toward a way to transcend the dichotomy between consequentialism and deontology? On the basis of both the theory of value sketched here and the theory of action that best fits it, the next chapter explores this possibility.

12   Consequentialism and Deontology

We have considered illustrations of moral value, intrinsic and inherent. If intrinsic moral value is irreducible, we can see how it is possible for a deontologist to take moral value to be normatively more basic than reasons for action. A deontologist can view reasons to act as grounded in considerations of value and can see moral reasons as grounded at least partly in considerations of *moral* value. There are many kinds of grounds of reasons. Think of happily contemplating the aesthetic pleasures of attending a concert or of eagerly anticipating a soccer match. These forward-looking experiences can ground reasons to attend the anticipated events. Similarly, a morally gratifying experience in reflecting on the satisfaction of helping malnourished children can be a ground of a moral reason to volunteer for service. If a state of affairs has (overall) intrinsic value or, more broadly, something is (overall) intrinsically or inherently good, there is some (objective if defeasible) reason to bring it about or in some way act positively toward it, as in the case of protecting it or honoring it – modes of action applicable to both inanimate objects of inherent value and, importantly, to persons.

1   Results, Effects, and Moral Value

An important addition I am making to the general idea that goodness is a source of (normative) reasons for action is that there are irreducibly morally good and bad things – not only experiences but many kinds of objects, actions, and persons themselves. Consider lying. It is not only prima facie wrong but also (inherently) bad (strictly, inherently bad-making), thus bad in itself, apart from its effects. Its wrongness, however, is not grounded in its badness. Even its moral badness is not brute but grounded in what it is, a kind of breaking faith with someone to whom one gave one's word. Consider, too, the experience of being lied to, with awareness of the lying character of what is said. I find this an intrinsically bad experience, as I find bad even the experience of vividly imagining lying to someone who trusts me. It does not follow that lying can never be inherently less bad overall than truth-telling, as in the case of murderers at the door seeking victims. But that is to be expected given the organicity of moral value, intrinsic and inherent. It might be recognized even apart from that view of value and even on a version of Kantian ethics.[1]

If the theory I am developing implies that in one way the good is more basic than the right, it nonetheless accommodates the deontological view that some act-types, e.g. killing and promise-breaking, are by their very nature wrong-making. Being wrong-making is a normative property, though it does not entail overall wrongness. But these points leave open that there is moral experience and moral intrinsic value. Suppose it is true that reasons for action normatively depend on value. Is a kind of utilitarianism now our only option? No. Moreover, if consequences of events are conceived causally (as seems the main construal for most non-technical uses of 'consequence' as applied to events[2]), we need not

---

1 An indication of how this is possible for Kant is provided in my (2018b).

2 Cf. a passage in which Sidgwick says, regarding commonsense morality, that in such maxims as "truth should be spoken without regard to consequences, that justice should be done 'though the sky should fall' [quoting Kant]... it is implied that we have the power of seeing clearly that certain kinds of actions are right and reasonable in themselves, apart from their consequences" (1907: 180). Causal consequences are apparently intended, but Sidgwick immediately refers to an earlier passage (96–97) which perhaps anticipates the distinction between results and causal consequences. Detailed analysis of Sidgwick's utilitarianism (1907) is provided by Crisp (2015b) and Skelton, *Sidgwick's Ethics* (forthcoming). For an indication of how consequences may be conceived causally (in epistemology as well as ethics) see Berker (2013); he notes that "Consequentialism in ethics is famously *forward-looking*: it ties an

even be consequentialists. But suppose we call lying a consequence of stating a falsehood intended to deceive someone, since lying is conceptually entailed by it. Then consequentialism may be more broadly conceived and my view can accommodate what is best in it. Terminologically, I prefer to call lying a result of what one does in so speaking. Similarly, a result, but not a causal consequence, of breaking a promise is failing to keep one's word; and a result of pulling a child from the path of a speeding car is preventing the child's being run over by it. Including results among consequences that may be intended in acting, provides wider options. Acting contrary to one's word has an intrinsically wrong-making result.

The view I am proposing – call it *consequencism* – incorporates deontological notions, particularly the notion of certain acts as wrong in themselves, but, regarding the *structure* of action, it is (as explained in Chapter 10) teleological (and "consequentialistic"). If there is moral intrinsic value, then the moral badness consequent upon – resultant from but not caused by – a lie or an injustice can (normatively) greatly outweigh the non-moral, say hedonic, goodness of its causal consequences.[3] Those causal consequences are important for determining final obligation, but they are not the only morally relevant variables. These and other ideas will be developed in this chapter.

2   Consequencism and Deontological Reasons

Historically, consequentialists, especially utilitarians, have taken value to be more basic than obligation, and they tend to take the

action's, or rule's, or institution's ethical merit to the value of the states of affairs it helps bring about" (377).

3 An early presentation of the distinction between results and causal consequences is in von Wright (1963: 39–41) and (1971), e.g. 66–69. Cf. McCann: "When an action is the bringing about of a certain change, that change is called the *result*" (1998: 76). For an insightful use of the notion of non-causal consequences in clarifying consequentialism, see Sosa (1993). Sosa shows how using this notion clarifies conceiving certain deontologists as including morally significant results of action and thus qualifying as consequentialists. More is said below about how this should be understood.

valuable to be the source of reasons for action and rightness to be equivalent to maximizing whatever they view as intrinsically good. Deontologists, including traditional intuitionists, oppose that position and many take reasons – including obligations, which are or at least entail reasons – as the most basic normative elements.

Consequencism gives weight to results as well as causal consequences. It focuses on conduct as central in moral education and as correspondingly important in moral deliberation. It countenances reasons for action that are appropriate to the intrinsic character of conduct; and it conceives the overall weight of reasons as organic rather than additive. It accommodates the view, often held by non-consequentialists and confirmed by the work of this book, that what we ought overall to do is what there is "most reason" for us to do; but it is pluralistic about reasons and rejects quantitative conceptions of their normative force. As a conduct view, it takes account of thick moral questions (described in Chapter 6) in determining our obligations. These questions focus on not only eligible act-types, but also one's possible conduct and the experience of deliberatively anticipating it in relation to both the projected motivation underlying one's options and the foreseeable manner of their performance.

The sense in which consequencism may be deontological can also be seen by considering situations of choice in which there are agent-relative factors (also called prerogatives). Imagine that terrorists (whom I somehow know to be reliable on the point) tell me that only my executing one innocent person will prevent their executing ten innocent people. Must doing this moral wrong be valuationally preferable to allowing ten comparable ones, in which others will be compelled to do what I am asked to do? It would be preferable on Bentham's hedonic calculus and could be for more sophisticated versions of consequentialism.[4]

---

4 See Bentham (1789), esp. ch. 1. I find no indication of his taking account either of incommensurability of certain elements in pleasure and pain or of the apparent organicity of intrinsic value.

But here we must again look to an action-theoretic description of the case. Let me elaborate.

I face a thick moral question. I am reflecting on and choosing between two types of conduct, not comparing, in the abstract, two states of affairs (actual or hypothetical), such as one innocent person's being sacrificially killed as opposed to ten people's being sacrificially killed. Viewed in isolation, the latter is worse. But a deontologist who grants this may still deny that *my* executing one to prevent ten similar wrongs presents me with a truly quantitative or even straightforward comparison. As consequencism sees it, the comparison is between incommensurables. More specifically, an instance of the first kind of conduct would entail – and have as a result, thus as an intrinsic element – killing an innocent person as an intended and morally tainted means to save other innocent people, and an instance of the second kind of conduct entails refusing to kill in that instrumental way and reflectively rejecting cooperation with malicious people.[5] For me, the inherent value of the sacrificial conduct would be negative and incalculably high, and anticipating it is a repugnant experience. My decision whether to sacrifice is, then, not a matter of enhancing value impersonally conceived, nor is it quantitative. Its moral soundness depends partly on the value both of my anticipation of the contrasting kinds of conduct and of those options themselves.

The causal consequences of the proposed murderous conduct-token (if the sacrifice is made) may figure in how I conceive my

---

5 The case is of course underdescribed and deserves more space than I have here. Must S be treating the victim *merely* as a means? This depends on S's operative motivation and attitudes in the contemplated conduct – which highlights the importance of considering what one's conduct would be, rather than only the consequences of the relevant deeds conceived as instancing act-types. In my view 'merely' is very strong, and some who kill would treat the victim mainly, but not merely, as a means (e.g. making the execution as nearly painless as possible). This does not preclude adhering to a consequencist version of the humanity formula (which requires treating persons as ends and never merely as means), nor is this treatment question the only relevant moral question here. My (2016) provides an account of the *merely*, but here I do not rely on that account as an element in the consequencist view.

choice. It would likely be with indefinite probabilities, a serious complication in itself. From a deontological perspective, in calling on me (in such morally important cases) to conceive my options as conduct and in terms of moral value (without excluding other kinds of value), consequencism respects my agent-centered autonomy, and my choice can and should have inherent value as an exercise of conscientious autonomous judgment.[6] The inherent value may be manifested partly in my own experience of my choice. It may also be seen in the consequences of my choice viewed in numerous ways. The sacrificial conduct in question, if realized, could have indefinite and incalculable inherent value, in my life and other lives over time, and it would have consequences with value and disvalue of multiple kinds. The same holds for the conduct in which, partly for moral reasons, one refuses to execute. Overall obligation cannot be determined in abstraction from the particulars relevant to the agent's choice.

3 Moral Deliberation Without Absolutist Constraints

There are two significant but extreme positions that consequencism avoids: a deontological absolutism and a consequentialist maximalism. On a strict Pauline deontology, one simply "may not do evil that good may come" (Romans 3: 8). This is action motivated by doing evil as a means to good, and the deontological element in consequencism grants its moral darkness but rejects the absolutism of the prohibition. By contrast, for classical utilitarianism and various other consequentialist views, if sacrificing some lives to save others is one's only way to maximize the good, it is obligatory. There will be epistemic uncertainty in any real decision case; but if

6 This case calls for far more discussion than space permits and is meant only to suggest some of the options possible given my view. For analysis of cases like these and extensive consideration of consequentialism in relation to deontology, see Sosa (1993) and Portmore (2011), esp. ch. 4. For a different perspective on "consequentializing," see Dreier (2011). What I call consequencism is not equivalent to any of the main kinds of consequentialism Dreier considers, but the generic description of consequentialism he develops is so encompassing that I leave this open.

the maximization judgment is true, the obligation follows. A practical result is to force on the agent a calculation that, even if it does not yield knowledge, may yield a probability high enough to cushion any objective error with the excuse of having known or justifiedly ascribed the high probability. On my theory of reasons and values, the needed reflection requires weighting moral values and judging what one would bring about – from results to expectable causal consequences – in the light of an organic conception of overall value, intrinsic and inherent, and of overall reasons for action.

It is important to see that, in a context of deliberation on an important and difficult moral question, one may properly contemplate – and in some cases should contemplate – what conduct one would be engaging in. In the example before us, one must have the terrible experience of killing an innocent person and, likely, of thinking of this as treating the person's life instrumentally, as a means to saving others. It is natural to feel moral revulsion in reflecting on such a case. The revulsion may be expected to rise if one must kill violently, say by shooting, and to rise further still if one must fatally stab. The manner of action is important, too. There is also a question of whether one will see refusing as morally cowardly or, instead, as expressing integrity, which one may take to have great inherent value. Such hypothetical cases are difficult to resolve, in part because they are not specified in terms of all the relevant variables. It is not even possible to be sure of *identifying* all of the values that should be appraised (that has not been done here, but we can see how to develop the example if further issues require that). It is clear, however, that in important matters we should think about our projected conduct. We may give great if indefinite weight to a reflective intuitive appraisal of that conduct, and we may resist stepping into a morally repugnant stream that may run unendingly in unforeseeable directions.

Just how to weight the moral disvalue of the proposed execution against whatever value is entailed by that execution (and whatever valuable consequences are foreseeably caused by it) is a matter of disputable normative judgment. Deontologists need not concur in all such hypothetical judgments and have typically considered such cases to require comparing incommensurables. Nor need they focus deliberation on values rather than reasons. The two realms are conceptually different in ways that can make deliberation on either side informative; and the normative priority of values does not entail that, in practice, decisions are always better guided by axiological reflection than by comparing reasons, obligations, fittingness, or indeed the demands of virtue.

In the difficult complex cases we have been considering, there is no additive formula for determining the overall (perhaps negative) value of the relevant conduct-tokens and their actual causal consequences. Consider an aesthetic analogy. A pink blotch in the wrong place might spoil a painting. How prominent must the blotch be? Will darkening it cancel its effect? Will shrinking it make it tolerable? Does disagreement on such questions entail that some cases permit no uncontroversial answers or even no right ones? These are eminently debatable questions. This is not to say that there are never good (even true) answers when enough is made clear or that there cannot be a case in which a "preventive" execution is morally permissible. The point is that deontology, at least in my version, attributes great moral disvalue to executing an innocent person; rejects quantitative formulas for weighting it against both non-moral value and even against the moral disvalue of forgoing the saving of innocent persons.[7] Consequencism does this too, and it also gives due weight to the agent-centered anticipation of the conduct in question and to the inherent as well as instrumental and intrinsic value of the conduct itself.

Consequencism does not, then, entail that no rational decision can be made in such cases. One might think this if one took incommensurability to entail incomparability, understood as precluding

---

7 Ross, e.g., says, "For the estimation of the comparative stringency of these *prima facie* obligations [including the obligation not to kill] no general rules can ... be laid down ... We can only say that a great deal of stringency belongs to the duties of 'perfect obligation'" (1930: 41). Unlike, Sidgwick, he did not (at least in [1930]) envisage the possibility that morality and rationality could call for incompatible actions, but he did not preclude a focus on conduct as central for moral deliberation.

rational choice. The view does not entail either incomparability or even the impossibility of there being some number of evil killings which, if one knows one can prevent them (and a great deal about the future as affected by one's conduct), makes it permissible to choose to kill preventively. More positively, it is plausible to hold that where practical reason clearly implies that *A*-ing is rational, morality does not clearly imply that it is (overall) morally wrong. But practical reason has high standards of justification and knowledge in such situations, and its deliverances tend to respect moral demands even if self-concern is also an ineliminable element in rational decision-making.

The broad action-theoretic idea underlying the possibility of a consequencist deontology is that in acting we bring about states of affairs, commonly with the important result that we experience the action or activity that is the vehicle of our conduct. In this broad sense, action has an instrumental structure, in which the total consequences of action include both what is intrinsic to it and what it causes. Why, then, shouldn't what we ought to do, and indeed what we have most reason to do, be in some way a matter of the value of what we stand to bring about, such as the keeping of a promise? This view need not lead to utilitarianism. The reason goes beyond what is entailed by the organicity and plurality of intrinsic value. Also central in the deontological point of view is the irreducibility of moral value and the positive or negative moral character intrinsic to certain act-types, such as killing and lying,[8] and indeed to the conduct-types that have the acts in question as vehicles. The obligatoriness of keeping a promise may make it the right act-type for me to aim at, but if I know I would be doing it for inherently immoral manipulative reasons and in a manner that I consider shameful, I may have

---

8 Extensionally, and as applicable to just act-types and not (as intended here) to conduct-types, consequencism might be equivalent to Parfit's triple theory: "An act is wrong just when such acts are disallowed by some principle that is optimific, uniquely universally willable, and not reasonably rejectable" (2011: 413).

overall reason to abstain. It may be that the deepest difference between deontological and (at least) causal consequentialist views is in the theory of value rather than in the theory of obligation. But beyond the point that rightness – and indeed permissibility and obligatoriness as well – are partly matters of *moral* value, consequencism retains the deontological idea that rightness is neither a kind of goodness nor reducible to or fully determined by any agent-neutral kind of goodness.

4   Consequencism as a Theory of Moral Conduct

There is at least one other reason why a consequencist deontology need not lead to utilitarianism or any similar maximizing consequentialism. The point is neutral with respect to the range of phenomena taken to be good in themselves and thus with respect to overall grounds for preferability. It also does not rest on difficulties of valuational measurement, though these raise a greater problem for maximizing consequentialism than for theories that, like my pluralistic view, neither require maximization of the good nor presuppose quantitative measurability of the good and the bad. What I propose instead as a rule of rational conduct is a *preferential standard*. This requires (at least) that when we are actually confronted with a necessary choice between acts *A* and *B* – or two projected conduct types, which in many cases of moral decision we should anticipate in detail – where one is discernibly better than the other, we should choose the better one.[9] This is an intuitively plausible standard many of us follow, and doing so is not in general unduly burdensome. (The standard readily extends to multiple alternatives.)

Adherence to this preferential standard does not commit one to adopting either the rule that in every decision to act, we should

---

9 As Chapter 6 explains, such conduct choices, as in pursuing thick moral questions, may in some cases take account of certain considerations of double effect. Other variables also need explication, e.g. discernibility and choices among multiple alternatives; and there are refinements in formulation, as well as alternative preferential principles, that cannot be pursued here.

seek to maximize the good, or the more specific rule that, in judging or acting in any morally important matter, we should maximize the good including the moral good.[10] Obeying such rules would often obligate one to explore possible options in ways that go beyond being morally conscientious. Internalizing a maximizing standard might be plausibly taken to require at least having good reason to believe that there is no available – some would say feasible – option preferable to the one we choose. It is often difficult or impossible to acquire such a reason. Our possibilities for future conduct are innumerable; even what is routine for us may encompass far more options than a morally conscientious agent need consider. Many rational decisions do not require even trying to consider them all, and some important decisions call for immediate action where assuming maximality is unjustified. On a maximizing view, we do wrong, even if excusably, when we fail to realize any "available" option that is better than our actual deed. The preferential standard is far more sensitive to our epistemic limitations, but is strong enough to sustain rigorous standards for judging conduct.

There is a range of more specific preferential principles that we need not pursue here, but adopting such principles in place of a maximization standard is neutral among substantive theories of value, thus concerning what consequences of behavior are relevant to moral and other rational decisions. Granted, proponents of a maximizing theory may, as Mill did (in chapter 2 of *Utilitarianism*), appeal to "secondary rules" for everyday life.[11] But at least where applications of these conflict, as where a promissory obligation conflicts with one of beneficence, a maximizing theory such as utilitarianism will lead to substantial differences in deliberation as compared with the consequencism proposed here, which embodies a preferential standard.

---

10 This is evidenced by Hooker's development of consequentialism in (2000). The preferential standard I suggest could be assimilated to a kind of satisficing view, but, for reasons to be indicated (among others), I doubt that this is a desirable project.
11 Mill (1861/2001).

Adopting the preferential standard embodied in consequencism also calls for a holistic judgment in such conflicts and precludes choosing discernibly inferior options. But it does not require (or always preclude) seeking maximization – which may be desirable in certain policy decisions – and it leaves open that one kind of conduct may be preferable to another because of the intrinsic character of either or both independently of causal consequences. In some cases, of course, causal consequences are crucial criteria.

It is a major question, moreover, when we should seek to ascertain options not apparent to us in a situation of moral decision. If our concern is just what to *do*, as it often is, this may or may not require reflection. If, as often holds, we should consider our prospective overall conduct, reflection may well be needed. Sometimes it is obvious what we should do, how we should do it, and why we would be doing it if we actually do. There, we should not delay by pondering alternatives to the expectable conduct. Too much seeking may misguide us, even disempower us; too little thought may cause us to overlook options preferable to some we take. There is much to be said about how to achieve a good balance between "instinctive" choice and reflective selection, but pursuing this complicated matter goes beyond the aims of this book.

If consequencism is not a maximizing theory, does it call for a kind of optimization or, as some would put it, satisficing – doing something that is overall satisfactory? Morality calls on us to achieve conduct that is at least overall satisfactory, but this satisficing formulation is not explicit enough to capture the force of consequencism. Suppose we do something morally and otherwise satisfactory where we readily – or readily enough relative to the importance of the case – could have done better. We will not have satisfied the preferential standard. If deliberation aims simply at satisfactory results – as is normal in much of ordinary life – the choices made will often fail to meet the preferential standard. It is a stronger constraint on action and provides – as is appropriate for morally important choices – higher standards of evaluation.

5   The Indispensability of Practical Wisdom and the Limitations of Master Principles

Given that the preferential standard embodied in the consequencist theory I have proposed focuses above all on *conduct*, and not just on *doing* conceived as simply realizing an act-type, it differs in another way from both satisficing and maximization theories. Not only is satisficing less demanding, and maximizing more demanding, regarding choice and action; both standardly focus on selection among act-types, though they can be developed to apply to conduct. Despite these differences with consequencism, one might wonder whether consequencism supports a master principle after all. If so, it is quite broad. We can realize conduct-types as well as act-types, but our conduct embodies our motivation, which we cannot control at will, and even act-types that we can realize at will may have manners we cannot realize – or suppress – at will. If consequencism has a kind of master principle, it is that we should realize the best conduct we can, where the 'can' has the kind of discretionary character needed for understanding the beneficence principle and where failure to live up to the rule is implied by inexcusable departures from the preferential standard but *not* by failures to meet the maximizing standard.

My view of obligation is pluralistic not only in affirming a number of different principles of prima facie obligation, but also in calling for understanding them and internalizing them in ways that enable us usually to avoid having to invoke any overarching standard in deciding what to do. There are times for such reflection; but in much of human life and, for some people, in nearly all of life, it is clear what obligations bear on the moment – or on a day's work – and, if the obligations do not conflict, we seek a good way to proceed. Deliberation may be needed, yet even then, thinking about achieving the best conduct we can achieve usually need not be global. Usually, we can ascertain realistic options, compare those, avoid choosing something inferior to another live option, and proceed.

We can, then, *act under* an overall consequencist standard of conduct without constantly *thinking of it*. One way this is possible is by our focally intending action salient in projected conduct while presupposing, in a certain responsible way, appropriate manner and motivation. Moral decision, like many other kinds of decision, is normally circumstantial. It may often require more thinking in the instrumental task of determining a good way to fulfill a salient obligation than in the moral task of resolving conflicts of obligation. Living morally does not require moral thinking at every turn. Practical wisdom enables us to achieve a great deal of unselfconscious good conduct, but stands ready to invoke principles and values when we need them. Here as elsewhere, consonantly with the preferential standard, we should achieve the best conduct we can.

In case one is inclined to see consequencism as a rough equivalent of Moore's ideal utilitarianism, I should indicate some major differences. First, Moore did not countenance, or anyway give a role to, the moral value of actions as a distinct kind of value. Contrary to my view, he took the value of actions to be determined by their consequences for non-moral good, particularly but not exclusively hedonic good.[12] Second, he held a maximizing theory of obligation and rightness, which I do not. Third, he did not specifically distinguish results from causal consequences, though nothing major in his view precludes doing this. This may partly explain a fourth difference. By focusing on action rather than the wider category of conduct, he also did not take into account the significance of manners of performance, which are intrinsic to conduct. Fifth, and related to this action-theoretic difference, he gave no major role to inherent goodness. Where moral value is a result of an action, however, it is an intrinsic property of it and so part of the basis of its non-instrumental value, often including positive or negative inherent value. The experience of that action, whether by the agent or someone it is "done to," may be appropriately focused on its intrinsic properties in such a way as to have intrinsic value. This is partly why inherent value can figure in grounding moral reasons for action. A final point of difference concerns metaphysical naturalism regarding moral properties:

12 See Moore (1903) and (1912/1965), which are discussed in some detail in my (2004), esp. ch. 1, and my (2003).

for reasons indicated in Chapter 9, rejecting naturalism is not essential to my overall view, as it is to Moore's.

These points also indicate some major differences between my view and Ross's, which I consider among the leading historically important positions in moral philosophy and with which my view has more in common than with Moore's. First, there are normative differences, as indicated in Chapter 3,[13] which proposes revisions in the characterization of the obligations detailed by Ross in presenting his list. Chapter 4 adds two further moral principles, one of liberty and the other of respectfulness (in manners of action). Second, there are differences between the two theories of value. The largest single difference is in the greater breadth of my theory, though in a direction Ross could have taken consistently with his overall view. The greater breadth is not just in countenancing inherent value as a distinct axiological category, which Ross did not,[14] but also in recognizing a wider range of things valuable in themselves than he does. Although he acknowledges the moral value of the complex pattern, acting from duty, he refuses to regard as good in themselves even actions that are right and amply fulfill moral obligation. Both theories countenance deontological reasons for action as having intuitively normative force even apart from causal consequences, and both conceive rightness as having grounds that determine obligation rather than antecedently depending on goodness. But my view differs in the way it identifies foundations of intrinsic value in the qualities of the experiences that ground it.

An epistemological difference from Ross derives from my account of self-evidence. He, like Moore and others, conceived self-evidence too narrowly. My account of it facilitates integrating commonsense intuitionism with a development of Kant's (rather

---

13 Here I refer to Ross's (1930). I have further differences from his departures from that position in his (1939).

14 Ross said, e.g., of a "universe in which mind is entirely absent," that "you will fail to find anything in it that you can call good in itself" (1930: 140). He adds that "the value of material things appears to be purely instrumental" (141), whereas I take such objects as beautiful sculptures to be sources of non-instrumental reasons for action.

skeletal) humanity formula.[15] This integration includes an explication and diverse applications of the notions of treating persons as
ends in themselves and, by contrast, merely as means, and it bears
on, among other things, how to view Rossian commonsense moral
principles as a unified framework. Treating persons as ends, for
instance, encompasses obligations of fidelity, veracity, reparation,
and gratitude; and avoiding treating persons merely as means
encompasses (in a more complex way) many characteristic *violations* of these obligations. Still another difference is perhaps expectable given this integration between treatment standards and prima
facie obligations viewed as mainly governing choice of act-types. It
concerns how to account for the permissibility of certain acts that
are not morally criticizable as failures to fulfill the obligation of
beneficence, which Ross considered a "prima facie duty to produce
as much that is good as we can."[16] In response to this beneficence
problem – inescapable in any serious ethics – Ross could perhaps
accept my partial account of permissibility and my additions to the
commonsense normative principles he accommodates, but he did
not sufficiently clarify either permissibility or supererogation.
Both terms apply to conduct-types as well as act-types; and in that
regard, my emphasis on the moral importance of manners of
action indicates a further contrast with Ross. We can do deeds
beyond the call of duty; but we can also do obligatory deeds in
better or worse ways. This includes doing them in a manner that is
itself supererogatory. These and related points indicate a further
difference from my theory: Ross did not (as I seek to do), take
adequate account of the relation between moral reasons for action
and non-moral reasons for it.[17]

---

15 The resulting Kantian intuitionism is presented in my (2004) and expanded
in my (2012), and the humanity formula – as I understand it in and taken
beyond Kant – is explicated in my (2016).

16 Ross (1930: 25); this is not an isolated description and, while of course
presupposing defeasibility, Ross here indicates no limitation of scope.

17 The views referred to here, on the relation between moral and non-moral
reasons, cannot be easily summarized and are developed and defended in my
(2001b) and (2010b). I should stress here, however, that there are non-moral
as well as moral reasons to reduce and to avoid causing suffering, and to

This is not the place for an account of supererogation, but it should be said that I have not meant to imply that there is no way Ross could accommodate supererogation. Suppose, regarding the beneficence problem, he thought that duties of self-improvement, for normal persons, often justify the leisure, or at least the discretion, to do (within limits) what they choose as for their own improvement, sometimes at the expense of forgoing beneficent deeds they could accomplish. This suggests that sometimes considerations of self-improvement (or other prima facie obligations) might put one in a position of moral parity between conflicting duties of self-improvement and beneficence in which one may permissibly prefer, without being overall obligated, to do beneficent deeds. One's beneficent but unrequired deeds that go beyond those needed simply to counterbalance the conflicting obligation are supererogatory and may be an admirable exercise of liberty. What I have added to the obligations Ross stressed is not only the obligations of liberty and respectfulness but also a morally acceptable place for non-moral reasons to operate in a realm of the purely discretionary and for those reasons to affect the manner of our actions and, sometimes, our motivation in doing them. Providing a significant place for non-moral reasons in determining our conduct (consistently with meeting our moral obligations) requires a weaker characterization of the obligation of beneficence than Ross offers but more readily provides for supererogation. Perhaps Ross could have accepted this position if he had viewed morality as I do in relation to practical reason conceived broadly. Practical wisdom is needed to decide what kind of situation calls for beneficent conduct, how far one should go in it, and – if this is important – what would be supererogatory.

––––––

At various points in this chapter and earlier ones, reasons for action, and implicitly for conduct, are viewed as axiologically

preserve, produce, and enhance enjoyment; and these as well as moral considerations bear on the treatment of animals and on planning for a future that includes (hypothetical) persons or other sentient beings or both.

grounded. Their normative force is possessed in virtue of the value of what the behavior in question – most importantly conduct – brings about. When consequences of action are thus understood to include entailed results and are preponderant in an agent's deliberative perspective, they represent states of affairs that, from this forward-looking perspective, may or may not be seen to have overall value that makes them worth realizing. Consequencism does not call for maximizing value but embodies a less demanding, preferentialist standard. It also does justice to the agential perspective in which options among kinds of conduct, and not just among acts, are considered. Moral deliberation should take into account not only intrinsic and inherent value in the abstract but also the agent's own place in realizing them. Realizations of moral value or disvalue can be intrinsic to our conduct – a point crucial for deontology. Realizing the good, understood pluralistically, is a central "aim" of practical reason, and *realize the good* – including moral good – is the central injunction of the consequencist view I am proposing. Conduct – and above all actions as its vehicles – should also be guided by beliefs (thus by theoretical reasons), and we may hope, and should try to ensure, that it is normally guided by true beliefs that are justified and constitute knowledge.

Realizing moral values does not exhaust the aim of practical reason but is essential for fully achieving that aim in normal human life. But so, too, is contributing to overall non-moral goodness. Deontological theories countenance the value of certain resultant realizations, as well as that of certain causal realizations, of both moral and non-moral goodness. These theories may, for instance, be Kantian or intuitionist or, indeed, an integration of Kantian and intuitionist notions – a kind of integration with much to recommend it.[18] They may, but need not, construe moral value as supreme relative to any potentially conflicting kinds of value. As the case of the witty sadist shows, one could have moral reasons to condemn sadistic activity and, in special cases, aesthetic reasons to tolerate it. Even if one thinks that given

18 This is argued in ch. 3 of my (2004) and developed further in my (2012).

equal strength, moral reasons override any opposing kind, one might allow that a minor moral reason might be outweighed by a major reason of another kind or at least by a coalition of reasons of other kinds. This is a question that belongs to normative value theory and may be left open here.

If the normative authority of reasons for action is axiologically grounded, it does not follow that reasons are reducible to values, nor should we endorse the converse reduction. In very general terms, a main argument proposed has been that normative reasons for action, as for conduct embodying it, depend on values – the overall value of consequences of conduct – that the rightness of an action is describable in terms of the reasons for it, and that reasons themselves depend, in the ways described, on qualities of experience, including moral qualities, that have a special grounding role. Action, however, is not the only element in our conduct, and appraising the value of conduct requires an even more comprehensive evaluation than the action it embodies.

In rationally responding to grounds for action, whether in realizing moral value or in realizing or increasing non-moral value, neither the weight of our reasons nor our success or failure is easy to determine. This is in part because of the organicity of value and in part because the causal consequences of our conduct, even if in principle identifiable empirically, go beyond our lifetimes and indefinitely into the future. These points indicate some of the reasons why moral decisions are so often difficult. They demand attention to both the agent-centered perspective on projected conduct and the impersonal point of view of values to be realized by one or another option. But this complexity does not make rational moral judgment or, in my view, even moral knowledge, impossible. Indeed, we can understand practical reasons best by viewing them as grounded in pluralistic considerations of value; and doing so is possible, in the ways outlined here, for moral theories that may be considered both deontological and fully responsive to the consequences of our conduct. The theory of conduct proposed in this book is of that kind, and it represents a path to convergence of deontological and consequentialist perspectives on the right and the good.

Conclusion

This book represents ethics as concerned not just with what we should do or even with that conceived as done for the kinds of reasons that, morally, befit what we should do. Ethics concerns our overall conduct. The ethical theory presented here stresses the three major dimensions of conduct: its matter – its act-type – the agent's motivation for acting, and the manner in which the agent does the thing in question. This theory has the important implication that moral obligation encompasses adverbial obligations, particularly those regarding the salient manners of what we do. The adverbial dimension of ethics deserves more explication than it has received, and this book is intended in part as a contribution to remedying that imbalance. The motivational dimension of moral conduct is also important, and it cannot be reduced to matters of obligation – by treating actions for reasons as act-types that are objects of obligation – nor can manners of action be fruitfully represented as act-types. Acting for a reason is not a manner of action but a compound phenomenon entailing both an action and an explanatory basis of it, and actions so conceived admit of indefinitely many manners of performance.

The importance of moral motivation is a topic belonging, in the main, not to the theory of obligation but to the theory of moral creditworthiness. This does not diminish its ethical importance. Indeed, if, in the way that bespeaks moral virtue, we clearheadedly and seriously care about why we do what we ought to do, we are more likely to do it both for an appropriate reason and in a manner that morally befits both the act-type and the circumstances of our

conduct. And if, in that way, we care about interpersonal relations – the main cases that call for moral conduct – then however
good we are at doing the right deeds, we must also care about the
manner in which we do them.

The importance of conduct as more than simply acting does
not imply that there is something wrong with centering ordinary moral deliberation, particularly in its initial stages, on what
should be done, thus on act-types that we consider eligible
options. Conduct has action as its essential vehicle, and a great
many moral decisions are focused on what our actions should
be. This is particularly so for institutional decisions or decisions
calling for cooperative agency. But a great deal of what we
deliberate about concerns what, as individuals, we anticipate
doing, often toward others in direct interactions. Here it is often
appropriate and sometimes essential to consider the thick question of what our conduct would be if we decide to do a particular
deed. This question should often lead to considering prospective
motivation for actions and envisaging manners of performance.
Agents are morally responsible in both cases: they have a high
degree of direct control of the manner of their actions and a
substantial degree of indirect control of their tendencies to act
for the reasons that they see, or should see, tend to motivate
their actions. The more important the acts in question, the
greater our responsibility for their manner and, in some cases,
their motivation.

Even a long book cannot describe our basic moral obligations
in the detail one might like. This book is not directly normative as
regards specific day-to-day actions, but it is intended to provide
understanding and clarification of the moral principles governing
much of ordinary life. In sketching part of a normative ethics,
I have identified a group of principles – concerning justice and
harm-avoidance, veracity and fidelity, beneficence and self-
improvement, reparation and gratitude, and, even more broadly,
liberty and respectfulness. These may be unified – some would say
derived from – one or another kind of comprehensive position.
Kant and Mill offered master principle theories. Aristotelian virtue
ethics is also comprehensive; it allows both for a vast range of

virtues and for a multitude of ethical principles – possibly some not grounded in virtues but having external normative force.

In arguing for the unifying potentiality of a reconstructive account of Kant's humanity formula in (2004), I described the unification of the commonsense principles that is possible under its injunctions to treat persons as ends and avoid treating them merely as means. Equally important is the clarification that commonsense principles derivable (with some regimentation) from those injunctions give to those lofty imperatives as candidates for comprehensive standards governing moral conduct. Even that Kantian master principle, however, is not monistic: it is double-barrelled, constituted by wide-ranging positive and negative imperatives. If this or some other abstract "axiom" in some sense unifies the everyday normative theorems, its own meaning is not clear apart from an account of their broad content and their concrete applications. Part I is intended to provide much of what is essential in such an account. We can study ethics from the top down, as master principle theorists have often sought to do, or from the bottom up, as intuitionists have often sought to do; but by itself, neither approach it likely to yield an adequate overall theory. We need a comprehensive understanding of action, obligation, and value to frame and apply ethical theory, a reflective equilibrium to justify its content, and an epistemological and metaphysical account of its objective soundness.

A further aim of this book is to develop an ethical theory that is both highly comprehensive in the normative standards it formulates and philosophically adequate to account for knowledge of their truth and applications. An ethical theory should be pursued partly in relation to the content, epistemology, and metaphysics of the normative standards it countenances. With this aim in view, one aspect of the ethical theory presented here is epistemological, another ontological. The moral epistemology is a moderate rationalism that takes the kinds of moral principles described in Chapters 4 and 5 to be a priori, though our justification for them is defeasible and our beliefs of the singular judgments made under their guidance are fallible. The moral ontology is realist. It countenances moral facts but does not foreclose the possibility that they could turn out to be natural facts. It firmly anchors moral properties in the natural world – indeed mainly in grounds whose perceptibility underlies moral perception. We perceive promises, hear assertions, receive gifts, notice distributions of resources, and sometimes witness brutality. The realism includes both internal and external realities – pain and pleasure, the rewarding experiences of the arts, challenges of the intellectual realm, the excitement of sports, the social activities of life with family and friends, and the multitude of objects and events we know in the natural world.

Still another aspect of the three-dimensional theory of conduct presented here is axiological: to provide an account of value that enhances understanding of action, especially action that fulfills the moral standards we have explored. Here we need a conception of value that does justice to its place in experience. Experience is fundamental for philosophical understanding in ethics as elsewhere in philosophy. It embodies and responds to the qualities of life we most deeply care about. Even apart from its epistemological and metaphysical importance in ethics, its qualities provide a basis for explaining how we distinguish good from bad practical reasons. Its richly plural forms clarify how fulfilling our intentions realizes the good. And understanding its forms and qualities enables us to do justice to the plurality of things – in experience or outside it – that are good or bad.

Some of what is said here can be seen in another way from a developmental perspective, a viewpoint often adopted on earlier pages. We are born helpless but sentient, ignorant but teachable. As sentience grows into percipience, we encounter right and wrong. Comprehension of both comes as we see right and wrong in what is done toward us, in loving care when we need it, and in stern rebuke when we err. We experience promises kept and broken, the satisfaction of helping others, and the benefits of good things done for us. We gradually come to discern our obligations and, with greater or lesser success, we internalize moral standards. Throughout this development, we experience the good and the bad – moral as well as hedonic, aesthetic, intellectual, or of some other kind. There are countless combinations of values. For most of us, maturity brings sensitivity to what is valuable and responsiveness to the reasons it gives us: reasons to seek, to promote, or to honor what is good and, in the dangerous world we inhabit, reasons to resist and reduce what is bad. We are constantly at the mercy of circumstance, and we are regularly subject to both the pressures of our individual desires and the moral demands of interpersonal life.

This developmental picture might invite viewing normal human experience as mainly a kind of self-consciousness, but it is far more an awareness of people and places, sights and sounds, acting and reacting, speaking and listening, the social and the solitary, and much more. Many of these objects of experience are inherently good; too many are inherently bad. These good and bad elements in life have the power to give us good and bad experiences, and we ourselves have the power to bring good and bad things into existence. Here our conduct is a major element. We should try in our conduct to realize the good. The scope of this range of obligations includes not just what is good in the abstract, independently of relationships; it also ranges to personal relations and to upholding our own integrity.

A unifying ethical idea in this broadly moral perspective is that moral conduct is properly oriented toward the good conceived in a comprehensive way that takes account of intrinsic moral value as a major kind and incorporates inherent value as a major axiological dimension. Consequences of action – intrinsic as well as causal – are crucial in this perspective, but not in the aggregative way characteristic of some utilitarian theories or in any monistic or hedonistic way represented by theories of value less pluralistic than the axiology of this book. Ethics concerns agency in a holistic way, and it respects our autonomy. Living up to its standards, for mature moral agents, is not just a matter of overt action, of doing the right things toward others, but of overall conduct. We should cultivate the tendency to fulfill our obligations by the right deeds, for the right kinds of reasons, and in the right manner. The scope of morality also ranges over the internal realm. There, we should do the right things in thinking and planning. Ethics is personal as well as social. In both realms, moral standards are fully met only by realizing them in all three dimensions of conduct: in what we do, why we do it, and how we do it.

References

Ameriks, Karl (2020). "The Fate of Dignity: How Words Matter." In Y. Kato and G. Schönrich, eds., *Kant's Concept of Dignity, Kant-Studien Ergänzungshefte* 209. Berlin: de Gruyter, 263–284.

Anderson, Elizabeth (1993). *Value in Ethics and Economics*. Cambridge, MA: Harvard University Press.

Anscombe, G. E. M. (1958). "Modern Moral Philosophy." *Philosophy* 33, 124, 1–19.

(1963). *Intention*, 2nd ed. Oxford: Blackwell.

Aristotle (2019). *Nicomachean Ethics*, trans. Terence Irwin. Indianapolis: Hackett Publishing Co.

Audi, Paul (2012). "Grounding: Toward a Theory of the *In-Virtue-Of* Relation." *Journal of Philosophy* 109, 12, 685–711.

(2013). "How to Rule Out Disjunctive Properties." *Noûs* 47, 4, 748–766.

Audi, Robert (1973). "Intending." *Journal of Philosophy* 70, 13, 387–403.

(1974). "Moral Responsibility, Freedom, and Compulsion." *American Philosophical Quarterly* 11, 1, 1–14.

(1986). "Acting for Reasons." *Philosophical Review* 95, 4, 511–546.

(1988). "The Axiology of Moral Experience." *Journal of Ethics* 2, 4, 355–375.

(1993a). *Action, Intention, and Reason*. Ithaca, NY: Cornell University Press.

(1993b). "Ethical Naturalism and the Explanatory Power of Moral Concepts." In Steven Wagner and Richard Warner, eds. *Naturalism: A Critical Appraisal*. Notre Dame: University of Notre Dame Press, 95–115.

(1993c). *The Structure of Justification*. Cambridge: Cambridge University Press.

(1996). "Intuitionism, Pluralism, and the Foundations of Ethics." In Walter Sinnott-Armstrong and Mark Timmons, eds., *Moral Knowledge?* Oxford: Oxford University Press, 101–136.

(1997). *Moral Knowledge and Ethical Character*. Oxford: Oxford University Press.

(1999). "Self-Evidence." *Philosophical Perspectives* 13, 205–228.

(2001a). "A Kantian Intuitionism." *Mind* 110, 439, 601–635.

(2001b). *The Architecture of Reason: The Substance and Structure of Rationality.* Oxford: Oxford University Press.

(2002). "Prospects for a Naturalization of Practical Reason: Humean Instrumentalism and the Normative Authority of Desire." *International Journal of Philosophical Studies* 10, 3, 235–263.

(2003). "Intrinsic Value and Reasons for Action." *Southern Journal of Philosophy* 41, Supplement, 30–56.

(2004). *The Good in the Right: A Theory of Intuition and Intrinsic Value.* Princeton: Princeton University Press.

(2005). "Wrongs Within Rights." *Philosophical Issues* 15, 121–139.

(2006a). "Ethical Generality and Moral Judgment." In James Dreier, ed., *Contemporary Debates in Moral Theory.* Oxford: Blackwell, 285–304.

(2006b). *Practical Reasoning and Ethical Decision.* London: Routledge.

(2010a). *Epistemology: A Contemporary Introduction to the Theory of Knowledge.* London: Routledge.

(2010b). "Practical Reason and the Status of Moral Obligation." *Canadian Journal of Philosophy* 37, Supplementary vol. 33, 197–229.

 (2012). "Kantian Intuitionism as a Framework for the Justification of Moral Judgments." In Mark Timmons, ed., *Oxford Studies in Normative Ethics*, vol. 2, 128–151.

(2013a). "Knowledge, Justification, and Normativity." *Res Philosophica* 90, 2, 125–145.

(2013b). *Moral Perception.* Princeton: Princeton University Press.

(2013c). "The Practical Authority of Normative Beliefs: Toward an Integrated Theory of Practical Rationality." *Organon* F 20, 4, 527–545.

(2015a). "Intuition and Its Place in Ethics." *Journal of the American Philosophical Association* 1, 1, 57–77.

(2015b). "On Mary Glover's 'Obligation and Value'." *Ethics* 125, 2, 525–529.

(2016). *Means, Ends, and Persons: The Meaning and Psychological Dimensions of Kant's Humanity Formula.* Oxford: Oxford University Press.

(2017a). "On Intellectualism in the Theory of Action." *Journal of the American Philosophical Association* 3, 3, 284–300.

(2017b). "Role Modeling and Reasons: Developmental and Normative Grounds of Moral Virtues." *Journal of Moral Philosophy* 14, 6, 646–648.

(2018a). "Doxasticism: Belief and the Information-Responsiveness of Mind." *Episteme* 17, 4, 542–562. DOI: 10.1017/epi.2018.53

(2018b). "Methodological Reflections on Kant's Ethical Theory." *Synthese* 198, Supplement 13, 3155–3179. DOI: 10.1007/s11229-018-01977-x

(2020a). *Seeing, Knowing, and Doing: A Perceptualist Account.* Oxford: Oxford University Press.

(2020b). "Toward an Epistemology of Moral Principles." *Res Philosophica* 97, 1, 69–92.

(2021). "Are Reasons Normatively Basic?" *Noûs*. DOI:10.1111/nous 12377

(2022). "The Phenomenology of Moral Intuition." *Ethical Theory and Moral Practice* 25, 53–69.

(forthcoming). "Normative Priority, Fittingness, and Grounds of Normativity." In David Copp and Connie Rosati, eds., *The Oxford Handbook of Metaethics*, Oxford: Oxford University Press.

Bentham, Jeremy (1789). *An Introduction to the Principles of Morals and Legislation*. London: T. Payne.

Bergqvist, Anna, and Robert Cowan, eds. (2018). *Evaluative Perception*. Oxford. Oxford University Press.

Berker, Selim (2013). "The Rejection of Epistemic Consequentialism." *Philosophical Issues* 23, 1, 363–387.

Birondo, Noell, and Stewart Braun, eds. (2017). *Virtue's Reasons: New Essays on Virtue, Character, and Reasons*. London and New York: Routledge.

Boyd, Richard (1988). "How To Be a Moral Realist." In Geoffrey Sayre-McCord, ed., *Essays on Moral Realism*. Ithaca: Cornell University Press, 181–228.

Bradford, Gwen (2015). *Achievement*. Oxford: Oxford University Press.

Brandom, Robert (1998). *Making It Explicit: Reasoning, Representing, and Discursive Commitment*. Cambridge, MA: Harvard University Press.

Brandt, Richard B. (1979). *A Theory of the Good and the Right*. Oxford: Clarendon Press.

Brandt, Richard, and Jaegwon Kim (1963). "Wants as Explanations of Actions." *Journal of Philosophy* 60, 15, 425–435.

Bratman, Michael (2018). *Planning, Time, and Self-Governance: Essays in Practical Rationality*. Oxford: Oxford University Press.

Brink, David O. (1989). *Moral Realism and the Foundations of Ethics*. Cambridge: Cambridge University Press.

Broad, C. D. (1930). *Five Types of Ethical Theory*. London: Routledge & Kegan Paul.

Burge, Tyler (2010). *Origins of Objectivity*. Oxford: Oxford University Press.

Buss, Sarah, and Nandi Theunissen, eds. (2023). *Rethinking the Value of Humanity*. Oxford: Oxford University Press.

Butchvarov, Panayot (1989). *Skepticism in Ethics*. Bloomington and Indianapolis: Indiana University Press.

Chang, Ruth (2013). "Commitments, Reasons, and the Will." In Russ Shafer-Landau, ed., *Oxford Studies in Metaethics*, vol. 8. Oxford: Oxford University Press, 74–113.

Chisholm, R. M. (1986). *Brentano and Intrinsic Value*. Cambridge: Cambridge University Press.

Copenhaver, Rebecca (2014). "Reid on Moral Sense." *Canadian Journal of Philosophy* 41, Supplementary vol. 1, 80–101.

Crisp, Roger (2005). "Value, Reasons, and the Structure of Justification: How to Avoid Passing the Buck." *Analysis* 65, 1, 80–85.

(2006). *Reasons and the Good*. Oxford: Clarendon Press.

(2015a). "A Third Method of Ethics?" *Philosophy and Phenomenological Research* 90, 2, 257–273.

(2015b). *The Cosmos of Duty: Henry Sidgwick's* Methods of Ethics. Oxford: Clarendon Press.

Cullity, Garrett (2017). "Moral Virtues and Responsiveness for Reasons." In Noell Birondo and Stewart Braun, eds., *Virtue's Reasons: New Essays on Virtue, Character, and Reasons*. London and New York: Routledge, 11–31.

(2018). *Concern, Respect, and Cooperation*. Oxford: Oxford University Press.

(2023). "Reasons and Fit." In Chris Howard and R.A. Rowland, eds., *Fittingness: Essays in the Philosophy of Normativity*. Oxford: Oxford University Press, 151–175.

Curren, Randall, and Richard M. Ryan (2020). "Moral Self-Determination: The Nature, Existence, and Formation of Moral Motivation." *Journal of Moral Education*. DOI: 10.1080/03057240.2020.1793744

Dancy, Jonathan (1993). *Moral Reasons*. Oxford: Blackwell.

Darwall, Stephen E. (in preparation). "Normativity in Contemporary (and the History of) Ethics."

Davidson, Donald (1963). "Actions, Reasons, and Causes." *Journal of Philosophy* 60, 23, 685–700.

(1971/1980). "Agency." In *Essays on Actions and Events*. Oxford: Oxford University Press, 43–62.

(1967/1980). "The Logical Form of Action Sentences." In *Essays on Actions and Events*. Oxford: Oxford University Press, 105–148.

(1980). *Essays on Actions and Events*. Oxford: Oxford University Press.

Dreier, Jamie (2011). "In Defense of Consequentializing." In Mark Timmons, ed., *Oxford Studies in Normative Ethics*, vol. 1. Oxford: Oxford University Press, 97–119.

Dretske, Fred I. (1981). *Knowledge and the Flow of Information*. Cambridge, MA: MIT Press.

Feldman, Fred (2000). "Basic Intrinsic Value." *Philosophical Studies* 99, 3, 319–346.

(2019). "Two Visions of Welfare." *Journal of Ethics* 23, 2, 99–118.

Fischer, John (2011). "Frankfurt-Type Examples and Semicompatibilism: New Work." In Robert H. Kane, ed., *The Oxford Handbook of Free Will*, 2nd ed. Oxford: Oxford University Press, 243–265.

FitzPatrick, William (2012). "Intention, Permissibility, and Double Effect." In Mark Timmons, ed., *Oxford Studies in Normative Ethics*, vol. 2, 97–127.

(2022). *Ethical Realism*. Cambridge: Cambridge University Press.

Först, Rainer (2012). *The Right to Justification*. New York: Columbia University Press.

(forthcoming). "Justice; Procedural and Substantive." In Richard Bellamy and Jeff King, eds., *The Cambridge Handbook of Constitutional Theory*. Cambridge: Cambridge University Press.

Gert, Bernard (2004). *Common Morality*. Oxford: Oxford University Press.

(2007). "Two Conceptions of Morality." In Mark Timmons, John Greco, and Alfred R. Mele, eds., *Rationality and the Good: Critical Essays on the Ethics and Epistemology of Robert Audi*. Oxford: Oxford University Press, 54–63.

Gert, Joshua (2004). *Brute Rationality*. Cambridge: Cambridge University Press.

Ginet, Carl (1990). *On Action*. Cambridge: Cambridge University Press.

Glover, Mary (1938). "Obligation and Value." *Ethics* 49, 1, 68–80.

Goldman, Alvin I. (1970). *A Theory of Human Action*. Englewood Cliffs, NJ: Prentice-Hall.

(1986). *Epistemology and Cognition*. Cambridge, MA: Harvard University Press.

Haidt, Jonathan (2001). "The Emotional Dog and Its Rational Tail." *Psychological Review* 108, 4, 814–834.

Hempel, Carl G. (1965). *Aspects of Scientific Explanation and Other Essays in the Philosophy of Science*. New York: Free Press.

Hooker, Brad (2000). *Ideal Code, Real World*. Oxford: Clarendon Press.

Horgan, Terry, and Mark Timmons (2022). "Expressing Gratitude as What's Morally Expected: A Phenomenological Approach." *Ethical Theory and Moral Practice* 25, 1, 139–155.

Hume, David (1777/1975). *Enquiries Concerning Human Understanding and Concerning the Principles of Morals*, ed. P. H. Nidditch. Oxford: Oxford University Press.

Hurka, Thomas (2001). *Virtue, Vice, and Value*. Oxford: Oxford University Press.

Hursthouse, Rosalind (1999). *On Virtue Ethics*. Oxford: Oxford University Press.

Isserow, Jessica (2020). "Moral Worth: Having It Both Ways." *Journal of Philosophy* 117, 10, 529–556.

Kagan, Shelly (1994). "Me and My Life." *Proceedings of the Aristotelian Society* 94, 309–324.

Kane, Robert (2011). *The Oxford Handbook of Free Will*, 2nd ed. Oxford: Oxford University Press.

Kant, Immanuel (1785/1997). *Groundwork of the Metaphysics of Morals*, trans. Mary Gregor. Cambridge: Cambridge University Press.

(1788/1996). *Critique of Practical Reason*, trans. Mary Gregor. Cambridge: Cambridge University Press.

Korsgaard, Christine M. (2008). *The Constitution of Agency*. Oxford: Oxford University Press.

Lackey, Jennifer (2021). *The Epistemology of Groups*. Oxford: Oxford University Press.

Lemos, Noah (1994). *Intrinsic Value: Concept and Warrant*. Cambridge: Cambridge University Press.

Lewis, C. I. (1946). *An Analysis of Knowledge and Valuation*. La Salle, IL: Open Court.

(1955). *The Ground and Nature of the Right*. New York: Columbia University Press.

Littlejohn, Clayton (2018). "Being More Realistic About Reasons: On Rationality and Reasons Perspectivism." *Philosophy and Phenomenological Research*. DOI: 10.1111/phpr.12518

Lord, Errol (2018). *The Importance of Being Rational*. Oxford: Oxford University Press.

Luco, Andres (2019). "How Moral Facts Cause Moral Progress." *Journal of the American Philosophical Association* 5, 4, 429–448.

Maguire, Barry (2018). "There Are No Reasons for Affective Attitudes." *Mind* 127, 507, 779–805.

McGrath, Sarah (2019). *Moral Knowledge*. Oxford: Oxford University Press.

McCann, Hugh (1998). *The Works of Agency*. Ithaca: Cornell University Press.

McConnell-Ginet, Sally (1982). "Adverbs and Logical Form: A Linguistically Realistic Theory." *Language* 58, 1, 144–184.

(2019). *Moral Knowledge*. Oxford: Oxford University Press.

Mele, Alfred R., ed. (1997). *The Philosophy of Action*. Oxford: Oxford University Press.

Mill, J. S. (1859). *On Liberty*. London: J. W. Parker and Son.

(1861/2001). *Utilitarianism*, ed. George Sher, 2nd ed. Indianapolis: Hackett Publishing Co.

Moore, G. E. (1903). *Principia Ethica*. Cambridge: Cambridge University Press.

(1912/1965). *Ethics*. Oxford: Oxford University Press.

Murray, Samuel (2020). *Vigilance: Self-Control for Planners* (doctoral dissertation). Notre Dame: University of Notre Dame, Indiana.

Nagel, Thomas. (1986). *The View from Nowhere*. Oxford and New York: Oxford University Press.

Nelkin, Dana Kay (2011). *Making Sense of Moral Responsibility*. Oxford: Oxford University Press.

Oliveira, Luis R. G. (2016). "Rossian Totalism About Intrinsic Value." *Philosophical Studies* 173, 8, 2069–2086.

O'Neill, Onora (1989). *Constructions of Reason: Explorations of Kant's Practical Philosophy*. Cambridge: Cambridge University Press.

298   REFERENCES

Parfit, Derek (2011). *On What Matters*, vol. 1. Oxford: Oxford University Press.

Parsons, Terence (1970). "Some Problems Concerning the Logic of Grammatical Modifiers." *Synthese* 21, 320–334.

Phillips, David K. (2019). *Rossian Ethics: W. D. Ross and Contemporary Moral Theory*. Oxford: Oxford University Press.

Portmore, Douglas (2011). *Commonsense Consequentialism*. Oxford: Oxford University Press.

Price, Richard (1787/1974). *A Review of the Principal Questions in Morals*. London. T. Cadell; and (in modern orthography), in D. D. Raphael (1974).

Prichard, H. A. (1949). *Moral Obligation: Essays and Lectures*. Oxford: Clarendon Press.

Quinn, Warren S. (1989). "Action, Intention, and Consequences: The Doctrine of Double Effect." *Philosophy and Public Affairs* 18, 4, 334–351.

Raphael, D. D., ed. (1974). *A Review of the Principal Questions in Morals*. Oxford: Clarendon Press.

Railton, Peter (2014). "The Affective Dog and Its Rational Tail: Intuition and Attunement." *Ethics* 124, 4, 813–859.

Reid, Thomas (1863/1983). *An Inquiry into the Human Mind on the Principles of Common Sense*. Reprinted in Ronald Beanblossom and Keith Lehrer, eds., *Thomas Reid: Inquiry and Essays*. Indianapolis: Hackett Publishing Co.

Ross, W. D. (1930). *The Right and the Good*. Oxford: Oxford University Press.
   (1939). *Foundations of Ethics*. Oxford: Oxford University Press.
   (1954). *Kant's Ethical Theory*. Oxford: Oxford University Press.

Rowland, Richard (2016). "In Defense of Good *Simpliciter*." *Philosophical Studies* 173, 5, 1371–1391.

Russell, Bruce (1977). "On the Relative Strictness of Negative and Positive Duties." *American Philosophical Quarterly* 14, 2, 87–97.

Scanlon, T. M. (1998). *What We Owe to Each Other*. Cambridge, MA: Harvard University Press.
   (2014). *Being Realistic About Reasons*. Oxford: Oxford University Press.

Sidgwick, Henry (1907). *The Methods of Ethics*, 7th ed. London: Macmillan & Co.

Sinnott-Armstrong, Walter (2006a). "Moral Intuitionism Meets Empirical Psychology." In Terry Horgan and Mark Timmons, eds., *Metaethics after Moore*. Oxford: Oxford University Press, 339–365.
   (2006b), *Moral Skepticisms*. Oxford: Oxford University Press.

Skelton, Anthony (forthcoming). *Sidgwick's Ethics*. Cambridge: Cambridge University Press.

Smithies, Declan (2019). *The Epistemic Role of Consciousness*. Oxford: Oxford University Press.

Sosa, David (1993). "Consequences of Consequentialism." *Mind* 102, 405, 101–122.

Stratton-Lake, Philip (2000). *Kant, Duty and Moral Worth*. London: Routledge.

(2011). "Recalcitrant Pluralism." *Ratio* 24, 4, 364–383.

Stroud, Sarah (2017). "Lying as Infidelity: A Quasi-Rossian Account." In Mark Timmons, ed., *Oxford Studies in Normative Ethics*, vol. 7, 79–97.

Stuchlik, Joshua (2021). *Intention and Wrongdoing: In Defense of Double Effect*. Cambridge: Cambridge University Press.

Sturgeon, Nicholas (1985). "Moral Explanations." In David Copp and David Zimmerman, eds., *Morality, Reason, and Truth*. Totowa, NJ: Rowman & Allanheld, 49–78.

(2006). "Moral Explanations Defended." In James Dreier, ed., *Contemporary Debates in Moral Theory*. London: Routledge, 241–262.

Swanton, Christine (2001). "A Virtue Ethical Account of Right Action." *Ethics* 112, 1, 32–52.

(2003). *Virtue Ethics: A Pluralistic View*. Oxford: Oxford University Press.

Theunissen, L. Nandi (2020). *The Value of Humanity*. Oxford: Oxford University Press.

Thomson, Judith Jarvis (1973). "Rights and Deaths." *Philosophy and Public Affairs* 2, 2, 146–159.

(1990). *The Realm of Rights*. Cambridge, MA: Harvard University Press.

(1997). "The Right and the Good." *Journal of Philosophy* 94, 6, 273–298.

(2008). *Normativity*. Chicago and La Salle: Open Court.

Timmons, Mark (2021). *Kant's Doctrine of Virtue: A Guide*. Oxford: Oxford University Press.

Timmons, Mark, John Greco, and Alfred R. Mele (2007). *Rationality and the Good: Critical Essays on the Ethics and Epistemology of Robert Audi*. Oxford: Oxford University Press.

Tuomela, Raimo (1995). *The Importance of Us*. Stanford: Stanford University Press.

von Wright, Georg Henrik (1963). *Norm and Action*. London: Routledge & Kegan Paul.

(1971). *Explanation and Understanding*. Ithaca: Cornell University Press.

Wagner, Steven, and Richard Warner, eds. (1993). *Naturalism: A Critical Appraisal*. Notre Dame: University of Notre Dame Press.

Wedgwood, Ralph (2007). *Normativity*. Oxford: Oxford University Press.

Williamson, Timothy (2000). *Knowledge and Its Limits*. Oxford: Oxford University Press.

Yablo, Stephen (1992). "Mental Causation." *Philosophical Review* 101, 2, 245–280.

Zagzebski, Linda (2017). *Exemplarist Moral Theory*. Oxford: Oxford University Press.

Zhao, Michael (2019). "Solidarity, Fate-Sharing, and Community." *Philosophical Imprints* 19, 46, 1–13.

Zhong, Lei (2019). "The Hard Problem for Soft Moral Realism." *Journal of Philosophy* 116, 10, 555–576.

Index

act-description, 44
adverbial obligation, 287
aesthetic perception, 179–180
altruism, 79, 116
Ameriks, Karl, xv, 250, 292
Anderson, Elizabeth, 252
Anscombe, G. E. M., 12
Aquinas, Thomas, 4, 59
aretaic integration. *See* integration, aretaic
Aristotle, xii–xiii, 4–6, 22, 52, 59, 73, 89, 94, 125, 198, 221, 237, 240
Audi, Paul, 205
autonomy, 99–100, 105, 161–162, 253, 273, 291

basic action, 16–17, 44, 49, 129
beneficence problem, 106, 283–284
benevolence, 78–79, 143, 156, 203
Bentham, Jeremy, 265, 271, 294
Bergqvist, Anna,, 170, 294
Berker, Selim, xv, 269, 294
Birondo, Noell, 156
Boyd, Richard, 141, 204, 294
Bradford, Gwen, 78
Brandom, Robert, 161
Brandt, Richard, 161, 212, 294
Bratman, Michael, 59
Braun, Stewart, 156
Brentano, Franz, 259, 294
Brink, David O., 141
Broad, C. D., 36

Burge, Tyler, 181
Butchvarov, Panayot, 200

Chang, Ruth, 229
Chisholm, R. M., 260, 294
cluster concept, 162
consequencism, 270–273, 277–281. *See also* preferential standard
consequentiality, 142, 167. *See also* grounding
contributory value, 263
control, 11–12, 16–18, 22, 25–26, 29, 37–38, 54, 64, 71, 97, 111, 118, 120, 125, 133, 245, 280, 288
Copenhaver, Rebecca, 179
Cornell Realism, 161
Cowan, Robert, 170, 294
creditworthiness, 1, 18, 23, 32, 34–37, 40, 53, 79, 114, 134, 156, 207, 245, 258, 287
Crisp, Roger, xv, 156, 223–224, 269, 295
Cullity, Garrett, xv, 36, 66, 109, 114, 143, 156–157, 212, 224, 250, 259, 266, 295
Curren, Randall, 52

Dancy, Jonathan, xv, 143, 295
Darwall, Stephen E., 252
Davidson, Donald, 221

301

For EU product safety concerns, contact us at Calle de José Abascal, 56–1°, 28003 Madrid, Spain or eugpsr@cambridge.org.